RESEARC[...]
HAPPIN[...]

Qualitative, Biographical and Critical Perspectives

Edited by
Mark Cieslik

BRISTOL
UNIVERSITY
PRESS

First published in Great Britain in 2021 by

Bristol University Press
University of Bristol
1–9 Old Park Hill
Bristol
BS2 8BB
UK
t: +44 (0)117 954 5940
e: bup-info@bristol.ac.uk

Details of international sales and distribution partners are available at
bristoluniversitypress.co.uk

© Bristol University Press 2021

British Library Cataloguing in Publication Data
A catalogue record for this book is available from the British Library

ISBN 978-1-5292-0612-8 hardcover
ISBN 978-1-5292-0613-5 paperback
ISBN 978-1-5292-0616-6 ePub
ISBN 978-1-5292-0615-9 ePdf

The right of Mark Cieslik to be identified as editor of this work has been asserted by him in
accordance with the Copyright, Designs and Patents Act 1988.

Cover design: blu inc, Bristol
Front cover image: Mark Cieslik/Theo's Vans, Dornoch, 2019
Bristol University Press uses environmentally responsible
print partners.
Printed and bound in Great Britain by CMP, Poole

Contents

List of Figures and Tables

Figures

Tables

Notes on Authors

David Beel is Senior Lecturer in political economy at Manchester Metropolitan University, UK. He has conducted several studies on various aspects of wellbeing in community settings in the UK.

Mark Cieslik is Senior Lecturer in sociology at Northumbria University, Newcastle Upon Tyne, UK. He has undertaken biographical research into life-course transitions since the late 1990s, publishing articles and books in youth studies and education and more recently around happiness and wellbeing. His most recent book, *The Happiness Riddle and the Quest for a Good Life*, was published by Palgrave in 2017. He is currently researching the long-term impact of mindfulness on wellbeing and also undertaking a comparative biographical/life-course project investigating happiness in the Netherlands and UK.

Sarah Coulthard in Senior Lecturer in international development at the University of Northumbria, Newcastle Upon Tyne, UK. She has conducted wellbeing research in different developing societies and in particular has explored the nature of happiness in fishing communities around the world.

Richard Gibbons is a doctoral researcher at Northumbria University, Newcastle Upon Tyne, UK. He worked in the music industry and civil service before his research career. His PhD study draws on biographical methods exploring the nature of wellbeing in relation to the body and how bodily practices can frame the experiences of wellbeing.

Nicholas Hill is an early career researcher at the RMIT University, Melbourne, Australia. His PhD explored the intersection of happiness and wellbeing in contemporary life. His broader research interests are in the areas of emotions and society, therapeutic and self-help culture, and experiences of health and illness, particularly mental health. He is co-editor of the volume *Critical Happiness Studies* (Routledge, 2020).

Barbara Holthus holds two PhD degrees (University of Trier, Germany and University of Hawaii at Manoa). She is deputy director of the German Institute for Japanese Studies Tokyo. Her research is on marriage and the family, childcare, wellbeing, media, gender, as well as demographic and social change. Her publications include 'Parental Well-being in Japan' (*DIJ Miscellanea*, 19, 2015), as well as the co-edited volumes *Life Course, Happiness and Well-being in Japan* and *Happiness and the Good Life in Japan* (both with Wolfram Manzenreiter, Routledge, 2017).

Kelly Johnson is a doctoral researcher at Northumbria University, Newcastle Upon Tyne, UK. Her PhD examines the wellbeing of residents living in a coastal town in the North East of England. Prior to university Kelly was a community activist and researcher.

Wolfram Manzenreiter is Professor of Japanese Studies at the Department of East Asian Studies at the University of Vienna, Austria. His research is mostly concerned with sociological and anthropological aspects of sports, emotions, work and migration in a globalizing world. Currently, he is working on migration networks and the Japanese diaspora in South America, rural wellbeing, the Tokyo 2020 Olympic Games, and gambling cultures. His most recent book-length publications include *Sport and Body Politics in Japan* (Routledge 2014), the *Contemporary Japan* (2017, 29(2)) edited special issue on 'Squared diaspora: representations of the Japanese diaspora across time and space', and the co-edited volumes *Happiness and the Good Life in Japan* and *Life Course, Happiness and Well-being in Japan* (both with Barbara Holthus, Routledge, 2017).

Ilona Suojanen is a happiness researcher based in Delft, the Netherlands, and has published widely around happiness. She has also been a positive safety researcher at the Erasmus University Rotterdam, the Netherlands. Her PhD at the University of Edinburgh, UK explored happiness at work among generation Y, drawing on a range of visual methods. She is also the author of *Onnellisuuspaineen alla* (Gaudeamus, 2021).

Neil Thin is an anthropologist based at the University of Edinburgh, UK and has written extensively around development and wellbeing in different cultural and policy contexts. He is the author of *Social Happiness* (Policy Press, 2012) and *A Research Agenda for Social Wellbeing* (Elgar, 2020). He has been particularly interested in the practical application of wellbeing research.

David Tross is Associate Lecturer at Birkbeck College, University of London, UK and doctoral researcher. His PhD examines Mass Observation data around the everyday experiences of happiness, utilizing biographical narrative methods.

Claire Wallace is Professor of Sociology at the University of Aberdeen, UK. She has published widely across many different areas of sociological research including digital society and social quality. In recent years she has conducted various projects into the nature of wellbeing in the UK and in other societies culminating in the book (with Pamela Abbott and Roger Sapsford) *The Decent Society: Planning for Social Quality* (Routledge, 2016). She is currently working on an Horizon 2020 project about cultural tourism and is part of a Digital Working research centre organized by the University of Sussex, UK.

Brianne Wenning is Lecturer in global health at Keele University, UK. Her doctoral research in anthropology engaged with wellbeing, happiness and the use of narratives among asylum seekers and refugees in Cameroon, the UK and the Gambia. Currently, she is exploring the experience, stigma and overarching syndemics of cutaneous leishmaniasis in Brazil, Ethiopia and Sri Lanka.

1

Introduction: Developing Qualitative Research into Happiness and Wellbeing

Mark Cieslik

Sociology and qualitative research into happiness/wellbeing

There are always difficulties choosing cover images for books, particularly for one on wellbeing given the elastic, ephemeral nature of happiness. It is important for the image to be appealing, conveying something of the contents and attracting readers. Many happiness books employ banal symbols of fun, joy and leisure pursuits. Bright yellow covers, smiley emojis, dancers, beaches and mountains, fairgrounds and clowns all feature on recent texts. Such common-sense images of fun obscure the complexities of people's lives and the life-long struggle to live well. Hence the less obvious cover image selected for this book. What does a pair of legs hanging lazily over the side of bridge say about this book and how we study happiness? The image taken of my 14-year-old son Theo, who was staring into a Scottish stream, encapsulates many of the themes we explore across the following eleven chapters. With a little bit of interpretative effort we can read this image as one about 'having time', to sit and enjoy the wonders of nature. Hidden in this shot are family members so the book is also about these pivotal relationships that carry us through life. The book is concerned with these nourishing and restorative moments that inform wellbeing in real time and imaginatively as we hold on to these memories through life. These moments are often about connections, to people, places and activities that are ingredients of a good life – that which makes life worth living. Hence the book is very much about 'social happiness' and using qualitative or ethnographic techniques to document the flow of relationships and evolving identities central to wellbeing. In investigating the spectrum of experiences and emotions important for wellbeing (from suffering to the sublime) the book is also curious about being human – what humans need to feel alive and how we create better societies that foster these experiences. The running waters of the stream that so captivated Theo symbolizes another important theme of this book around the notion of movement and journeys – people's daily routines; moving places seeking happier lives; people aging, moving through stages in life all shaping the ebb and flow of wellbeing. The book also examines how individuals and their happiness are conditioned by the environments in which they live, social policies and their social backgrounds. Finally, the various chapters document the imaginative and creative ways people work together to fashion their wellbeing often resisting and modifying these wider processes that impinge on them.

In 2009 I helped establish the British Sociological Association Happiness Study group to promote sociological research into happiness and wellbeing. At the time, there were few sociologists researching happiness/wellbeing and since then we have seen a modest growth in studies and publications (Hyman, 2014; Frawley, 2016; Cieslik, 2017), yet it still remains a marginal topic in sociology. Partly this is because sociologists are more interested in structural processes than subjectivities and social problems rather than living well (Veenhoven, 2014; Bartram 2015). These priorities colour the relatively narrow focus of some research into the happiness industry and new forms of consumer capitalism (see Cieslik, 2015). This book calls for a broader understanding of happiness/wellbeing and a more ambitious research programme into the complexities of happiness. This should encompass the everyday, lived experiences of living well, the collaborative and conflictual relationships this implies and how these are embedded in personal biographies and evolving sociocultural contexts.

Since 2009 we have seen some undergraduate programmes and doctoral researchers exploring happiness/wellbeing but these are still rare in university sociology departments. This book therefore continues the effort to promote sociological research into happiness illustrating the important contribution it can make to key debates in the social sciences. It seems unusual that happiness should remain a niche topic in sociological research for wellbeing is integral to social identities, the fabric of social practices and popular cultures we see today.[1]

This book in particular illustrates the use of qualitative techniques such as ethnographic, critical, life history and biographical approaches (although several contributors combine these with quantitative data, adopting a mixed-methods perspective). Qualitative studies are under-represented in happiness research as influential economists and psychologists and their quantitative methodologies have shaped much of the work in the field, even that by noted sociologists like Ruut Veenhoven (2000). In a wider discipline now dominated by qualitative research there are curiously very few sociological studies of happiness/ wellbeing that utilize ethnographic or qualitative research techniques. There remains a clear gap in the current sociological literature on happiness/wellbeing and a pressing need for further study into the everyday experiences of living well.

The contributors to this book offer insights into the key empirical findings from their studies as well as discussing some of the research techniques they used in their work. The book offers readers a sense of the richness and diversity of the meanings and experiences around happiness while also detailing some of the challenges of undertaking ethnographic and biographical research into happiness/wellbeing.

To date much happiness research has been restricted in its scope and ambition by the numerical methodologies of survey techniques and the interest sociologists have with social problems. This volume transcends these constraints by showing happiness emerging from shared social practices; situated in community traditions; evolving with our identities as we age; and struggled over because of the classed and gendered divisions in modern societies. Over the next few pages I introduce some of the principles of qualitative research into happiness, setting out some of the themes that structure the chapters in this book. I also discuss some of the challenges we faced developing our qualitative research projects and show how these were managed by contributors. The aim was to create a text that would inspire you to undertake your own studies and offer some guidance as you research happiness/wellbeing.

Although this is a text about the sociological investigation of happiness/wellbeing I hope the growing popularity of such studies presents an opportunity for sociology more generally. Developing my own studies and teaching happiness/wellbeing to my students has rekindled my enthusiasm for research as I have been forced to draw on readings and ideas well beyond the usual terrain of mainstream sociology (see Cieslik, 2017). This perhaps has made me a better sociologist? My engagement with the work of philosophers, historians, economists, psychoanalysts and psychologists pushed me to question the over-specialization and disciplinary conventions that often limits sociological research. Qualitative researchers also draw inspiration from literature, art, journalism, music and social media in their efforts to understand the human condition and flourishing.[2] I have conducted research driven simply by a curiosity about people and how they live in all their richness and diversity (see Brinkmann, 2012). To research what the Japanese refer to as 'Ikigai', 'that which makes life worth living', is intriguing and life affirming, and so very different to the usual focus on the social problems of people and societies and social policy 'solutions' (Mathews and Izquierdo, 2010; though see Gibbons in this volume). The chapters in this book therefore are examples of a broader, more balanced sociological imagination that offer the freedom to study 'people in the round' where we investigate not only people's problems but also their strengths, talents and nourishing experiences important for wellbeing. Rather than endlessly documenting the problems of modernity this approach holds out the possibility of producing really useful knowledge, learning from our research subjects as they document their travails and victories, sharing their insights into how to live well and their 'skills for life' acquired over their lifetimes.

Some issues to consider when conducting qualitative research into happiness/wellbeing

In developing qualitative techniques to study happiness/wellbeing we visualize and model people, their behaviours and social relations rather differently to the more common quantitative and critical perspectives that dominate existing research. We deploy rather different ontological assumptions (how we conceive and define what we study) which in turn influences how we conduct our studies – the epistemological features of our work.

Definitions of happiness/wellbeing in qualitative research

There are numerous definitions of happiness and wellbeing in social research, reflecting the questions and design of particular projects. How one defines happiness/wellbeing will direct attention to what one studies – the sorts of experiences, settings and events in participants' lives. As a sociologist the definitions of happiness/wellbeing should also reflect the principles and priorities of sociological research. I take this to mean, following foundational writers (Mills, 1959), that accounts of wellbeing experiences and how these are patterned should be sensitive to the interplay of structural processes and agency of groups and individuals.[3] A sociological definition of happiness/wellbeing then has a subjective dimension, as wellbeing is integral for social identities but these are shared through cultures and other networks that bind people together and imply inequalities, (dis)advantages and struggle that reflect how power operates through these relationships. This broad processual definition of happiness/wellbeing helps us focus attention on the micro interactional encounters significant for subjectivities, how these evolve in biographical time and how these are influenced by wider institutional and structural (such as socio-economic) contexts. This approach often involves combining qualitative research techniques such as focus groups and interviews with the use of secondary data and other network mapping to generate this wide range of data. This broad sociological definition of happiness should also help us generate insights that have the potential to empower or enhance lives. By systematically investigating differences in wellbeing research studies can offer practical guidance on living well.

Despite this aim to develop broad conceptualizations of wellbeing, happiness is sometimes defined more narrowly to convey positive emotions and experiences as we see in popular culture, consumer lifestyles and advertising. Some critics of the happiness industry (Furedi, 2004; Davies, 2015) utilize these understandings of happiness, allowing them to construct happiness as a rather superficial subjective state they contrast with more sophisticated, meaningful and socially aware ways of living. Qualitative researchers are sensitive to these types of definitions but usually draw on additional features to create broader conceptions of living well. For example, some economists and psychologists unpack a range of dimensions often viewing happiness itself as a lay term and the notion of wellbeing to denote a more precise technical understanding of quality of life. Wellbeing is then subdivided into a subjective dimension (SWB) (which in turn comprises the balance and experience of positive and negative feelings/emotions as well as a reflective/evaluative aspect – life satisfaction) and an objective dimension (OWB) such as income, housing, employment and marital status (Argyle, 2001; Layard, 2005). Some sociologists, drawing on these ideas, have developed quantitative research (using Likert scale-type questions) that surveys these enduring and importantly measurable notions of life satisfaction, 'the degree to which an individual judges the overall quality of his/her life favourably' (Veenhoven, 2009: 49). Qualitative researchers sometimes utilize these definitions in their research, investigating how participants reflect on their lives and come to judgements about their wellbeing (see Hyman, 2014); or study the everyday patterns of positive/negative emotions

(Cieslik, 2017); or the way that more objective community resources influence subjective wellbeing (see the chapter by Wallace and Beel).

Some qualitative research (see the chapter by Gibbons) draws on classical understandings of happiness whereby Hedonia denotes everyday ephemeral emotions and experiences significant for wellbeing while Eudaimonia implies more durable understandings (such as contentment) and embodied practices (such as meaningful activities) that constitute a good life (McMahon, 2006; Aristotle, 2009).

Given the wide range of influences on qualitative research we therefore are open to an eclectic mix of conceptions and definitions of wellbeing, sensitive to both more inductive lay accounts as well as more technical definitions from the research literature – hence, happiness and wellbeing are often used interchangeably or as happiness/ wellbeing. The interest in lay accounts stem from an understanding of wellbeing emerging from everyday relationships that evolve as people age together. The focus on 'social happiness' (Thin, 2012) implies techniques from anthropology (such as participant observation, narrative and biographical research) and attention to how happiness is expressed and lived through historically and spatially specific rituals, talk and images (see chapter by Holthus and Manzenreiter). Hence, researchers will often spend time embedded in communities, developing close relationships with participants in order to understand their distinctive interpretations and understanding of wellbeing – see the chapter by Johnson and Coulthard as an example of this approach.

'Social happiness': understanding happiness as a social process

A key ontological principle guiding the research in this book is that we understand happiness as emerging out of the everyday social relationships that constitute people's lives. Although subjective wellbeing is experienced and articulated by individuals it is also produced through our relationships with others. Hence, to research this 'social happiness' (Thin, 2012) we need to understand the complex social relationships of our research subjects. In our studies, therefore, we need to map these social networks and observe these relationships as they happen to investigate how they influence the wellbeing of respondents (Scott, 2017). This approach is rather different to mainstream happiness studies that often understand happiness/wellbeing in terms of life satisfaction based on the judgements people make when they are asked in surveys to reflect on the quality of their lives. These techniques are problematic as they focus on 'average' individuals that are decontextualized from the surroundings in which they live.

There are several other implications that flow from this principle of social happiness. As we map a respondent's social relationships we often find they are involved in many different networks in various institutional settings that differ in scale and complexity – from intimate partnerships to extended family, friendship groups, waged employment, neighbourhood and social media groups. All of these relationships and the experiences that flow from them influence wellbeing, positively and negatively, in different ways over time. It is useful therefore to employ theories and concepts to help understand how these various relationships influence wellbeing. So one may employ interactionist theories to investigate how impression management and emotions feature in some of the small-scale relationships (Goffman, 1956; Hochschild, 2003). By assuming that wellbeing is 'co-produced', researchers need to attend to how people's relationships involve trade-offs, negotiations, compromises and conflict over everyday affairs like work, care, budgets, parenting, ambitions, and past events that all influence happiness/wellbeing. In intimate relationships, for example, notions of gender, sexuality and class may be significant so concepts developed by feminist researchers (Skeggs, 1997) may be useful to reveal how everyday interactions involve subtle (and not so subtle) power relationships which influence happiness. As the scale of social networks increases one may have to deploy concepts such as alienation (Marx, 1983), anomie (Durkheim, 2014) or rationality (Weber, 1990) to help illuminate how employment experiences, for example, influence the personal wellbeing of research subjects.[4]

This principle of social happiness implies that researchers endeavour to situate research subjects in the web of social relationships that constitute their lives. By studying people in situ, rather than in the abstract, we generate wellbeing narratives that are connected to some of the social relationships that are the source of that wellbeing. In doing this we develop a 'thicker' description of wellbeing (Geertz, 1973) than the 'thin slice' approach adopted by many other techniques. The principle of social happiness also reflects some of the key tenets of the sociological imagination whereby, for example, we are sensitive to how other people in networks condition the lives of our research subjects. At its simplest this can be about the reciprocal relationships in life – the responsibilities we have to those we love or more impersonal contracts with employers, neighbours and so on. These structuring processes and then how individuals experience these and adapt and manage them (their agency) are at the heart of 'doing sociology' and integral to researching the ebb and flow of wellbeing.

Talking to people over many years about living well one soon discovers the importance of belonging and 'fitting in', being accepted and valued in a local community. The principle of social happiness therefore also directs us to investigate the communities of our research subjects and their influence on their wellbeing. The work of anthropologists and sociologists like Durkheim and Bourdieu can help us investigate how growing up in a particular community with its rituals and practices shapes beliefs, values, expectations, morality and ethics that all influence the quality of people's lives. People often hold on to distinctive understandings of what happiness is and how to lead a good life and these often subtle subjective interpretations can be gleaned and made intelligible if we research the community cultures of the people we study.

Biographies, subjectivities and self-identity

Another key principle of qualitative research into happiness is the acknowledgement of the multifaceted, dynamic and socially constructed nature of humans. The chapters in this book, for example, explore the messy emotions of wellbeing; psychic depths to the self and its effect on happiness and how wellbeing is experienced both mentally and bodily. In embracing this complexity and agency the contributors challenge existing approaches that often view people as rather passive bearers of wellbeing in life-satisfaction research (Blanchflower and Oswald, 2004; Clark et al, 2018) or as people subjected to powerful forces of neo-liberalism in other studies (Furedi, 2004; Ahmed, 2010; Cederström and Spicer, 2015; Davies, 2015).

The treatment of people as active agents is a counterpoint to the role we afford social relationships and place in our analysis of happiness/ wellbeing. These dimensions or principles work together, echoing Mills' insights into the biographies (agency) and social processes (structures) that constitute the notion of the sociological imagination (1959). All of the studies in this book recognize the role of interpretative processes in the way people make sense of the their lives, trying to live well. Wellbeing is inherently subjective and so one would expect any research to offer some narratives from the researched of how life experiences generate different feelings and emotions (and their intensity, duration, frequency and sources) that frame more durable notions of life satisfaction. Yet often research attends more to the latter understandings of life satisfaction than the events and emotions that inform them (Veenhoven, 2000) creating curiously decontextualized, disembodied accounts of people's wellbeing. In contrast, authors in this book employ concepts such as internal conversations, cognitive functions and reflexivity or the psyche to offer more dynamic conceptions of the self, interrogating how people engage creatively with social constraints to fashion their wellbeing. Where existing research will have the simpler modelling of the self and social processes this book utilizes life history data, personal narratives, ethnographic observations and participants' images to reflect the flow of experiences, events and emotions, how they are internalized and function to constitute people's subjective accounts of wellbeing.

Another reason why happiness researchers need to acknowledge the complexity of the self and being human is because by posing questions about living well we also raise questions about the needs or conditions necessary for good wellbeing. These questions have been explored since classical times (McMahon, 2006; Aristotle, 2009) informing, for example, research by Maslow (Maslow, 2013) and Marx's work on human nature, 'self-estrangement' or alienation (Marx, 1983). At its simplest, modern happiness researchers do need to reflect on what they mean by happiness, wellbeing or living well and how these assumptions inform the empirical questions shaping their work (see, for example, Nussbaum and Sen, 1993). Johnson and Coulthard employ a three-dimensional model of wellbeing (involving material, relational and subjective elements) in their chapter which reflects recent thinking in international development on the nature of essential needs for good wellbeing. In my own research, for example, I have drawn on Aristotle (2009), Marx (1984) and Csikszentmihalyi (2002) to guide my understanding of the basic ingredients of flourishing or living well (Cieslik, 2017). Hence, as humans we all have some fundamental needs that have to be satisfied if we are to develop and be satisfied with life – culturally specific material needs, social relationships, implying care and intimacy, connections to our bodies, meaningful relationships with the natural world and opportunities to learn, create and be productive.

The notions of individuals and the self, employed by contributors here, acknowledge the temporality of being human and so concepts of aging, life-course transitions and generations and their impacts on wellbeing are explored in various chapters. Although people's identities are shaped in early life, forming values, ethical frameworks and expectations that influence wellbeing, these features evolve as we age transforming understandings of wellbeing. One of the challenges noted by respondents about living well was how to monitor their changing lives and shifting expectations about happiness. Their confusion about their changing lives and its effect on their efforts to live well is one of the strange paradoxes of happiness – the so-called issues of adaptation and fallibility. Despite the popularity of happiness in popular culture many people struggle to make informed choices about how best to live well. In early life with simpler social networks participants often viewed happiness in cruder materialistic ways whereas by later life many interviewees had more nuanced, philosophical interpretations of living well. But the transformation of these views was often uneven and experienced in problematic and troubling ways.

Theories and methods in qualitative happiness research

The focus on social happiness and the complex self has a range of implications for how qualitative researchers conduct their work and, in particular, the theories and methods they deploy. To access the subjective interpretations around happiness and the social relationships that generate them means that researchers often study wellbeing in situ, using ethnographic techniques to observe and participate in the social practices of respondents. Researchers map respondents' social networks to assess how different relationships and activities across various life domains (such as family, employment and friendships) contribute to the overall wellbeing of research subjects. Theories from those like Bourdieu (1977; 2010) on social capital, field, habitus and practice are used to explore how networks can generate resources and opportunities, shaping patterns of wellbeing between people and at different points in the life course (see Cieslik, 2017). Other chapters (Gibbons) discuss how theories on embodiment can help us research the place of the body in everyday wellbeing. Theories on community relationships and identities are employed in other chapters (Wallace and Beel) to illuminate the impact of social networks on personal wellbeing.

Although much data is based on what people articulate about wellbeing, ethnographers also investigate behaviours (what people do – their practices and rituals) and other sources such as visual representations of wellbeing (see Suojanen chapter in this volume). As people can hold contradictory, hidden or tacit understandings of wellbeing and struggle to acknowledge its deep sources in biographies and relationships one does need multiple sources of data to adequately investigate happiness/wellbeing. It is often more fruitful for happiness researchers to discuss the changing lives of interviewees and the feelings they have about employment, their love life and caring responsibilities than to quiz people about their wellbeing. A key paradox of happiness research therefore is that one often discovers more about a person's wellbeing by *not* directly enquiring about their happiness!

Qualitative research into happiness can discern some of the ambiguities and nuances around the meanings that people have of wellbeing that can be lost when people are interviewed or surveyed in isolation from the social practices that constitute their lives. For example, the chapter by Holthus and Manzenreiter discusses the difficulties traditional Western wellbeing surveys have investigating the complex cultural understandings that the Japanese have around living well. Ethnographic research has shown that many Japanese regard happiness as a familial or collective phenomenon rather than something that is experienced individually as in the West. Hence, traditional wellbeing surveys in Japan tend to misrepresent the Japanese as being particularly unhappy when in fact they experience other notions of happiness neglected by popular survey questions. I found similar examples in my own research where I was initially surprised to discover relatively disadvantaged respondents reporting good wellbeing. After spending some time with these participants I learned they had developed complex nurturing social networks that allowed them to live 'thrifty' happy lives outside the usual consumerist lifestyles that are popular today (Cieslik, 2017: 100–6).

As researchers need to employ techniques to discern the nature of social happiness so they also need to utilize theories and methods to investigate the complex self and its significance for wellbeing. At the very least researchers need to access some of the subjective experiences and interpretations that respondents have of wellbeing – fleeting emotions and feelings as well as more durable dispositions around contentment, satisfaction or problems such as anxiety and depression. Theories of emotions (Hochschild, 2003) and work by psychologists on cognition (Boniwell, 2012) can be useful here as can the research into reflexivity and agency developed by sociologists (Archer, 1988; Sayer, 2010). Similarly, psychoanalytical theory may be useful to explore how experiences are internalized and influence wellbeing often in ways that seem opaque to respondents (Craib, 2001). To research the complex subjectivities around wellbeing usually involves small samples of individuals that are interviewed several times, preferably in their communities to allow for some observations and participation in cultural activities. To access the more fleeting as well as more durable aspects of wellbeing it helps to deploy several data-generation techniques. As well as interviews and observations, respondents can complete diaries (recorded on their smartphones) and use cameras to document their wellbeing experiences through the day and week. Insights into the patterning of wellbeing – the sorts of activities people undertook and the intensity of associated emotions/feelings, and their duration, frequency and location – will all help map the wellbeing of respondents.

A key dimension of the complex self is the evolving biographical nature of individuals and hence some researchers employ life-course theories and methods such as life-history narrative and mapping techniques to generate data on respondents' histories and their significance for wellbeing. Researchers are often sensitive to processes of socialization and the role of values and ethical frameworks (such as those around faith and spirituality) on wellbeing. In my own work I have drawn on Bourdieu and concepts like habitus and symbolic violence (Bourdieu and Passeron, 1990) to investigate how people grow up as classed and gendered subjects which have a bearing on their wellbeing through life.

As with the principle of social happiness, the fallibility of respondents can be an issue when conducting biographical research so investigators will have to be sensitive to the tacit or hidden aspects of wellbeing in the lives of those they research. In my own studies I have encountered many examples where respondents seem surprised and confused about their wellbeing at key points in life, unable to account for the sources of their good or bad wellbeing at the time. It was only after much reflection and several interview discussions that respondents were able to discern how their wellbeing had been influenced by earlier events (see Cieslik, 2017: 106–10, for examples).

Outline of the book

All of the chapters in this book illustrate the contribution that qualitative research can make to happiness studies. By reflecting on the shortcomings of existing survey and polemical studies contributors call for a broader understanding of happiness as a social, collaborative practice. The different authors document some key findings from their projects whilst offering insights into the methods and theories informing their research. The chapters are organized into three sections highlighting some of the different features of qualitative research into happiness/wellbeing.

In the first section, on theories, debates and issues, Thin's chapter is distinctive in offering a polemical discussion of the many barriers that have hindered the development of qualitative research into social happiness. In particular the obsession of social science with social problems and narrow individualistic conceptions of wellbeing that thwart efforts to promote a more positive study of people's efforts to live well together. Hill's chapter makes similar points about the neglect of happiness by sociologists illustrating how life history narratives can be employed to study people's wellbeing and notably how happiness is rooted in biographies and emotions associated with them, evolving through dense social relationships. In particular, he focuses on the way that life stories are used by his participants to make sense of the complex emotions that frame key moments in life, reflecting the dialogue that interviewees have with researchers through the research process. The final chapter in this section by Tross discusses the use of data from the UK Mass Observation Archive to investigate the happiness of participants in this longitudinal study. Although a large-scale survey, participants completed lengthy written responses to questions allowing Tross to compile a nuanced account of the meanings and understandings around happiness/wellbeing. Participants also noted the impact of shifting economic and political fortunes on their wellbeing, particularly experiences of insecurity and disenchantment in recent years.

The second section of the book focuses on community research and the study of biographies and identities. The first two chapters by Cieslik and Gibbons explore the way that wellbeing is experienced across personal biographies influenced by class and gender relationships. Both chapters document how people access different opportunities and resources as they age, shaping personal wellbeing. Individuals develop different lifestyles and bodily practices reflective of gender/ class dynamics that can sometimes be problematic for happiness, yet at key moments in the life course people often become aware of their wellbeing, changing their lives in an effort to live differently and happier. Both chapters illustrate how early life experiences cast a long shadow over wellbeing. A key challenge faced by the authors was how to generate reliable data on participants' life-course events stretching over many years across complex social networks and domains.

The two chapters by Johnson and Coulthard and Wallace and Beel document the complex mixed methods needed to investigate wellbeing in community settings. Both studies employ surveys and ethnographic techniques to research large numbers of community residents, (the former in North East England and the latter in Scotland) illustrating how wellbeing experiences can be stratified by age, class and gender. There are tensions between residents around different interests and agenda that influence wellbeing across these communities. Wallace and Beel examine wellbeing through a focus on heritage projects in two Scottish fishing communities. They show how residents' involvement in festivals, archives and craft workshops produce wider social, economic and cultural benefits that enhance wellbeing in often surprising and unintended ways. Johnson and Coulthard document the challenges facing de-industrialised communities in the UK and how limited employment opportunities and public services frame much of the poor wellbeing we see in such areas today. Yet residents are often resilient, drawing on long established social networks to help them manage some of the privations they experience. In the chapter by Wenning the author recounts the difficulties of African migrants and their efforts to mitigate the trauma of losing their homes and families. Mainstream research often depicts refugees as damaged victims of global social forces but Wenning offers a more nuanced account of their wellbeing emerging from their journeys. The author shows how African cultural traditions, particularly those around faith, spirituality and belonging are mobilized enabling migrants to recreate positive narratives of identity and life journeys. She documents the paradoxical optimism and hopefulness of her interviewees that is seldom reported in migration research.

The final section discusses methodological aspects of qualitative happiness research. Holthus and Manzenreiter report on their research undertaken in Aso, a small community in the Southern Islands of Japan. The authors document how the Japanese have more collective, social understandings of happiness than the more personal, individualised conceptions common in Western societies. The Japanese are hence often reticent about public discussion of personal wellbeing, particularly with outsiders. The authors discuss some of the ways they overcame these challenges during the research process. They reflect on their fieldwork roles, access, gatekeepers and problems of rapport, discussing the development of a board game as a key tool for generating rich data with participants. The board game techniques allowed the researchers to map in a participative way the social networks and complex meanings ascribed to wellbeing/ happiness by Japanese interviewees. As participants constructed numerous tokens for the game, which symbolized different aspects of wellbeing, the authors were able to explore the diverse ways that wellbeing is understood and experienced by the Aso community. The final chapter of the book by Ilona Suojanen discusses her study of happiness in the workplace and how she combined visual methods with traditional interview techniques to map the experiences of young workers in Edinburgh. She charts the embedded nature of wellbeing and the complex visual representations of happiness in various aspects of workplace relationships. She goes on to evaluate the usefulness of photography and visual methods for documenting happiness experiences in everyday life.

Notes

[1] Although one might argue that cuts to public services and state benefits in the UK following the banking crisis of 2008, the so-called period of austerity, has encouraged attention on traditional sociological research questions around poverty and inequality.

[2] In my own work I have been inspired by Charles Dickens, Aldous Huxley, Tim Winton and Lisa Taddeo to name but a few, who have all written evocatively about the human condition – how people are shaped by life events, struggling to live well as they journey through life.

[3] I have argued elsewhere (Cieslik, 2020) that some other sociological research into happiness has tended to neglect aspects of this principle of structure/agency; for example, critics of the happiness industry (Cederström and Spicer, 2015; Cabanas and Illouz, 2019) emphasize the structuring of subjectivities by corporations and some survey research (Veeenhoven, 1984) portrays wellbeing as a function of the social characteristics of individuals rather than as a product of more social, creative practices.

[4] Although happiness researchers must be mindful when using traditional sociological concepts as they are often biased towards the analysis of poor wellbeing rather than strengths and virtues.

References

Ahmed, S. (2010) *The Promise of Happiness*, London: Duke University Press.

Archer, M. (1988) *Culture and Agency: The Place of Culture in Social Theory*, Cambridge: Cambridge University Press.

Argyle, M. (2001) *The Psychology of Happiness* (2nd edn), London: Routledge Press.

Aristotle (2009) *Nicomachean Ethics*, Oxford: Oxford University Press.

Bartram, D. (2012) 'Elements of a sociological contribution to happiness studies', *Sociology Compass*, 6(8): 644–56.

Blanchflower, D. and Oswald, A. (2004) 'Wellbeing over time in Britain and the USA', *Journal of Public Economics*, 88, July: 1359–87.

Boniwell, I. (2012) *Positive Psychology in a Nutshell: The Science of Happiness* (3rd edn), Milton Keynes: Open University Press.

Bourdieu, P. (1977) *Outline of a Theory of Practice*, Cambridge: Cambridge University Press.

Bourdieu, P. (2010) *Distinction*, London: Routledge.

Bourdieu, P. and Passeron, J.C. (1990) *Reproduction in Education, Society and Culture*, London: Sage Press.

Bourdieu, P. et al (1999) *The Weight of the World: Social Suffering in Contemporary Society*, Stanford: Stanford University Press.

Brinkmann, S. (2012) *Qualitative Enquiry in Everyday Life: Working with Everyday Life Materials*, London: Sage.

Cabanas, E. and Illouz, E. (2019) *Manufacturing Happy Citizens: How the Science and Industry of Happiness Control Our Lives*, Cambridge: Polity Press.

Cederström, C. and Spicer, A. (2015) *The Wellness Syndrome*, London: Polity.

Cieslik, M. (2015) 'Not smiling but frowning: sociology and the problem of happiness', *Sociology*, 49(3): 422–37.

Cieslik, M. (2017) *The Happiness Riddle and the Quest for a Good Life*, London: Palgrave.

Cieslik, M. (2020) 'Sociology, biographical research and the development of critical happiness studies', in N. Hill, S. Brinkman and A. Peterson (eds) *Critical Happiness Studies*, London: Routledge, pp 144–61.

Clark, A., Fleche, S., Layard, R., Powdthavee, N. and Ward, G. (2018) *The Origins of Happiness: The Science of Well-Being Over the Life Course*, Woodstock, Oxfordshire: Princeton University Press.

Craib, I. (2001) *Psychoanalysis: A Critical Introduction*, Cambridge: Polity Press.

Csikszentmihalyi, M. (2002) *Flow: The Classic Work on How to Achieve Happiness*, London: Harper and Row.

Davies, W. (2015) *The Happiness Industry: How the Government and Big Business Sold Us Wellbeing*, London: Verso.

Dickens, C. (1984 [1843]) *A Christmas Carol*, London: Penguin.

Durkheim, E. (2014) *The Division of Labour in Society*, New York: Free Press.

Frawley, A. (2016) *Semiotics of Happiness: Rhetorical Beginnings of a Public Problem*, London: Bloomsbury.

Furedi, F. (2004) *Therapy Culture: Cultivating Vulnerability in an Uncertain Age*, London: Routledge.

Geertz, C. (1973) *The Interpretation of Cultures: Selected Essays*, London: Basic Books.

Gilbert, D. (2006) *Stumbling on Happiness*, London: Harper Perennial.

Goffman, E. (1956) *The Presentation of Self*, Edinburgh: Edinburgh University Press.

Hochschild, A. (2003) *The Managed Heart: The Commercialisation of Human Feeling* (2nd edn), Berkeley: University of California Press.

Huxley, A. (1994 [1932]) *Brave New World*, London: Vintage.

Hyman, L. (2014) *Happiness: Understandings, Narratives and Discourses*, London: Palgrave.

Layard, R. (2005) *Happiness: Lessons from a New Science*, London: Penguin.

Marx, K. (1983) *Alienated Labour, The Portable Karl Marx*, Kamenka, E. (ed), New York: Penguin.

Marx, K. (1984) *Marx: Early Writings*, Harmondsworth: Penguin.

Maslow, A. (2013) *A Theory of Human Motivation*, London: Merchant Press.

Mathews, G. and Izquierdo, C. (eds) (2010) *Pursuits of Happiness: Well-Being in Anthropological Perspective*, Oxford: Berghahn Books.

McMahon (2006) *Happiness: A History*, New York: Grove Press.

Mills, C. Wright (1959) *The Sociological Imagination*, Oxford: Oxford University Press.

Nussbaum, M. and Sen, A. (eds) (1993) 'Introduction', *The Quality of Life*, Oxford: Clarendon Press.

Sayer, A. (2010) 'Reflexivity and habitus', in M.S. Archer (ed) *Conversations About Reflexivity*, London: Routledge, pp 108–22.

Sayer, A. (2011) *Why Things Matter to People: Social Science, Values and Ethical Life*, Cambridge: Cambridge University Press.

Scott, J. (2017) *Social Network Analysis* (4th edn), London: Sage.

Skeggs, B. (1997) *Formations of Class and Gender*, London: Sage.

Taddeo, L. (2019) *Three Women*, London: Bloomsbury Circus.

Thin, N. (2012) *Social Happiness: Theory into Policy and Practice*, Bristol: Policy Press.

Veenhoven, R. (1984) *The Conditions of Happiness*, Lancaster: Kluwer Academic Publishers.

Veenhoven, R. (1999) 'Quality of life in individualistic societies: a comparisons of 43 nations in the early 1990s', *Social Indicators Research*, 48: 157–86.

Veenhoven, R. (2000) 'The four qualities of life: ordering concepts and measures of the good life', *Journal of Happiness Studies*, 1(1): 1–39.

Veenhoven, R. (2009) 'How do we assess how happy we are? Tenets, implications and tenability of three theories', in A.K. Dutt and B. Radcliff (eds) *Happiness, Economics and Politics: Towards a Multidisciplinary Approach*, Cheltenham, UK: Edward Elgar, pp 45–69.

Veenhoven, R. (2014) 'Why sociological theory of happiness falls short', *Social Indicators Network News*, May–August, 119–20: 1–4.

Weber, M. (1990) *The Protestant Ethic and the Spirit of Capitalism*, London: Allen & Unwin.

Winton, T. (2009) *Breath*, London: Picador.

PART I

Qualitative Research into Happiness/Wellbeing: Theories, Debates and Issues

2

Living Well Together: On Happiness, Social Goods and Genuinely Progressive Sociology

Neil Thin

Introduction

Life is short. As a social researcher or social reformer, do you really want to spend your days in adversarial mode, treating society as if it were your enemy? Are social inequalities, disruptive traumas, inter-ethnic hatred and crimes really more interesting and more worthy of your attention than conviviality, love, and positive social engagement? Why not choose – unlike most social scientists and social activists – to make the positive promotion of happiness and social goods your core concern?

This chapter is mainly intended as an opinion piece, and the opinions I ask you to consider are these:

- that the deliberate and explicit adoption of a 'happiness lens' in social scholarship and planning would achieve benign outcomes;
- that these improvements would derive from making our learning strategies more appreciative and our social plans more aspirational and uplifting; and
- that social researchers and social planners can't claim to be 'ethical', or 'progressive', or even 'politically engaged' if they don't make happiness an explicit and central concern in their work.

This last claim, which may seem unnecessarily provocative, is probably the most challenging one for social scholars, given that happiness has since the late 19th century so rarely been an explicit concern in social studies. Yet I take it as axiomatic that happiness is what matters most to humanity, and that no-one can be ethical or politically engaged without addressing the things that matter most. So the strong claim here – a provocation to mainstream sociology, but also potentially an inspiration and a wake-up call – is that social disciplines could be radically disrupted, in good ways, by adopting some of the militant positivity that we have seen for 20 years in the positive psychology movement.

When I tried to define the happiness lens in my 2012 book *Social Happiness*, I whittled its characteristics and potential benefits down to five:

- **Positivity** (appreciating people's strengths and enjoyments)
- **Empathy** (respecting and sharing other people's subjective experiences, and viewpoints)
- **Holism** (considering people as wholes, their interactions and relationships)
- **A lifespan perspective** (happiness through the life course, how experiences are anticipated and remembered)
- **Ethical transparency** (using happiness evidence/theories to clarify assumptions about what is good and why)

This can be further simplified to three aspects: *positivity*; *appreciative empathy*; and *life integration*. Thinking about individuals, to consider happiness or wellbeing systematically and overtly entails thinking about good feelings, and whole lives. Thinking about the kinds of society that would be good to live in, a happiness lens means considering social goods, collective experiences, and the social contexts and processes through which we achieve the sense of having a 'life' or a 'biography', and of being a well-integrated, whole 'person'.

This chapter's main concern is what it might mean for social scholars and planners to embrace deliberate positivity by focusing more on synergies between happiness and social goods. By the end of this chapter I hope you will have a stronger and more systematic appreciation of using a happiness lens to become more *genuinely* 'progressive', as opposed to 'progressive' in the lazy senses that are all too common today. It will be an illustration of my claim that a happiness lens can make our work not only more positive, empathic, and integrative, but also more 'ethically transparent'. We can't hope to adopt a plausibly evaluative approach to societies and cultures of the present, past, or future, without paying substantial attention to happiness and wellbeing (Johnson, 2013).

Happiness, social qualities, and moral progress

'The inability of mankind to imagine happiness except in the form of relief, either from effort or pain, presents Socialists with a serious problem' (Orwell, 1943).

The Greatest Happiness Principle – along with reason, science, industry, freedom, democracy, and progress – was utterly crucial to the Enlightenment's moral influence on the world. Academic interest in both happiness and progress was suppressed in the 20th century, but began to be reborn in the closing decades until a global whoosh of interest in the early 21st century. We are yet to see its truly radical potential as a disruptive clusterbomb of an idea, but perhaps its time has come. And if, in social science and social planning, we could somehow persuade ourselves to rekindle our interest in aspirational forms of progress (ie progress that goes beyond remedial action and production of goods and services), then we may yet find ways of establishing an era of social happiness – one in which individuals flourish by living well together in really good societies. The social sciences, however, have yet to find a common language for talking intelligently about social goods in aspirational terms.

If you wanted to identify a tipping-point on the road to modernity, it was Francis Hutcheson's recommendation that 'the greatest happiness of the greatest number' (Hutcheson, 1725) should be the criterion for moral decisions. To be sure, other social goals proved hard to unseat such as the alleviation of harms (removing want, fighting crime). But the happiness principle was in the forefront of European and North American social philosophy for nearly two centuries until it was suppressed by the unashamed miserabilism of 20th-century social research.

By highlighting the moral centrality of happiness, Hutcheson also paved the way for a uniquely novel universalistic and democratic approach to social improvement. Since humans value happiness and the happiness of other people, here was a platform for global collaboration. Yet, scholars and social leaders will often continue to be distracted by other concerns. But today we are at last seeing the fruit of the Enlightenment with global agreement that good governments and societies facilitate happiness, and that good scholars research how to live well.

Figure 2.1: Ngram Viewer: 'moral progress'

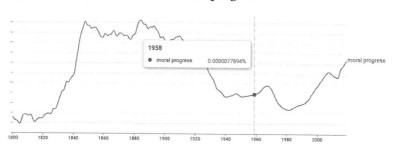

According to Google's Ngram Viewer, 2020 marks the centenary of a 100-year steep decline in interest in moral progress in Anglophone countries, and the bi-centenary of the initial steep increase that began in 1820.[1]

If we use the Ngram Viewer to compare interest in moral progress with interest in various other kinds of progress, we can see that moral and social progress received declining attention from 1920, whereas interest in cultural progress continued to rise until the 1940s, and interest in scientific, economic, and technical progress continued to rise until the 1960s before all of these declined too. In modern Anglophone countries, faith in progress in our *ultimate* values were damaged by the two world wars, whereas faith in *instrumental* progress survived until the challenges of the 1960s and 1970s.

But the Ngram Viewer also tells us something even more unsettling: throughout most of that 200-year period – an age of quite astonishing progress worldwide in most of the goods and social qualities that humans have reason to value (longevity, health, democracy, freedom, education, equality, opportunity, peace, technical capabilities) – we see a steady decline in interest in happiness, truth, justice, beauty, virtue, and wisdom. Perhaps it's just that we take them more for granted. Also, these concerns seem too aspirational and holistic for an age in which people attend to more mundane and pathological concerns.

If we do want to rekindle scholarly and public interest in happiness and social quality, then our purposes must have something to do with moral progress. Yet that term has fallen surprisingly out of favour as the social sciences lag behind the business world and concepts of 'corporate social responsibility', 'business ethics' and 'values–driven business' (Cohen and Warwick, 2008; Painter et al, 2018). For academics, 'research ethics' are still precautionary – about avoiding harms in the research process (Wiles, 2013).

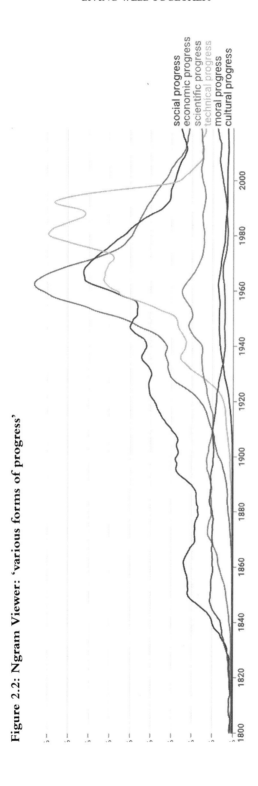

Figure 2.2: Ngram Viewer: 'various forms of progress'

Figure 2.3: Ngram Viewer: 'truth, justice etc'

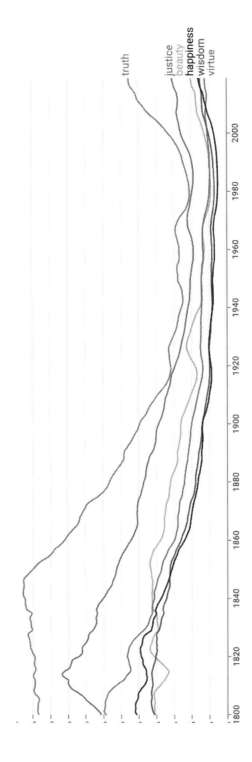

Happiness concerns take us to the heart of what moral debates are ultimately for. Unfortunately, the neglect of happiness is still the norm rather than the exception in scholarly and public ethical debate. As more social scientists study happiness, we can look forward to linking social research with moral compasses. But what is it that makes moral discourse so weak and so constrained in social science and public discourse?

Orwell points the way. Were you to replace the word 'socialists' with 'sociologists' in Orwell's quote cited earlier, the gist of the message would remain valid. Too many sociologists restrict their moral gaze to pathological and remedial concerns. They look below what we might as well call the 'OK line', below the level at which individual lives and social qualities become acceptable, to understand things that go wrong with society. Scholars are remarkably reluctant to acknowledge or appreciate things that go right. Sociologists have made little progress towards enriching understanding of human happiness, or social goods. As it was in Orwell's day, the discipline is inspired by cultural pessimism and victimology. It remains mired in declinist worries, remedialisms and social antagonisms. We need to go back to the early Enlightenment to rediscover the happiness focus that eventually led to sociology (Thin, 2014).

Happiness and genuinely 'progressive' sociology

Whereas in the UK all political parties call themselves 'progressive', in the US it can mean the opposite. Conservatives use this as a term of abuse, disparaging 'woke' culture, 'political correctness' and virtue-signalling. What they usually mean is that 'progressive' policies and practices make society worse, not better. I am going to assume that even if you do not identify as politically progressive, you do believe in both the possibility and the desirability of some forms of significantly benign social change. But what does 'social progress' mean to you?

Usually it means removing poverty, fighting for justice, reducing violence and hate, or upholding human rights. All of these can be about making societies better. Yet they all indicate constrained visions of society. Their gaze is too pathological, their aspirational horizon too modest; shouldn't we be fostering social goods like empathy, kindness, and conviviality? Their gaze is also unrealistic – is it possible or desirable to eliminate all deprivations, offences and inequalities?

By reviewing uses of the term 'progressive' over the past century, we can establish a better way of understanding it today that avoids pathologism. In the past there were a variety of positive uses of 'progressive':

- **Aspirational, utopian:** envisaging future happiness
- **Cumulative improvement:** building on new knowledge, learning from successes and failures
- **Innovative and creative:** progressive science, progressive music, progressive art, progressive business
- **Anti-tradition:** modernizing, progressive religion, schooling, peace and reconciliation; reforming state institutions

Of these senses, only the first points inspirationally towards a wonderful world. The rest are either ethically neutral, or about instrumental goods or about fighting perceived harms. In order to become more articulate about 'progress', we could benefit from a simple analytical model, based on two distinctions:

- Progress that happens below an 'OK line', versus progress that happens above it.
- Means versus ends.

The first is a distinction between 'negative' (or 'protective') avoidance goals and 'positive' approach goals. Avoiding miseries, coping better with them, or preventing them are all forms of progress, but they are minimalist rather than aspirational. Making progress below the OK line tends to be more urgent and more morally compelling. Global progress since the 1950s in reducing poverty, warfare and disease has been an unprecedented success. But should we really be restricting our aspirational horizon to a line of minimal acceptability? Surely we want to know not only that most people are eating well and surviving, but also living well in good societies?

The second is a distinction between progress towards instrumental goods (providing people with the means to pursue a good life) and progress towards ultimate or intrinsic goods (people actually living better). You can imagine a world with excellent systems with high-quality goods and services, but where this has not led to flourishing. Although people might still use the misleading term 'high living standards' to describe those conditions, it would be clear that the population wasn't actually living well. What humans ultimately value is mainly mental (enjoying life, having purpose or growth) and relational (living well with other people and nature).

Figure 2.4: 'Four kinds of progress'

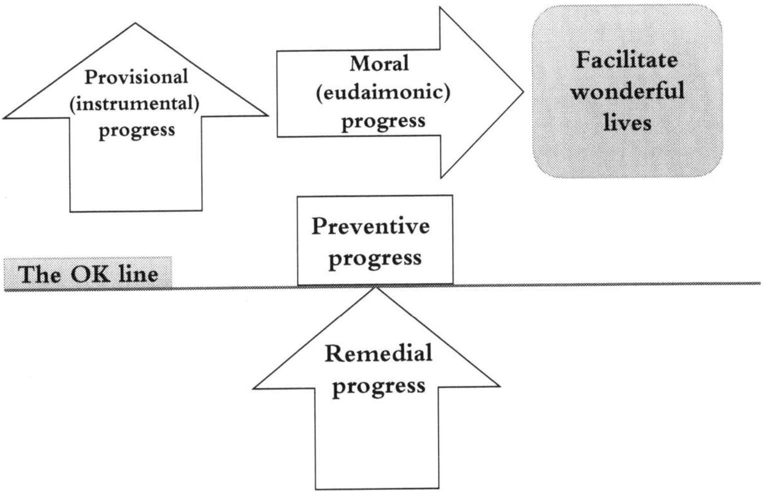

Figure 2.4 provides an analytical model for different kinds of progress that planners might focus on. The vertical axis depicts movements from bad to good, and the horizontal axis represents shifts of attention from means to ends, or from living conditions to the quality of life. The 'OK line' represents a concept of minimal adequacy, below which people suffer deficits and harms. Thinking about dividing lines is an important and effective way of distinguishing pathological and remedial thinking from appreciative and aspirational thinking.

Remedial progress happens when people make successful efforts to mitigate those harms. In anticipating harms, societies plan protective measures. A second kind of progress is *preventive progress*, which would include things like preventive health measures, crime prevention, and war prevention.

As economies grow, and people escape poverty, increased productivity and provision of services becomes the main category of progress. This is more aspirational, yet may not translate into good lives. So we can call this general category *provisional progress* but 'provisional' includes the double meaning of providing goods and being an intermediate step towards wellbeing. Provisional progress is about resources, services, social arrangements, and efficiencies.

Our ultimate aim is to bring about happiness and social flourishing, and if this is achieved, then we can confidently describe it as *moral progress* (happiness scholars might want to call it 'Eudaimonic progress' (Tomer, 2011; Vitterso, 2016). Happiness scholars have made great strides in conceptualization and measurement of self-reported happiness and life satisfaction, meaning, and satisfactions with specific domains and activities. Yet there has been little progress in the measurement or analysis of positive social qualities. In the next two sections, we will explore this challenge and consider what might be done about it.

Social progress in public rhetoric

Although most social scientists doubtless think of themselves and their disciplines as 'progressive', attention to the meanings around progress have been piecemeal and half-hearted, and strongly biased towards remedial rather than aspirational challenges. Social science seems a lot more enthusiastic about studying and dismantling social harms than about appreciating and fostering social goods.

Since you're currently reading a text on social happiness, I assume you are interested in people living well, and the issue of social qualities. Few social researchers or social planners even get that far. Worse, many who claim to be 'progressive' confuse this notion with a lazy sense of belonging on the 'left wing' of the political spectrum, and being 'caring' and 'egalitarian'. Even Joseph Stiglitz (2019), the distinguished economist who has done much to promote happiness research, explores progress in antithetical and remedial terms rather than the aspirational; capitalism becomes 'progressive', in this view, mainly by reducing the inequality, instability, unemployment, crime, pollution, and corruption.

My aim is to rescue the concept of 'progressiveness' from shallow virtue signalling. I wish to empower people to articulate an evaluative concept of moral progress that is plausible and inspirational. Concepts of social goods, and visions of social progress, need to be rational, and constructive, providing a universalistic basis for intercultural cooperation. However, notions of social progress are often problematic as I now illustrate.

In the UK, a 'Progressive Alliance', led by the Compass Organization, offers an explicit vision of a 'good society'. They explored a variety of abstract labels for social goods (pluralism, liberty, egalitarianism, culture of citizenship), settling on three: *equality*, *democracy*, and *sustainability* (Compass, 2018). There is a astonishing lack of ambition in this vision. Equality and democracy are both instrumental values – good insofar as they help people live better, but not good in themselves. Sustainability doesn't even have instrumental value; it's essentially a practical question rather than a value. If anything is valuable, we should ask ourselves how long will it last, and whether our use of it may impact on other people's use of it in future. So this triad of values fails to offer any serious vision for social progress at all.

This is a curiously inadequate but not usual example of work from seasoned politicians, academics and journalists, all of whom genuinely want to enhance how we live. Something is inhibiting their ability to articulate a 'vision' of genuine social progress involving happy, loving, engaged human beings. There is more substance to the Alliance's 2016 essay collection, 'The Alternative: Towards a New Progressive Politics'. There are statements about what 'progressive' people have in common: building 'better systems' offering 'equality', 'inclusion' and social justice, civil liberties, human rights and responsibilities; progressives are 'radicals' reimagining society, fighting social isolation and environmental degradation, redistributing power and wealth, and resisting 'the politics of fear and division'. Even here, however, the discussion focuses on fighting, mending, and producing vaguely instrumental goods like wealth and freedom.

Turning now to a very much larger effort to define social progress for the whole world, the United Nations Sustainable Development Goals (SDGs), finalized in 2015, initially appears more aspirational and complex than the earlier Millennium Development Goals (MDGs). As the United Nations agreed in 2011 Resolution 65/ 309: 'Happiness: towards a holistic approach to development', we would expect the SDGs to reflect this aspiration. But do the SDGs show more interest in happiness or flourishing than the MDGs?

Certainly, the SDGs are more thematically comprehensive than the MDGs, with 17 goals, 169 targets, and more than 300 indicators. They are more ambitious in their diversity, aiming above the 'OK line' (Costanza et al, 2016; Thin, 2016; Iriarte and Musikanski, 2019). The MDGs were designed to inspire and describe remedial progress achieved by people in poorer countries. In contrast, the SDGs have been drafted for all of humanity, and although roughly half of them are about remedial or preventive action, there are several which in theory could be used to promote and monitor much more aspirational social progress.

Many of the goals and targets, understandably, do focus on minimizing human suffering and ending poverty, hunger, and avoidable illness (goals 1, 2, 3, 5, 8, and 11). Others are about minimizing planetary harms to stabilize climate and protect oceans, terrestrial ecosystems, and biodiversity (goals 12, 13, 14, and 15). But there are also several goals that seem more aspirational, looking at life above the OK line. Goals 6, 7, 9, and 11 are about better provision of resources and infrastructure. But most importantly here are those that aim at positive social qualities: lifelong learning, peace, social inclusion, justice, cooperation, and decent work and sustainable production and consumption (goals 4, 5, 7, 8,10, 16, and 17).

The indicators for monitoring the two goals directly relevant to happiness and social flourishing are Goal 3 ('health and wellbeing') that implies that wellbeing, (which logically includes happiness), is not the same as health. One can hope that behind the selection of this two-part label there were genuine intentions to promote interest in examining how well people live, not just whether their bodies are free from disease and impairments. Sadly, as is so often the case with health agency rhetoric, the 'and wellbeing' part has not been taken seriously. There are no proposed targets or indicators for this goal that are linked to wellbeing in a positive sense but instead are concerned with diseases and ailments.

The most overtly 'social' goal is Goal 16 ('Peace, justice, and strong institutions'). Unlike the 'wellbeing' Goal, there is little pretence in the Goal title about getting beyond remedial and preventive progress. Hence, the targets and indicators are either remedial (reduce violence, trafficking, corruption) or preventive (restrict global arms trade, improve legal institutions), although some (rule of law, access to justice, accountable institutions, participatory decision-making) do blend into the provision of instrumental social goods.

This last category, participation, could potentially refer to intrinsically valuable social goods, since active, benign, and interested social engagement is what it means to live well together with other people. But it is clear from the indicators that monitoring will be mainly designed to look at basic functionality of participatory process, and not at outcomes in terms of enhanced lives. It is similarly clear from the biennial *Report on the World Social Situation* by the UN Department of Economic and Social Affairs (UN-DESA, 2018) that the UN has no appetite for considering social progress aspirationally. These reports also focus on social pathologies and remedial action for disadvantaged minorities rather than aspirational social progress.

Although these are just two brief sketches of rhetoric on progress, similarly restrictive thinking is ubiquitous among nations, civil society organizations and 'progressive' businesses. This is not a criticism of their efficacy, just a recognition there widespread reluctance or inability to systematically consider positive social quality that we – as private individuals – know is crucial for personal and social flourishing.

If we wish to assemble a more persuasive, informative, inspirational platform for 'progressive' political action we must change the script.

We must make positive visions of a better world more explicit. To find ways of talking about how personal happiness and positive social qualities are mutually supportive. Electoral tactics, fighting harms and producing instrumental goods are still important. But these would be secondary to conversation about what we really care about.

Social qualities: more than an absence of pathology?

The World Health Organization famously declared, in 1947, that its conception of 'health' was 'more than an absence of disease'. As if this idea wasn't ambitious enough, it also declared that health meant 'a state of complete wellbeing'. More than seven decades later, people are still talking about this aspirational rhetoric as if it served as a meaningful philosophical guide, and yet no-one has succeeded in clarifying either what the 'more than an absence' means in practical or policy terms, or what wellbeing might look like if it were 'complete'.

Perhaps it just really was the case, all along, that the pursuit of health is and always will be mainly an avoidance goal, not an aspirational 'approach goal'. Certainly, this is how the term has always been used in English.

Still, the fact that public health commentators have tended not to reject these ideas outright implies that they have fulfilled some useful function in persuading people to consider health-related policies in more positive terms. Have we seen versions of this in social policy? It must be admitted that above-the-OK-line positivity is extremely rare in sociological and social policy discourse. Consider the following questions we might reasonably ask of most of the major categories of social goals:

- Is 'welfare' more than protection against poverty and illness?
- Are 'human rights' more than an absence of wrongs?
- Is 'social justice' more than an absence of injustice?
- Is 'equality' more than an absence of inequality?
- Is 'freedom' more than an absence of constraint?
- Is 'democracy' more than an absence of unfair governance?
- Are 'peace' and 'security' more than an absence of war and violence?
- Are 'diversity', 'tolerance', and 'multiculturalism' more than an absence of cultural chauvinism?
- Is 'social inclusion' more than an absence of exclusion?
- Is 'sustainable development' more than an absence of unsustainability and environmental harm?
- Is 'social trust' more than the absence of suspicion?

First, if these questions have rarely been asked, we must conclude that social researchers and planners have been even less concerned with wellbeing and positive social qualities than health planners have. Second, if the answer to all or most of these questions is 'no' (Spicker, 2014), then we must admit to ourselves that this set of collective social ambitions is largely concerned with remedial or at best preventive policies and actions. This doesn't mean, of course, that these social goals are worthless. But unless we believe that most of humanity still lives in a world utterly dominated by social pathologies, then it looks as if the 'social' dimensions of happiness need to be made a lot clearer and a lot more salient in research and in policy.

So if we were to try to come up with more aspirational, positive categories of social goods, what labels and indicators might we use? We would need concepts that can genuinely be understood to be part of what it means to live well together. Ironically, the most positive social quality label is probably 'conviviality', which on the face of it is a purely neutral term. Although etymologically it translates simply as 'living together', in practice this term tends to be understood more positively as 'living *well* together'. This is certainly the sense conveyed when, for example, people refer to an occasion or a place as 'convivial' (Shaftoe, 2008). It is the sense of the French movement for 'convivialité', which promotes socially innovative ways of overturning the loneliness and alienation of modernity, replacing these with ways of living that open everyone up to multiple forms of benign social contact with other people (Caillé, 2013; Les Convivialistes, 2019). It was also the sense conveyed by several of the papers in an anthropological collection on conviviality in Amazonia (Overing and Passes, 2000).

But conviviality is also, perhaps more commonly, used by sociologists as a rubric for exploring the *difficulties* of living together. For example, a recent book about online conviviality is actually all about giving and taking offence (Tagg et al, 2017). Paul Gilroy's book about 'convivial culture' is mainly about racism. At the start he makes clear that in his usage 'conviviality ... does not describe the absence of racism or the triumph of tolerance. Instead, it suggests a different setting for their empty, interpersonal rituals' (Gilroy, 2004: xi–xii). Inspired by his social pathologism, two recent collections of sociological essays on 'conviviality' are actually all about the difficulties and opposition faced by immigrant communities (Burchardt and Michalowski, 2015; Wise and Noble, 2017). The latter editors say they prefer the Spanish term *convivencia*, because it 'doesn't infer [sic] happy, festive, fun togetherness' (Wise and Noble, 2017: 203). It sometimes seems as if sociologists feel

Table 2.1: Remedial versus aspirational social planning

Pathological, remedial and defensive concerns	Appreciative interests and aspirations
Welfare, poverty reduction, social protection	Social cohesion, harmony, kindness, belonging
Human rights, justice, equality	Social participation, responsibilities, opportunities, social mobility
Freedom from constraint	Freedom to achieve and innovate
Democracy	Civic engagement/participation; employee engagement
Peace, security, safety	Prosocial support, love, friendliness, neighbourliness
Inclusion, tolerance, diversity, multiculturalism	Conviviality, belonging, intercultural empathy
Sustainability, environmental protection	Sustainable wellbeing, environmental enhancement

obliged to refer to conviviality, but are worried that their reputations might be damaged if they show interest in anything so trivial as people getting along well and enjoying themselves.

If we examine Table 2.1, the right-hand column is just a small selection of terms we use to discuss social goods. Given the failure of sociology to discuss social qualities in aspirational terms, we must acknowledge the practical challenges facing attempts to develop a more appreciative and aspirational social science. In particular:

- Can we specify categories of positive social goods that are broad and flexible enough to attract universal interest without being vague or meaningless?
- Can we specify indicators for categories of social goods that are measurable and amenable to qualitative evaluation?
- Qualitative research on social goods must be local and specific to provide detailed descriptions and narratives, but how can we extrapolate and generalize from these studies to have wider relevance?

From the early 1990s there emerged non-pathological social research on the theme of 'social capital', collaborative capabilities, and trust (Putnam, 1993; Fukuyama, 1995; Helliwell, 2001). This made important steps towards depathologizing applied social research, particularly in the fields of international development, urban planning, business studies, and community studies. Referring to our 'progress' model, this research was appreciative as it looked above the 'OK line', but tended to be restricted to provisional forms of social good. The term 'social capital', like related concepts such as 'human capital' and 'human resources', explicitly instrumentalizes people and relationships, treating them as good as they facilitate other values such as productivity (Pierce et al, 2016), profit (Ng et al, 2015), or health (Nyqvist and Forsman, 2015; Folland and Nauenberg, 2018). 'Social quality' research, too, instrumentalizes positive social qualities by treating them as potential causes of other values such as productivity and academic performance (Dijkstra et al, 2018).

Remarkably little of the research literature on social capital explicitly recognizes social relationships as intrinsically good. Even when explicitly linked to happiness, social capital research treats the bonds between people as a means to an end – as a way of becoming happy, rather than as a constitutive part of the good life (Bartolini et al, 2016; Munzel et al, 2018; Helliwell et al, 2018). It may be that researchers who observe the way that happiness is shaped by social relations also think of these relations as a dimension of happiness. But prospects for appreciative social research would be enhanced if positive social relationships were de-instrumentalized, recognizing them as constitutive of happiness (Pena-Lopez et al, 2017).

But we can take heart from recent developments in appreciative enquiry (Whitney et al, 2002; Lewis, 2016); positive organizational scholarship (Cameron et al, 2003; Cameron and McNaughtan, 2014; Ferreira Vasconcelos, 2018; Redelinghuys et al, 2019), positive school climate (Cohen, 2013; Sibnath, 2019), and kindness (Hamrick, 2002; Brownlie and Anderson, 2017; Wallace and Thurman, 2018; Unwin, 2018; Cotney and Banerjee, 2019). These researchers see social goods as intrinsically valuable and interesting, a part of what makes life go well. The focus is not on avoiding harms, or simply on promoting instrumental goods, but rather on more aspirational promotion of things that have intrinsic value.

Confirmatory versus disruptive uses of the 'happiness lens'

Would you say it was 'left-wing' or 'right-wing' to argue for greater salience for happiness in policy discourse or ethical debate? Or, if you're North American, is happiness a 'liberal' thing, or 'progressive', or maybe 'Conservative'? When one takes these questions seriously, one recognizes the disruptiveness of the happiness lens comes from its ability to undermine naïve political polarizations. The happiness lens disrupts traditional political oppositions and cultural parochialisms, by drawing attention to common agreements on what we all hope for – happy societies that respect and support diverse ways of pursuing the good life. It disrupts evaluative procedures by offering a radically democratic way of assessing social progress: asking people how they feel and evaluate their lives (Unanue, 2017). By adopting happiness as our focal interest, we learn to evaluate societies and policies not only by aesthetic criteria and resource distribution, but also through what people enjoy and how well they live together.

If you associate 'left-wing' or 'progressive' or 'liberal' politics with egalitarianism, you might look to happiness research to support justification for egalitarian reform. If you're in favour of redistributive policies you might, like Richard Layard (2006), hope that higher taxes would benefit poor people at little hedonic cost to richer people. You might also hope that by discouraging status-related conspicuous consumption, overwork and greed, you can make benign contributions to social quality by reducing the drivers of envy (Lane, 2000; Kasser, 2002). You might also bolster public support for redistributive welfarism by showing positive correlations between happiness and the generosity of governments (Radcliff, 2013).

In using happiness to challenge naïve beliefs about the value of economic growth and wealth, these authors believe they use happiness research disruptively. It may well be that happiness research exerts benign social influence by making wealthier people more generous towards poorer people, by highlighting the dangers of greed and toxicity of status display. Yet too often these authors confirm and justifying their pre-existing political and moral beliefs. This is all too easily achieved through the selective use of research data.

The research evidence, however, on happiness and financial inequality and welfare state generosity is highly variable. Money does bring diminishing returns, but it correlates positively with happiness all the way up the wealth spectrum (Wolfers and Stevenson, 2013; Lindqvist et al, 2018). It may be that financial inequality is bad for European happiness but not in less egalitarian societies (Delhey and Dragolov, 2014). Although evidence suggests progressive taxation can make poorer people happier in rich countries (Oishi and Diener, 2014; Oishi, Kushlev, and Schimmack, 2018), there is also considerable evidence that welfare state generosity and 'progressive' taxation does not necessarily make populations happier, due to unintended effects like crowding out private effort, reducing freedom, and slowing economic growth (Veenhoven, 2000; MacCulloch, 2018). A more disruptive consequence of happiness research might be instead of levying high taxes to reduce envy (Layard's prescription), we might consider better educating people to not envy the rich and their lifestyles (Wilkinson, 2006).

For egalitarians, the more genuinely disruptive influence of a happiness lens comes from shifting our attention from means to ends, from resources (as indicated by proxies such as income and wealth) to valued outcomes (life satisfaction or happiness). Moral egalitarians, rather than resource egalitarians, do keep unequal resource distribution in perspective, focusing more on people's beliefs about inequalities than on the issue of unequal access to resources.

A different logical conclusion from the evidence of diminishing returns is the 'sufficientarian' argument – namely, we should worry less about financial inequalities above a relatively modest, 'sufficient' level of income (Frankfurt, 2015; Deveaux, 2018). Just as there are diminishing returns to increased income for individuals, so too there are likely to be diminishing social benefits from redistribution of money beyond that needed to reduce poverty. The focus instead should be on the inequalities of power, opportunity and capability that matter more for happiness. Once our gaze shifts to happiness outcomes, we should favour social outcomes that spread happiness more evenly, provided that we can do so without lowering average happiness. This makes sense in principle, but once again the crucial empirical test is actual influence on happiness. Despite 'objectively' mattering less, financial inequalities between moderately and very well-off people may still matter if they damage self-esteem and social quality. An example of the happiness lens is provided by the economist Carol Graham. She shows how increasing prosperity gaps in the US really do matter because they are linked to an 'optimism gap', creating a generation whose beliefs, hopes, and aspirations are suffering long-term damage, which is undermining overall social quality in the US (Graham, 2017).

So here's the disruptive challenge posed by the introduction of a happiness lens into social and political discourse: if your approach to ethics is purely negative, or purely remedial, or purely protective, or purely instrumental, it isn't really ethical is it? Ethics can only be both honestly transparent and morally benign if a happiness lens is involved. If anyone engages you on an ethical matter, advocating 'progress', check if they have some theory about how people's lives get better. Also explore if their happiness theory attends to positive social qualities, rather than considering the happiness of individuals.

Happiness research and moral progress

No serious scholar of happiness could fail to recognize its social embeddedness (Fitzpatrick, 2018; Helliwell et al, 2018; Appau et al, 2019). Although qualitative social researchers have been slow to develop happiness scholarship, psychologists, quantitative sociologists, and economists have explored how happiness is influenced by social factors. It is much less clear, however, whether they have grasped how happiness is socially *constituted*, rather than merely 'influenced' by social factors. Societal happiness is more than the mere sum of individuals' happiness (Sirgy, 2011; Spicker, 2014). But how can we make sense of and use the concept of 'social happiness', if people think happiness is something that happens in the heads of individuals?

There are two main ways to think of happiness as socially constituted: from a first-person perspective, and from a sociological perspective. From a first-person perspective, social life and social qualities are part of what we understand by living well, so we must appreciate these as social components of happiness and not just extraneous causes. When we act in 'prosocial' ways we know we aren't simply being 'altruistic', because we appreciate that society is a part of us.

From the sociological perspective, observing society, we recognize happiness as a loose term that people use to describe individual flourishing and also more widely as positive social qualities. The elusive entity that we call 'happiness' seems to 'happen' not only inside people's heads but in the social atmosphere, through social movements, culturally scripted occasions, places, and particular kinds of organization. The 'happiness' of a festival, or of a pub, a good school or business is not an aggregate of the happiness of the individuals who participate in these social entities but an emergent property of them.

'Social issues', therefore, are not just causes of happiness among others such as money, nutrition, and cleanliness. Research on wellbeing recognizes that self-transcendence – the ability to understand and feel strong connections between ourselves and our social and physical environment – is crucial to a mature sense of living well (Koltko-Rivera, 2006; Elzanowski, 2013; Frey and Vogler, 2018). Happiness means living well not just in the mind, but in the body, in society, and in the environment. When people use the term 'spiritual wellbeing', they are waving in a vague sense towards this idea of connectedness or joined-up, non-individualistic wellbeing.

When people think about their lives going well or badly, not only do they think about whether they live in a good society, but also their ability to appreciate their own happiness is itself culturally and socially facilitated. This happens through cultural scripts, concepts and key terms; through relationships with socially significant others; and through social institutions and events (Umanath and Berntsen, 2013; Koppel and Berntsen, 2014).

'Conviviality', as the collective disposition and ability to live well together, is probably our best term for the social qualities that enable happiness (Overing and Passes, 2000; Shaftoe, 2008; Caillé, 2013). Yet the treatment of 'sociocultural factors' in wellbeing research continues to be problematic as it treats these as external causes rather than as constituents of the good life. The potential for a social happiness and of notions like conviviality are also hindered by a culture and society that are overwhelmingly concerned with social pathologies.

Conclusions

For the social researcher, perhaps the most life-changing advantage of adopting a happiness lens is that it can help you shake off your disapproval addiction. If you work in the social sciences, you are complicit in institutionalized pathologism. You may sometimes study wellbeing or look at relatively neutral social phenomena, but this will not be true of most of your colleagues. The courses your students take and the textbooks and journals they read assumes that what is interesting about society is its rottenness, not its decency or its joys. When your students choose their dissertation topics, will a majority of them choose topics like love, awe, flow, friendliness, cooperation, fun, or happiness? Some may, most will not.

The academic disciplines established to study society, originally for the purpose of promoting happiness, have learned to treat social phenomena with suspicion or disdain. Distracted by obsessive attention to the ills of modernity, throughout the 20th century these disciplines looked mainly at troubles and harms. In a century of dramatic ups and downs, the second half was for most an astonishingly wonderful five decades of social progress, and still most social researchers cling to their cultural declinist dogmas. No doubt in their private lives, they enjoyed the fruits of social progress, yet they learned that it would not advance their careers if they chose to admire and cherish social goods.

When we study cultural differences, we are more likely to be looking at racism, ageism, and intolerance than appreciating the joys of diversity. When we study gender, we are more likely to be looking at segregation, stigma, sexism, and inequalities than to appreciate gender progress or the fascination of gender differences. When we study businesses and workplaces, we more likely explore strains, exploitations, and sufferings than to appreciate work as an interesting and satisfying way of spending time, not just an act of self-sacrifice in exchange for money.

By deliberately trying to adopt a happiness lens in order to learn about social goods in more appreciative ways, you won't of course need to give up on disapproval altogether. The happiness lens is a move towards rationality, balance, and ethical transparency, not a denial of the many evils of the world. It is a recognition that if our mission as social researchers is to make a benign difference in the world, we must appreciate how people and societies improve and learn if we are to investigate and debate those improvements more explicitly.

Note
[1] Google's Ngram Viewer is available at books.google.com/ngrams. It provides instant visualization of the relative frequency of words or phrases in the several million books in Google's archive. Although it is possible to narrow searches to shorter time periods and/or to books in US or British English, the searches presented here are all based on Anglophone books. Users interested in the numerical frequencies can check these for themselves, but the illustrations here are only intended to show trends in relative frequency.

References
Appau, S., Churchill, S. and Farrell, L. (2019) 'Social integration and subjective wellbeing', *Applied Economics*, 51(16): 1748–61.

Bartolini, S., Bilancini, E. and Sarracino, F. (2016) 'Social capital predicts happiness over time', in S. Bartolini, E. Bilancini and F. Sarracino (eds) *Policies for Happiness*, Oxford: Oxford University Press.

Brownlie, J. and Anderson, S. (2017) 'Thinking sociologically about kindness', *Sociology*, 51(6): 1222–38.

Burchardt, M. and Ines, M. (eds) (2015) *After Integration: Islam, Conviviality and Contentious Politics in Europe*, Dordrecht: Springer.

Caillé, A. (2013) *Manifeste Convivialiste: Declaration d'Interdependence*, Lormont, France: Editions Le Bord de l'eau.

Cameron, K., Dutton, J. and Quinn, R. (2003) *Positive Organizational Scholarship: Foundations of a New Discipline*, San Francisco: Berrett-Koehler.

Cameron, K. and McNaughtan, J. (2014) 'Positive organizational change', *Journal of Applied Behavioral Sciences*, 50(4): 445–62.

Cohen, B. and Warwick, M. (2008) *Values-Driven Business: How to Change the World, Make Money, and Have Fun*, San Francisco, CA: Berrett-Koehler.

Cohen, J. (2013) 'Creating a positive school climate: a foundation for resilience', *Handbook of Resilience in Children* (2nd edn), Dordrecht: Springer, pp 411–26.

Compass (2018) *The Common Platform: An Inquiry into a Good Society*, London: Compass. https://www.compassonline.org.uk/wp-content/uploads/2019/03/Compass_AnnualReport2018.pdf

Costanza, R., Daly, L., Fioramanti, L., Giovannini, E., Kubiszewski, I., Fogh Mortensen, L., Pickett, K., Vala Ragnarsdottir, K., De Vogli, R. and Wilkinson, R. (2016) 'Modelling and measuring sustainable wellbeing in connection with the UN Sustainable Development Goals', *Ecological Economics*, 130: 350–5.

Cotney, J. and Banerjee, R. (2019) 'Adolescents' conceptualisations of kindness and its links with well-being: a focus group study', *Journal of Social and Personal Relationships*, 36(2): 599–617.

Delhey, J. and Dragolov, G. (2014) 'Why inequality makes Europeans less happy: the role of distrust, status anxiety, and perceived conflict', *European Sociological Review*, 30(2): 151–65.

Deveaux, M. (2018) 'Re-evaluating sufficientarianism in light of evidence of inequality's harms', *Ethics and Social Welfare*, 12(2): 97–116.

Dijkstra, A., Daas, R., De la Motte, P. and Ehren, M. (2018) 'Inspecting school social quality: assessing and improving school effectiveness in the social domain', *Journal of Social Science Education*, 16(4): 75–84.

Elzanowski, A. (2013) 'Moral progress: a present-day perspective on the leading Enlightenement idea', *Argument*, 3(1): 9–26.

Ferreira Vasconcelos, A. (2018) 'Positive organizational scholarship concept: an overview and future studies', *Revista Eletrônica de Administração*, 24(1): 85–128.

Fitzpatrick, T. (2018) *How to Live Well: Epicurus as a Guide to Contemporary Social Reform*, Cheltenham, UK: Edward Elgar.

Folland, S. and Nauenberg E. (eds) (2018) *Elgar Companion to Social Capital and Health*, Chichester, UK: Edward Elgar.

Frankfurt, H. (2015) *On Inequality*, Princeton, NJ: Princeton University Press.

Frey, J. and Vogler, C. (2018) *Self-Transcendence and Virtue: Perspectives from Philosophy, Psychology, and Theology*, London: Routledge.

Fukuyama, F. (1995) *Trust: The Social Virtues and the Creation of Prosperity*, New York: Free Press.

Gilroy, P. (2004) *After Empire: Melancholia or Convivial Culture?* London: Routledge.

Graham, C. (2017) *Happiness for All? Unequal Hopes and Lives in Pursuit of the American Dream*, Princeton, NJ: Princeton University Press.

Hamrick, W. (2002) *Kindness and the Good Society: Connections of the Heart*, New York: State University of New York Press.

Helliwell, J. (ed) (2001) *The Contribution of Human and Social Capital to Sustained Economic Growth and Well-Being*, Ottawa: Human Resources Development Canada and the OECD.

Helliwell, J., Aknin, L., Shiplett, H., Huang, H. and Wang, S. (2018) 'Social capital and prosocial behaviour as sources of well-being', in E. Diener, S. Oishi, and L. Tay (eds) *Handbook of Well-Being*, Salt Lake City, UT: DEF Publishers.

Hutcheson, F. (1725) *Inquiry into the Original of our Ideas of Beauty and Virtue*, Indianapolis, IN: Liberty Fund, https://oll.libertyfund.org/quotes/426

Iriarte, L. and Musikanski, L. (2019) 'Bridging the gap between the sustainable development goals and happiness metrics', *International Journal of Community Well-Being*, 1: 115–35.

Johnson, M. (2013) *Evaluating Culture: Wellbeing, Institutions and Circumstance*, London, UK: Palgrave Macmillan.

Kasser, T. (2002) *The High Price of Materialism*, Cambridge, MA and London: MIT Press.

Koltko-Rivera, M. (2006) 'Rediscovering the later version of Maslow's hierarchy of needs: self-transcendence and opportunities for theory, research, and unification', *Review of General Psychology*, 10(4): 302–17.

Koppel, J. and Berntsen, D. (2014) 'The cultural life script as cognitive schema: how the life script shapes memory for fictional life stories', *Memory*, 22(8): 949–71.

Korn, R. and Elliot, A. (2015) 'Avoidance and approach motivation: a brief history', in J. Wright (ed) *International Encyclopedia of the Social & Behavioral Sciences* (2nd edn), Amsterdam: Elsevier, pp 326–31.

Lane, R. (2000) *The Loss of Happiness in Market Democracies*, New Haven, CT: Yale University Press.

Layard, R. (2006) 'Happiness and public policy: a challenge to the profession', *The Economic Journal*, 116: C24–33.

Les Convivialistes (2019) *Why the World Needs Convivialité*, http://www.lesconvivialistes.org

Lewis, S. (2016) *Positive Psychology and Change: How Leadership, Collaboration, and Appreciative Inquiry Create Transformational Results*, Hoboken, NJ: Wiley.

Lindqvist, E., Östling, R. and Cesarini, D. (2018) 'Long-run effects of lottery wealth on psychological well-being', NBER *National Bureau of Economic Research*, Working Paper 24667.

MacCulloch, R. (2018) 'How political systems and social welfare policies affect well-being', in E. Diener, S. Oishi and L. Tay (eds) *Handbook of Well-Being*, Salt Lake City, UT: DEF, DOI: nobascholar. com/chapters/57

Munzel, A., Galan J.-P. and Meyer-Waarden, L. (2018) 'Getting by or getting ahead on social networking sites? The role of social capital in happiness and well-being', *International Journal of Electronic Commerce*, 2: 232–257.

Ng, A., Abbas, M. and Ibrahim, M. (2015) *Social Capital and Risk Sharing: An Islamic Finance Paradigm*, London, UK: Palgrave Macmillan.

Nyqvist, F. and Forsman, A. (eds) (2015) *Social Capital as a Health Resource in Later Life: The Relevance of Context*, Cham: Springer.

Oishi, S. and Diener, E. (2014) 'Can and should happiness be a policy goal?', *Policy Insights from the Behavioral and Brain Sciences*, 1: 195–203.

Oishi, S., Kushlev, K. and Schimmack, U. (2018) 'Progressive taxation, income inequality, and happiness', *American Psychologist*, 73(2): 157–68.

Orwell, G. (1943) 'Why socialists don't believe in fun', http://www.k-1.com/Orwell/site/work/essays/fun.html, first published in *Tribune*, 20 December 1943, under the name of John Freeman.

Overing, J. and Passes, A. (eds) (2000) *The Anthropology of Love and Anger: The Aesthetics of Conviviality in Native Amazonia*, London: Routledge.

Painter, M., Pouryousefi, S. and Hibbert, S. (2018) 'Sharing vocabularies: towards horizontal alignment of values-driven business functions', *Journal of Business Ethics* [advance online], 23 May, https:// link.springer.com/article/10.1007/s10551-018-3901-7

Pena-Lopez, J., Sanchez-Santos, J. and Membiela-Pollan, M. (2017) 'Individual social capital and subjective wellbeing: the relational goods', *Journal of Happiness Studies*, 18(3): 881–901.

Pierce, J., Lovrich, N. and Budd, W. (2016) 'Social capital, institutional performance, and sustainability in Italy's regions: still evidence of enduring historical effects?', *Social Science Journal*, 53(3): 271–81.

Putnam, D. (1993) *Making Democracy Work: Civic Traditions in Modern Italy*, Princeton: Princeton University Press.

Radcliff, B. (2013) *The Political Economy of Human Happiness: How Voters' Choices Determine the Quality of Life*, Cambridge: Cambridge University Press.

Redelinghuys, K., Rothmann, S. and Botha, E. (2019) 'Flourishing-at-work: the role of positive organizational practices', *Psychological Reports* [advance online], 20 February, DOI: 10.1177/0033294118757935

Shaftoe, H. (2008) *Convivial Urban Spaces: Creating Effective Public Spaces*, London: Earthscan.

Sibnath, D. (ed) (2019) *Positive Schooling and Child Development*, Cham: Springer.

Sirgy, J. (2011) 'Societal QOL is More than the Sum of QOL of individuals: the whole is greater than the sum of the parts', *Applied Research in Quality of Life*, 6: 329–34.

Spicker, P. (2014) 'Cohesion, exclusion and social quality', *International Journal of Social Quality*, 4(1): 95–107.

Stiglitz, J. (2019) *People, Power, and Profits: Progressive Capitalism for an Age of Discontent*, New York: Norton.

Tagg, C., Seargeant, P. and Brown, A. (2017) *Taking Offence on Social Media: Conviviality and Communication on Facebook*, Cham: Springer.

Thin, N. (2012) *Social Happiness: Research into Policy and Practice*, Bristol: Policy Press.

Thin, N. (2014) 'Positive sociology and appreciative empathy: history and prospects', *Sociological Research Online*, 19(2): 5, http://www.socresonline.org.uk/19/2/5.html

Thin, N. (2016) 'Social wellbeing: the global happiness epidemic', Public Lecture, University of Edinburgh, https://www.youtube.com/watch?v=fadcDZdK-RE&index=1&list=PL9E20C4BE37DEBC70

Tomer, J. (2011) 'Enduring happiness: integrating the hedonic and eudaimonic approaches', *Journal of Socio-Economics*, 40(5): 530–7.

Umanath, S. and Berntsen, D. (2013) 'Personal life stories: common deviations from the cultural life script', *Nordic Psychology*, 65(2): 87–102.

Unanue, W. (2017) 'Subjective wellbeing measures to inform public policies', in CDS (ed), *Happiness: Transforming the Development Landscape*, Bhutan: Centre for Bhutan Studies, pp 60–79.

United Nations DESA (2018) *Report on the World Social Situation*, New York: UN-DESA.

Unwin, J. (2018) *Kindness, Emotions, and Human Relationships: The Blind Spot in Public Policy*, Dunfermline, UK: Carnegie UK.

Veenhoven, R. (2000) 'Well-being in the welfare state: level not higher, distribution not more equitable', *Journal of Comparative Policy Analysis*, 2: 91–125.

Vittersø, J. (ed) (2016) *Handbook of Eudaimonic Wellbeing*, Dordrecht: Springer.

Wallace, J. and Thurman, B. (2018) *Quantifying Kindness, Collective Action and Place*, Dunfermline: Carnegie UK.

Whitney, D., Cooperrider, D., Trosten-Bloom, A. and Kaplin, B. (2002) *Encyclopedia of Positive Questions, Volume One: Using Appreciative Inquiry to Bring Out the Best in Your Organization*, Euclid, OH: Lakeshore Communications.

Wiles, R. (2013) *What are Qualitative Research Ethics?*, London: Bloomsbury.

Wilkinson, R. and Pickett, K. (2018) *The Inner Level: How More Equal Societies Reduce Stress, Restore Sanity and Improve Everyone's Wellbeing*, London: Allen Lane.

Wilkinson, W. (2006) 'Happiness is ... higher taxes. Is one man's productivity another man's pollution?', *Reason Online*, www.reason.com/news/show/36209

Wise, A. and Noble, G. (2017) *Convivialities: Possibility and Ambivalence in Urban Multicultures*, London: Routledge.

Wolfers, J. and Stevenson, B. (2013) 'Subjective well-being and income: is there any evidence of satiation?', *American Economic Review, Papers and Proceedings*, 101(3): 598–604.

3

Happiness as an Affective Practice: Self, Suffering and Biography

Nicholas Hill

Introduction

There has been a general reluctance on the part of sociology to engage substantively with happiness and the role it plays within people's everyday lives. While some notable exceptions exist (see Hyman, 2014; McKenzie, 2016; Cieslik, 2018), sociology has been suspicious of the topic because of a perceived emphasis within contemporary framings on positive subjective experience, the prioritization of inner potential, and its implication within neoliberal modes of government and the capitalist economy. This chapter argues that as a discipline we must transcend this critical lens because it obscures the socially situated and intersubjective aspects of happiness. By drawing on hermeneutic, interpretivist and phenomenological methods, sociology is well placed to offer an important corrective to the dominant research methods employed by positive psychology and happiness economics that emphasize the measurement of happiness and wellbeing and identification of determinants.

A limitation of quantitative methods used to explore happiness and wellbeing is that they obscure complex accounts of emotions, particularly the movement between and through different subjective experiences, such as emotions, feelings and thoughts, and how emotional experience is embedded in relationships between self and others, and self and world (Burkitt, 2014). Qualitative research methods work differently, drawing attention to ambivalent and contradictory understandings of happiness that are subject to 'interactive and situational variation' (Thin, 2018: 2–3). Interpretivist, phenomenological and hermeneutic informed approaches are, in contrast to positivist methods, better able to work with complex and provisional experiences and perspectives. Within these paradigms, research questions proceed differently. Instead of asking *how happy* a person is, they examine how people *think about*, *understand* and *work* at their happiness (Walker and Kavedžija, 2015; Thin, 2018). The relative lack of attention to people's own views and experiences is surprising since it is 'an experience-near concept' (Thin, 2012: ix), at once banal and yet simultaneously central to people's lives. Given the increasing scientific, policy and popular attention that happiness and wellbeing is receiving, further exploration of people's experiences and understandings of happiness is necessary.

Happiness is interwoven with ideas about the good life and in this way shapes perceptions of good (and happy) lives. A key starting point then is to recognize how happiness and emotional experience more generally are central to the production of self and the subject's evaluation of their place in the world. In what follows, I outline the methods I used to explore people's experiences of pursuing wellbeing through therapeutic and self-help practices framed by the happiness turn (Ahmed, 2010) in Melbourne, Australia for my PhD thesis, *Happiness as a therapeutic quest: the problem of suffering.* I begin by offering some theoretical and methodological reflections on what was a slippery and at times frustrating topic. I then demonstrate the utility of narrative methods for exploring experiences and understandings of happiness using examples from interview data collected as part of my research.

The need for a reparative reading of happiness

The resistance of sociology to researching happiness is traceable to a tradition of critique informed by what Paul Ricoeur (1977) memorably termed 'the hermeneutics of suspicion' that he identified with the work of Marx, Nietzsche and Freud. This disposition has generated a genealogy of theories and methodological approaches within sociology, but also anthropology, cultural studies, and so on that privilege what Eve Kosofsky Sedgwick (2003) terms a *paranoid reading*. Interrogations and explorations of happiness from within sociology and related fields have, for the most part, been conducted through this prism. These readings emphasize the commodification and reification of happiness, the growth of therapeutic and self-help culture, the use of happiness as a contemporary strategy of government and highlight the social and political problem of increasing atomization, depoliticization and narcissism resulting from present framings (see Binkley, 2014; Cabanas and Illouz, 2019; Cederström, 2019; Hill et al, 2020).

These approaches draw attention to significant limitations and highlight troubling currents within the turn to happiness (Ahmed, 2010), but in their rush to critique miss something fundamental. That is, how happiness is actively lived and pursued within the everyday realities of individuals and communities. As Ricoeur (1992: 179) reminds us, the 'good life is for each of us, the nebulous of ideals and dreams of achievements with regard to which a life is held to be more or less fulfilled or unfulfilled'. There is a need for what Sedgwick (2003) terms a *reparative* reading of happiness and the development of methodologies able to achieve this aim, approaches which allow for 'surprise, hope, and creativity.' In otherwords, feelings and dispositions essential to experiences of happiness and the quest for a good life.

The failure to take seriously the question of happiness is surprising given sociology's interest in how the personal and public are interrelated and the co-constitutive relationship between the individual and society. Happiness should be understood as an individual subjective experience but also as an ethical or moral aspect of everyday life. Rather than approaching happiness as an individual subjective experience, it is more productive to examine happiness as a social process implicated in the production and maintenance of self. To contextualize this argument, I offer a brief outline of my project before offering a theorization of happiness as an affective practice.

The project

My PhD research[1] focused on the 'happiness turn' in an attempt to understand how mental health is understood and experienced in a positive sense, rather than as the absence of disorder or suffering. My project examined the implications of the happiness turn for people's self-understanding and the social production of self. It also explored the different ways therapeutic and self-help framings of happiness and wellbeing are reshaping how people experience, understand and respond to anxiety and suffering. I conducted semi-structured narrative interviews with 13 women and eight men aged between 24 and 81 who were either participating in classes, workshops or courses, or were happiness practitioners such as psychologists, life coaches and yoga teachers who facilitated classes and workshops. The people I interviewed had diverse and long-standing – in life-history terms – engagements with self-care in the pursuit of happiness and wellbeing. Each participant's self-account demonstrated a significant investment in therapeutic and self-help practices including mindfulness, happiness science, wellbeing science, positive psychology, among others. Significantly, however, people did not limit themselves to 'evidence-based practices' which are often used to differentiate positive psychology and happiness economics from the allegedly less 'scientific' discourses of humanistic psychology and self-help (see Hill et al, 2020).

An important conceptual step was settling on a definition of happiness and the development of a methodological approach to grapple with this subject. This led to much despair and frustration as I was confronted with diverse conceptualizations and methodological approaches from the literature that did not match how my participants spoke about happiness and wellbeing. During those darker moments I often returned to Zadie Smith's (2013) essay, *Joy*, to remind me of what was at stake:

> It doesn't fit with the everyday. The thing no one ever tells you about joy is that it has very little joy in it. And yet, if it hadn't happened at all, at least once, how would we live? (Smith, 2013: np)

The experience of happiness, and related emotions, such as pleasure, joy and cheerfulness, but also delight, optimism, ecstasy, glee, jubilation, hopefulness and wellbeing are critical to the way people get on and go on within the context of their everyday life. The complexity and ephemerality of happiness requires the acknowledgement of elusive – and nonetheless frustrating – traits, particularly the way it is an embodied experience, but is simultaneously implicated in socially produced patterns of meaning and value (Wetherell, 2013; Burkitt, 2014).

As my research progressed and my thinking evolved, I found it increasingly difficult to separate happiness from its opposites, such as sadness, melancholy, depression, and suffering. The people I spoke to struggled to articulate how they experienced and understood happiness and wellbeing and often connected this to anxiety about their future happiness, or experiences of general unhappiness and suffering.[2] Ingrid, for example, offered this cautious definition:

> '[M]aybe I'm just misguided in my own definition of well-being, but I guess in terms of holding ourselves in a particular way day-to-day that is relaxed, with an open kind

of perspective; without, kind of, a focus on any physical or mental aches and pains.' (Ingrid, 32, married, trainee psychologist/musician)

There is an unfinished quality to Ingrid's understanding, with her definition settling on a disposition rather than a specific emotion or feeling. Suffering is central to her understanding with wellbeing defined metaphorically as an 'open perspective' in contrast to a 'focus' on 'aches and pains'. The instability and fluidity of subjective life was central to people's accounts, with reflection, labour and, where necessary individual and social adjustment (Hochschild, 2012) permeating people's descriptions and understandings of happiness and wellbeing. Significant attention within Ingrid's biography was given to the isolation and unhappiness she had experienced as a teenager, combined with an eating disorder and later, in her twenties, a significant health problem, drawing attention to the way people's experiences and understandings of happiness were linked to unhappiness, suffering and so on. We might read Ingrid's definition critically, drawing attention to how happiness and wellbeing are implicated in life projects and the development of 'good' habits (Morgan, 2020), but this does not empathetically respond to the significant experiences of suffering that permeated her biographical self-account. What is needed is a way to recognize the perpetually unfinished qualities of happiness and wellbeing and one that acknowledges the way positive and negative emotions are entangled.

Searching for a definition of happiness

Questions of happiness and the good life and to a lesser extent wellbeing are inseparable from the social imaginary because of their moral and ethical qualities. I draw on Charles Taylor's (2004: 23) definition of the social imaginary here: they are 'broader and deeper than the intellectual schemes' people use when thinking about their social existence. A social imaginary refers to how 'people imagine their social existence, how they fit together with others, how things go on between them and their fellows, the expectations that are normally met, and the deeper normative notions and images that underlie these expectations'. It is through the social imaginary that normative expectations and understandings of what constitutes good or pathological lives are produced and sustained. Emotions and feelings are central to a person's sense of being-in-the-world (Wetherell,

2013: 85). As Martha Nussbaum (2001: 5) notes, to have a sense of 'emotional health requires the belief that one's own voluntary actions will make a significant difference to one's most important goals and projects'. Thin (2014: np) further highlights how happiness is evident in the 'conversations we have about the goodness of life – not only the enjoyment of good feelings, but also the justification, anticipation, and sharing of our evaluations of how good people's lives are prudentially (i.e., for their sake)'. There is a need, as Svend Brinkmann (2020: 134) argues, to focus on *what happiness means*, rather than *how happy we feel*. If we are to understand how happiness shapes and directs human lives, we must focus attention on its intimate, moral and ethical aspects.

The trouble with happiness

Aristotle's (2005) assertion that happiness is the teleology of human life underpins research and animates debates today with contemporary happiness definitions falling on either side of the distinction between pleasure and the good life. It was Aristotle who elevated Eudaimonia to a higher plane, where happiness is tied to conduct and the development of one's character, and placed Hedonia, understood as experiences of good feeling or pleasure, on a lower rung. For Aristotle the god-like state of Eudaimonia was available only to philosophers and was achievable through a life dedicated to contemplation and study, whereas Hedonia resulted from slavish pleasures and was the preserve of women, servants and animals. This tension between feeling and conduct results in blind allies, and methodological impasses that are not easily resolved.

Claire Colebrook (2007/2008: 93) underscores this problem, arguing that we are constrained by two distinct modes of narrative happiness: 'one that maintains itself through time in the form of continuity and recognition, and a happiness that releases itself from all worldly recognition'. By the former she means a type of happiness that can be worked at and is implicated in the unfolding of a person's inner potential and development of character pointing to the socially situated and dialectical nature of happiness. The latter, however, arrives by chance and is synonymous with freedom and release from worldly constraints. The open disposition that Ingrid refers to in the earlier quotation indicates the importance of conduct because of the emphasis on 'holding herself' but also suggests that it is through this disposition that she can experience positive emotions and feelings. Elsewhere, she spoke about the freedom and release she experienced while running. This highlights the inadequacy of separating conduct and feeling and the need for a more dynamic and complex theorization of happiness, one that is able to examine how they are interrelated.

Within positive psychology and happiness economics – which claim to have 'discovered' the secrets of happiness – much work is focused on measurement and the identification of determinants (see Cieslik, 2018; Thin, 2018; Hill et al, 2020). The aim is to quantify experiences of happiness, demonstrate the benefits of positive emotions, develop policy and make available therapeutic resources that can be used to increase individual and collective happiness. Apart from neuroscientific measures which attempt to track happiness as it is experienced in real time, most methods rely on some form of self-reporting (Thin, 2012; Morgan, 2020). Research participants rate their happiness over a period of time or following a particular activity on a scale. These quantitative self-assessments rely on 'numerical reductionism', where happiness is subject to a methodological reification in the pursuit of scientific evidence (Thin, 2012: 318). Measurement, however, tells us little about how happiness is actually understood or experienced. Underpinning statistical techniques are 'blunt labels and fragile distinctions' 'between affective and cognitive wellbeing, or between Hedonic and Eudaimonic wellbeing' (Thin, 2018: 2), where the distinction between good and bad feelings is secure and there is little room for complex or ambivalent feelings, such as 'bitter sweet' emotions (Ahmed, 2010; Segal, 2017).

Claims by quantitative researchers to have discovered the 'truth' of happiness are dubious as they neglect the socially shaped and culturally particular ways people think about and pursue happiness (see Cabanas, 2018; Hyman, 2020). Conceptualizing emotions as programmed into bodies, and more significantly, 'as closed circuits entirely abstracted from their social context' (Wetherell, 2013: 17–18) fails to acknowledge the social and relational aspects of happiness. The problem is one of understanding emotion and feeling, as 'pre-social, located in the autonomic and central nervous system' (Burkitt, 2014: 28). Self-reports and the study of emotional behaviour under laboratory conditions do not effectively engage with 'the dialectic interactions of everyday life' (Thin, 2018: 14). Within my research, I needed a conceptualization of happiness able to address the socially situated and biographical nature of people's understandings.

Happiness and social life

Drawing on a tradition framed by the work of Charles Cooley and George Herbert Mead, increasing scholarship asserts that emotions are central to the way we locate ourselves socially and evaluate our place in the world (see Holmes, 2010; Burkitt, 2014; McKenzie, 2016). Ian Burkitt, for instance, explores how the self and emotions are produced through fluid and ongoing social relations, formed in dialogue between people in interaction but also in the relationship we have to our own selves (2014: 107). Mary Holmes similarly suggests that emotions are central to the way we navigate and negotiate everyday life (2010: 140). This was particularly important for the people interviewed as part of my research. All participants described how their ability to interact with others and undertake action in a socially meaningful and valued sense was dependent upon their wellbeing. Participants described significant attempts to improve their agency by altering their relationship between self and others and self and world at the level of emotion and feeling (see Hill, 2020). According to the people I interviewed, it was important for them to work at their (un)happiness, to be better able to participate socially in a meaningful and socially valued way.

Examining the way (un)happiness is experienced, performed, and understood intersubjectively reveals how some emotions are valued, while others are stigmatized. This process also points to the need for more complex understanding of the relational aspects of happiness and wellbeing. For example, Nussbaum (2008) utilizes geological metaphors to illustrate how emotions mark our social and mental lives and shape our moral decision-making and ethical judgements. Focusing on more negative emotions and feelings, Iain Wilkinson and Arthur Kleinman (2016: 9) illustrate the social consequences of suffering, arguing that the experience threatens the 'social constitution of our humanity' and is registered in the 'individual and collective body as a sadness, disorientation, anomie, and unfulfillable longing'. Turning back to my research data, we can see how Samantha's description of her desire for a more fulfilling life highlights how happiness and suffering are interwoven, shaping how people relate to the world.

> 'I want something more fulfilling in my life and – one thing is investment in the future and having, maybe living longer, but if not happy, then is it worth it? And just … having something … something more meaningful and fulfillment and contentment instead of this like … nagging discontentment.' (Samantha, 40, De facto, IT Specialist)

Elsewhere, Samantha described moving from the Philippines to the US at the age of nine, completing High School and studying at two different Ivy League universities. She later worked in the US and

New Zealand in Tech start-ups. Despite this professional success, her biography centres on difficult childhood experiences, family conflict, problems with her relationship and unhappiness at work. Economic and professional success does not compensate for the lack of meaning and value in other areas of her life. Samantha's account reflects wider concerns about contemporary life – that material success alone seldom guarantees meaningful, long-lasting happiness.

Understanding happiness as an affective practice

The work of Ian Burkitt (2014) and Margaret Wetherell (2013) were useful for theorizing emotions and producing a complex conceptualization of happiness. They offer a conceptualization of emotions that straddles the cognitive, neural and somatic particularities of subjective experience, while also highlighting the role of cultural, historical and social norms in shaping how emotions, feeling and thought are performed and understood. Their work centres patterns, practice and relations within practices and understandings of emotions and subjective life.

Burkitt (2014: 15) notes how emotions are composed of different but 'interrelated aspects of experience, such as the bodily, the psychological, the discursive or linguistic, and biographical'. 'What our emotions and feelings are the subject matter of', Burkitt (2014: 2) argues, 'are *patterns of relationships* between self and others and self and world'. He describes how '[o]ur feelings and emotions along with other bodily perceptions are the means by which we meaningfully orientate ourselves within a particular situation, as well as in relation to others who are part of that situation' (2014: 8). He contends that:

> A complex understanding of emotion allows us to understand how socially meaningful relationships register in our body-minds and, at some level of awareness, are felt. (2014: 15)

The organized and patterned way emotions are experienced and perceived highlights the need to recognize and understand the importance of interactions and relationships in any conceptualization of happiness.

Wetherell's definition of affective practice is particularly useful because it draws attention to the 'the way bits of the body ... get patterned together with feelings and thoughts, interaction patterns and relationships, narratives and interpretive repertoires, social relations, personal histories, and ways of life' (2013: 19). A focus on happiness as an affective practice generates insight into processes of development, routines of emotional regulation, and relational patterns and settling. Understanding happiness as an affective practice recognizes and allows for the improvisation that occurs within social action, yet at the same time, recognizes that the 'past and what has been done before, constrains the present and the future' (2013: 23). Within Wetherell's theorization of affective practice, emphasis is placed on 'ongoingness' and the patterns that exist within emotional experience and performance. This was useful for my project because of the way that the presence or absence of happiness shaped and directed my participant's lives but also their engagement with therapeutic and self-help practices. Theorizing happiness as an affective practice erases the tension between the two narrative modes that Colebrook (2007/2008) outlines because it posits that feeling and conduct are interwoven and mutually constituted.

People's definitions of happiness and their pursuit of wellbeing were grounded in their lived experience and often centred on significant junctures within their lives. There accounts focused on their attempts to maintain a certain emotional and mental trajectory in the face of significant life events and struggles. For example, Sam described how he had discovered a sense of meaning and value through his voluntary work after a 'shock' cancer diagnosis and treatment that precipitated his retirement. Here Sam outlines the different aspects of his wellbeing:

> 'So, we've got physical wellness, inspirational and emotional wellness, which is [therapeutic group]. And I've got a goodness campaign here, which is linked with my faith.' (Sam, 73, married, retired small-business owner/volunteer)

Within Sam's account, these four aspects – "physical", "inspirational", "emotional" and "goodness" – were interwoven and difficult to tease apart. This inseparability contrasts with assumptions underpinning quantitative measurements, which isolate and abstract these elements from a person's social context. According to Sam, working at his "physical" and "emotional" wellness and finding "inspiration" was necessary for his "goodness campaign". By goodness campaign, Sam meant his voluntary work, his attempts to remain positive and be kind to others in light of his cancer diagnosis, and the support he provided to his family, particularly his daughter who was experiencing mental health problems. Sam offers a grounded, contextual account of his experience and understanding of happiness. The metaphor of the "campaign" works symbolically to indicate how wellness and goodness are unfinished projects. Stability and 'ongoingness' in emotional and mental life are necessary for his relationships with others. Relationships, which, according to Sam, are sources of happiness and wellbeing.

The idea that happiness and wellbeing are individual projects with social significance was an important aspect of my participant's accounts. This might be simplistically explained away as an *effect* of therapeutic and self-help technologies that construct happiness and wellbeing as a 'problem' to be solved in the creation of 'happy subjects' (see Binkley, 2014: 18). A reparative reading of Sam's story, however, highlights the immediacy and complexity of the psychosocial (Moreno-Gabriel and Johnson, 2020). We see how his life experience and personal relationships drive his quest for an improved sense of wellbeing. Rather than simply an attempt to improve his happiness, his story is one of attempting to live a good and meaningful life following a cancer diagnosis and treatment. Other interviewees recounted efforts to improve their sense of 'being-in-the-world'; particularly, how they related both to themselves and others, pointing to the fluidity and labour involved in subjective and intersubjective life.

Happiness, reflection and biography

Emotions and reflection

A challenge in researching an ephemeral subjective state like happiness is the difference between identifying the emotion in the present and reflecting on it after the fact (McKenzie, 2018). The multiple factors and aspects involved in life satisfaction highlights the complexity and difficulty in researching happiness. Ruut Veenhoven (2006) explains that affective experience is often used to infer life satisfaction because it points to how much or how little an individual's innate needs are met within their immediate economic, political and social setting. This points to the role of reflection and self-evaluation. Reflection, however, as Alastair Morgan (2020) notes, presents methodological challenges because the feeling of happiness tends to disappear the moment we consciously reflect on what we are experiencing. The emphasis on reflective awareness within positive psychology and happiness economics potentially removes us from the actual experience of happiness. Thin (2012: 319) also draws attention to the limitations of relying on aggregated statistical analysis, noting that to begin conversations about a person's experience of happiness, researchers must 'suspend disbelief and treat numerical self-reports as if they were self-disclosures – i.e. revelations of actual selves and actual happiness – rather than temporary and provisional self-corrections'. Theorizing happiness as an affective practice highlights the relationship between unconscious experience and conscious awareness.

It is important then to acknowledge the relationship between the unconscious and conscious and the role of reflection in emotional performance. Burkitt (2014) highlights the importance of reflection within individual attempts to control and foster particular emotions. In all thought, he argues, there is a constant interplay between 'the reflective and unreflective, the conscious and unconscious, as explicit thinking and reflective action always occurs within the boundaries of the implied and the habitual' (2014: 106). This quotation from Susan, a clinical psychologist and yoga and meditation instructor, illustrates this point:

> 'I'm aware of the influence of the meditation coming through all the time. I'm rarely ever emotional in a way that I'm not proud of afterwards. I'm usually able to take a breath and think about it and not feel ashamed of myself after, because I've been you know, mean or furious or panicky or something like that.' (Susan, 47, married)

We see how emotional performance has consequences for Susan's self-presentation. It is by stopping and reflecting on what she was feeling that Susan was able to consciously maintain emotional control. Her account suggests that it is through embodying the principles of meditation that she is able to maintain her dignity within social interactions. It is through the act of reflection that we retrospectively assign emotional and moral value to an experience. Acknowledging the role of reflection is necessary if we are to effectively research happiness and wellbeing because personal histories and social norms shape how we interpret our emotions, influence our emotional performance and evaluate our place in the world.

Emotions, the self and biography

The emotions attached to significant events and banal episodes from our lives are formative because they shape how we interpret the events that we draw on when telling the story of our selves. Paul Ricoeur (1991) and Taylor (1989) note that the construction of a narrative identity is achieved through the weaving of interlocking and sometimes contradictory narratives about the self into a coherent whole, a process that Ricoeur refers to as *emplotting the self*. A narrative identity is produced and sustained through the way people make sense of and create purpose out of the configuration of disconnected episodes from their life in the form of a plot. Within my data, Tim's (Anglo-Australian, De facto, unemployed) account of why he had employed a life coach and participated in several therapeutic and self-help activities illustrates this point. Tim described how he had begun his "journey" of self-development following the breakdown of his marriage – which was precipitated by his affair with another woman – and the loss of his job because of "anger" issues at work. We see how Tim joins together different events retrospectively to explain why he felt it was "time for [him] to go on this journey".

A life story, however, is never entirely one's own and is necessarily a dialogical endeavour. The stock of stories, associated plot lines and narrative resources are deeply shaped by one's social and cultural context (Taylor, 1989; Butler, 2005). Butler (2005: 8) puts this succinctly: 'the "I" has no story of its own that is not also the story of a relation – or set of relations – to a set of norms'. The "I" constituted within a story is constructed through and against normative frameworks, what Taylor (1989) refers to as 'horizons of meaning'. Individual selves are socially produced, through a polyphonic and dialogic subjectivity that imaginatively reflects and refracts the various meanings it has for others, where the self appears only in (imaginary) dialogue with others (Burkitt, 2014: 171), as the emphasis on emotional performance in the quotation from Susan earlier suggests. A narrative approach to happiness (and its absence) is productive because of the way that normative ideas of what a life is if it is lived well are implicated in personal biographies (Taylor, 1989; Freeman and Brockmeier, 2001).

Autobiographical narratives should not be understood as a true depiction of self or the past but rather a reflexive construction, where personal experiences are selectively assembled and meaning attributed to them retrospectively (Freeman and Brockmeier, 2001). According to Jens Brockmeier (2001: 251), biographical stories involve an oscillation between two orders – the narrative event and the narrated event. A narrative event is the telling of a story in the here and now, whereas narrated events are the episodes used to propel the story forward in time. For a biographical account to make sense and hold significance for others there is necessarily an evaluative aspect to the act of self-interpretation. Schachter (2011) notes that self-narration is a goal-oriented and value-laden process that has consequences for how characters are positioned within stories. We will see this process at work in the excerpt from Edith in the next section. Focusing attention on the goals and values evident within biographical constructions draws attention to the affective value that different objects hold for people, such as relationships, life transitions and material goods (Ahmed, 2010). Burkitt (2014: 101) explains that these 'emotional-evaluative stances' are at the base of our self-feeling, or my feeling, and the way we feel about the world we live in. They say something about our relationship to our selves, others and the world-at-large.

Using narrative methods to examine experiences of (un)happiness

The interview

In using a semi-structured narrative approach to interviews I adopted the position that the interview experience was dialogical and the narratives co-produced (Kvale and Brinkmann, 2009). The stories within the interview setting drew attention to how 'the turn to happiness' is reshaping normative ideas of good and happy lives, and demonstrate how therapeutic and self-help ideals of the healthy, happy self are located socially. To encourage people to 'tell their own stories of their lived world' (Kvale and Brinkmann, 2009: 48), the initial question was open ended, to elicit a life story that would frame later questions around happiness and wellbeing practices. I included specific questions about: 'actively working on wellbeing'; 'the key aspects of wellbeing,' 'why it was important to work on wellbeing'; and 'whether wellbeing was related to happiness'.[3]

Analysis

My aim during analysis was to keep the stories intact by focusing on key themes (Riesmann, 2008) and examining the stories in their totality (Frank, 2012). I was particularly interested in how people positioned themselves within their stories (Schachter, 2011) and the broader social and cultural context (Squire, 2013). I employed Arthur Frank's (2012) Dialogical Narrative Approach (DNA) which focuses attention on how a story unfolds 'horizontally' in time, containing at a minimum a complicating event and resolution, and 'vertically' in terms of characters, points of view, genre, suspense and imagination.

Exploring subject positioning and standpoints within people's stories illustrated the evaluative components of people's stories. I analysed each interview transcript individually and jointly using an iterative method of reading and writing critical reflections that I gradually built up into the analysis chapters of my thesis.

After analysing several interview transcripts, it was apparent that people were constructing autobiographical narratives in dialogue with me around happiness and wellbeing. The metaphor of a "journey" that Tim used to describe his pursuit of happiness and wellbeing through therapeutic and self-help practices was common within people's accounts. I termed this plot line a 'therapeutic quest for happiness'. People presented themselves normatively, in a 'culture confirming' way (Bruner, 2001: 29) by describing how they responsibly and dutifully worked at their (un) happiness. Their biographical self-accounts tended to revolve around critical junctures, particularly moments of disruption and suffering. Bruner (2001: 32–3) asserts that these 'turning points' within biographies are significant because they are a step towards narrative consciousness, where a narrator describes how they have become free from their personal history. People described how they had turned to therapeutic and self-help technologies in the hope of regaining control over their – occasionally complex and chaotic – lives to achieve a happier and more socially connected self. Working at their happiness and wellbeing was a way to make sense of their present and past and imaginatively project themselves into a happier future. To illustrate my approach to analysis, I present a lengthy excerpt from Edith's biographical account.

Edith

Edith, 29, worked as a freelance writer. She was single and living alone after separating from her boyfriend three months prior to the interview. There was a strong emphasis within her self-account on prioritizing personal growth and improving her self-knowledge, illustrating the *happiness as a therapeutic quest* plot line. The explanation of why her relationship had broken down is an example: "It's just that I could see that together we weren't going to grow and then I'd grown a lot and then he wasn't growing." Edith explained that she was on an "experiential kind of journey" after the break-up, to "re-get to know me". The following excerpt is taken from a section of the interview where Edith described how her interest in wellbeing and happiness practices was connected to past experiences of anxiety.

Nicholas: Was it just around the anxiety that it became important for you to work on your internal life?

Edith: I think so. I wasn't really, I mean, there was always that curiosity and I guess a – but I don't think I was as practical as I am now, where I'm just like, "Actually, that's a better life". Like, I was much more reactive then. Whereas I'm much more proactive now. Ten years thankfully.

Nicholas: Could you unpack that a little more? That seems interesting – to move from being 'reactive' to being 'proactive'.

Edith: Well, I feel like it's, you know to get psychological about it, the pre-frontal cortex is kind of ruling when I'm younger. And I'm like, "Ooh, that looks good. I'll do that". And, "Ooh, that looks good, and I'll do that", and life is already exciting. Life is already moving along, and I'd fall into you know happiness pits and I'd climb amazing mountains and life was an adventure. And I lived it that way too. I'd find myself in great situations and terrible situations, but I was living vivaciously and so it was great. And then I guess as you get older and you start working and you stop studying you kind of go, "Well actually I have a choice now to make".

Edith's description of her emotional experience works temporally to illustrate her self-development and the fluidity and fleeting nature of happiness. Her story highlights how her understanding of happiness is socially situated and linked to her transition to adulthood. Edith illustrates her self-development temporally by using spatial metaphors to highlight the adventure and misadventure of her youth, as well as her transition to adulthood, which is marked by the seriousness of the choices she must now make. These choices carry moral weight within her account: "Actually, that's a better life".

There is reference to her past experience of anxiety, which indicates a key turning point in her biography. She employs what Thomas DeGloma (2014) describes as an awakening plot to describe this personal transformation. Neurological discourse is used to explain the shift from being "reactive" to "proactive". Evident here is an ambivalence or resistance towards happiness as an ideal, particularly where it is understood as akin to adventure, pleasure and excitement. It is constructed as a finite emotion that is linked to "great" and "terrible" situations. Elsewhere in her account Edith felt that peace rather than happiness was connected to wellbeing: "[H]appiness is almost like a peak that you may fall from, whereas peace is more a balance". Describing happiness as risky underscores the seriousness of the adult choices she was confronted with. There is an implicit acknowledgement that these decisions have implications for subjective and intersubjective life. Edith explained that it is through, "Quiet, reflective moments", that she was able to find the peace necessary for her wellbeing. She stated: "I'm always looking for that nice, gentle kind of padding and I feel as I've gotten older that that's more, it is more of my time spent there." The self here is positioned as being in need of insulation and protection from the ups and downs of everyday life. This recognition that both the self and one's happiness is vulnerable is a product of her growing self-awareness.

A paranoid reading of Edith's story might interpret this as her becoming a good, well-rounded citizen who makes responsible life choices. Elsewhere in her account, however, the choice to live well holds social significance because, according to Edith, her family's wellbeing is important for her own wellbeing. She described how it was necessary to work at her wellbeing to ensure she had the energy to support her Dad, brother and ex-boyfriend, all of whom experienced chronic depression. This resists criticisms that the pursuit of happiness and wellbeing is a solipsistic self-concern. Focusing attention on how happiness and wellbeing figured within individual biographies generates insight into the relationships and modes of being that hold meaning and value for people. We are able to see how lived experience shapes individual understandings of happiness but also shapes and influences the emotional and mental labour that people engage in. In other words, we see how happiness and wellbeing functions socially, shaping how people think about and understand their social existence, particularly their individual goals, ideals and relationships.

Conclusion

Sociology is well placed to draw out the both subjective and intersubjective aspects of happiness. In this chapter, I have argued that happiness is central to the social imaginary because of the way that it shapes human lives. Rather than theorizing happiness as individual subjective state I have argued for a more complex conceptualization. Theorizing happiness as an affective practice is useful because of the way it grounds emotion, feeling and thought within the routines and rhythms of personal conduct, life histories and everyday life. Happiness and wellbeing are central to the production of self because of the way their presence or absence are used to evaluate our place in the world and influences how we view, understand and pursue the things that hold meaning and affective value within our lives. Individual agency and self-feeling are central to people's experiences and understandings of happiness.

A reparative reading of happiness and wellbeing challenges paranoid and largely theoretical treatments because it generates insight into the moral and ethical aspects of happiness. Employing qualitative empirical methods informed by hermeneutic, phenomenological and interpretivist tradition draws attention to how individuals approach happiness within the complexity and messiness of their intimate lives. Narrative methods are useful because they help us to recognize the way normative expectations regarding what constitutes a good and happy life shape the stories that people tell about their lives. They also generate insight into the way individual understandings of happiness are located biographically. These methods centre experience, meaning and understanding in contrast to quantitative methods which attempt to capture how happy a person feels and render this into a numerically significant format.

Through the use of empirical examples from my PhD project I have demonstrated how lived experience shapes individual understandings and explanations of happiness and how these are necessarily socially situated. As social researchers we must begin any project focused on happiness and wellbeing by acknowledging their moral and ethical aspects. We must proceed sensitively and delicately in our research because, as Smith (2013) reminds us, how would we live without the possibility and promise that experiences like happiness and joy offer?

Notes

[1] Monash University Human Research Ethics Committee (MUHREC) – number CF14/514 – 2014000177 granted approval for this project. All data has been de-identified and participants have been assigned a pseudonym.

[2] I used wellbeing rather than happiness within the interviews because during my early field work where I participated in many happiness and wellbeing classes, workshops and courses, such as mindfulness, happiness science, positive psychology, laughter yoga and so on it became clear that happiness was a problematic term for many people.

[3] Interviews ran for a minimum of 90 minutes, though many ran longer, with one lasting three hours. Interviews were audio-recorded and professionally transcribed.

References

Ahmed, S. (2010) *The Promise of Happiness*, Durham: Duke University Press.

Aristotle (2004) *The Nicomachean Ethics*, London: Penguin.

Binkley, S. (2014) *Happiness as Enterprise: An Essay on Neoliberal Life*, Albany: SUNY Books.

Brinkmann, S. (2020) 'Living well and living right: aesthetic and ethical dimensions of happiness', in N. Hill, S. Brinkmann, and A. Petersen (eds) *Critical Happiness Studies*, London: Routledge, pp 131–43.

Brockmeier, J. (2001) 'From the end to the beginning: retrospective teleology in autobiography', in J. Brockmeier and D. Carbaugh (eds) *Narrative and Identity: Studies in Autobiography, Self and Culture*, Amsterdam: John Benjamins Publishing Company, pp 247–82.

Bruner, J. (2001) 'Self-making and world-making', in J. Brockmeier and D. Carbaugh (eds) *Narrative and Identity: Studies in Autobiography, Self and Culture*, Amsterdam: John Benjamins Publishing Company, pp 25–37.

Burkitt, I. (2014) *Emotions and Social Relations*, London: Sage.

Butler, J. (2005) *Giving an Account of Oneself*, New York: Fordham University Press.

Cabanas, E. (2018) 'Positive psychology and the legitimation of individualism', *Theory and Psychology*, 28(1): 3–19.

Cabanas, E. and Illouz, E. (2019) *Manufacturing Happy Citizens: How the Science and Industry of Happiness Control our Lives*, Cambridge: Polity.

Cederström, C. (2019) *The Happiness Fantasy*, Cambridge: Polity.

Cieslik, M. (2018) *The Happiness Riddle and the Quest for a Good Life*, London: Palgrave.

Colebrook, C. (2007/2008) 'Narrative happiness and the meaning of life', *New Formations*, 63: 82–102.

DeGloma, T. (2014) *Seeing the Light: The Social Logic Of Personal Discovery*, Chicago: University of Chicago Press.

Frank, A. (2012) 'Practicing dialogical narrative analysis', in J. Holstein and J. Gubrium (eds) *Varieties of Narrative Analysis*, London: Sage, pp 33–52.

Freeman, M. and Brockmeier, J. (2001) 'Narrative integrity: autobiographical identity and the meaning of the "good life"', in J. Brockmeier and D. Carbaugh (eds) *Narrative and Identity: Studies in Autobiography, Self and Culture*, Amsterdam: John Benjamins Publishing Company, pp 75–99.

Hill, N. (2020) '"It's the soul that needs the surgery"? The social life of (un)happiness', in N. Hill, S. Brinkmann, and A. Petersen (eds) *Critical Happiness Studies*, London: Routledge, pp 110–27.

Hill, N., Brinkmann, S., and Petersen, A. (2020) 'Critical happiness studies: an invitation', in N. Hill, S. Brinkmann, and A. Petersen (eds) *Critical Happiness Studies*, London: Routledge, pp 1–19.

Hochschild, A. (2012) *The Managed Heart: Commercialisation of Human Feeling*, London: University of California Press.

Holmes, M. (2010) 'The emotionalisation of reflexivity', *Sociology*, 44(1): 139–54.

Hyman, L. (2014) *Happiness: Understandings, Narratives and Discourses*, Basingstoke: Palgrave.

Hyman, L. (2020) 'Happiness: a societal imperative', in N. Hill, S. Brinkmann, and A. Petersen (eds) *Critical Happiness Studies*, London: Routledge, pp 98–109.

Illouz, E. (2008) *Saving the Modern Soul: Therapy, Emotions, and the Culture of Self-help*, Berkeley: University of California Press.

Kvale, S. and Brinkmann, S. (2009) *InterViews: Learning the Craft of Qualitative Research Interviewing*, London: Sage.

McKenzie, J. (2016) *Deconstructing Happiness: Critical Sociology and the Good Life*, New York: Routledge.

McKenzie, J. (2018) 'Is there such a thing as happiness in the present? Happiness and temporality', *Journal of Classical Sociology*, 18(2): 154–68.

Moreno-Gabriel, E. and Johnson, K. (2020) 'Affect and the reparative turn: repairing qualitative analysis', *Qualitative Research in Psychology*, 17(1): 98–120.

Morgan, A. (2020) '"The sickness unto health": self-reification, self-love and the critique of happiness in contemporary life', in N. Hill, S. Brinkmann, and A. Petersen (eds) *Critical Happiness Studies*, London: Routledge, pp 48–63.

Nussbaum, M. (2001) *Upheavals of Thought: The Intelligence of Emotions*, New York: Cambridge.

Ricoeur, P. (1970) *Freud and Philosophy: An Essay on Interpretation*, London: Yale University Press.

Ricoeur, P. (1991) 'Life in quest of narrative', in D. Wood (ed) *On Paul Ricoeur: Narrative and Interpretation*, London: Routledge, pp 20–33.

Ricoeur, P. (1992) *Oneself as Another*, Chicago: University of Chicago Press.

Riessman, C. (2008) *Narrative Methods for the Human Sciences*, London: Sage.

Schachter, E. (2011) 'Narrative identity construction as a goal-oriented endeavour: reframing the issue of "big vs. small" story research', *Theory and Psychology*, 21(1): 107–13.

Sedgwick, E. (2003) *Touching Feeling: Affect, Pedagogy, Performativity*, Durham: Duke University Press.

Segal, L. (2017) *Radical Happiness: Moments of Collective Joy*, London: Verso.

Smith, Z. (2013) 'Joy', *The New York Review of Books*, 60(1). Retrieved from http://www.nybooks.com/articles/2013/01/10/joy/

Squire, C. (2013) 'From experience-centred to socio-culturally oriented approaches to narrative', in M. Andrews, C. Squire, and M. Tamboukou (eds) *Doing Narrative Research* (2nd edn), London: Sage, pp 47–71.

Taylor, C. (1989) *Sources of Self: The Making of the Modern Identity*, Cambridge: Harvard University Press.

Taylor, C. (2004) *Modern Social Imaginaries*, Durham: Duke University Press.

Thin, N. (2012) *Social Happiness: Theory into Policy and Practice*, Bristol: Policy Press.

Thin, N. (2014) *Positive Sociology and Appreciative Empathy: History and Prospects, Sociological Research Online*, 19(2), DOI: 10.5153/sro.3230

Thin, N. (2018) 'Qualitative approaches to culture and well-being', in E. Diener, S. Oisihi, and L. Tay (eds) *Handbook of Well-being*, Salt Lake City: DEF Publishers.

Veenhoven, R. (2006) 'The four qualities of life: ordering concepts and measures of the good life', in M. McGillivray and M. Clarke (eds) *Understanding Human Wellbeing*, New York: United Nations University Press.

Walker, H. and Kavedžija, I. (2015) 'Values of happiness', *Journal of Ethnographic Theory*, 5(3): 1–23.

Wetherell, M. (2013) *Affect and Emotion: A New Social Science Understanding*, London: Sage.

Wilkinson, I. and Kleinman, A. (2016) *A Passion for Society: How We Think about Human Suffering*, Oakland: University of California Press.

4

Personal Happiness, Social Unhappiness: Understanding the Complexity of Individual Happiness Accounts

David Tross

Introduction

This chapter introduces the Mass Observation archive, its participant panel and its significance for qualitative happiness research. I outline key themes that emerge from my research before focusing on one significant finding: how disaffection with socio-economic conditions, political structures and 'selfish' social norms are embedded in happiness narratives. This was an unexpected finding, partly because the panel participants were not prompted to include a social dimension in their responses and also because in survey research individual (un)happiness is assumed to relate to an evaluation of personal wellbeing domains rather than wider social concerns (Thin, 2012; Pavot and Diener, 2013).

I situate this social dimension of happiness narratives in the context of political and sociological theories around democratic deficit and political disengagement in the UK (Norris and Inglehart, 2016; Curtice, 2018;). I also employ concepts of moral sentiment and lay normativity (Haidt, 2003; Sayer 2004; Smith, 2009) that view individuals as socially situated and sensitive to others' wellbeing as well as their own. I conclude with two considerations for future happiness research: first, the need to understand the interrelationship of societal and individual happiness and, second, the challenge of developing methodologies that can interrogate lay perceptions of happiness/wellbeing.

What is Mass Observation?

The Mass Observation Project represents 'a key national, qualitative, secondary data resource' (Lindsey and Bulloch, 2014: 3). Originally established in 1937, Mass Observation (relaunched as the Mass Observation Project in 1981) aims to provide a record of everyday life by eliciting written accounts about a diverse range of topics from ordinary people to gain access to the thoughts, feelings and behaviours of non-official voices in the UK. As a 'publicly available data set' (Dale, 1988: 7) the Mass Observation archive, owned by the University of Sussex, constitutes one of 'the major repositories of longitudinal qualitative social data for the UK' (Casey et al, 2014: 1).

Three-times-a-year 'Seasonal Directives' on a variety of topics are sent to a volunteer participant panel resident in the UK. These directives constitute a set of open questions that invite participants 'to write freely and discursively about their views and experiences on a range of subjects' (Casey et al, 2014: 1). The data set for my research comprised 200 accounts about happiness written by the participant panel in response to a 2013 Seasonal Directive, 'What Is Happiness?',[1] formed of six questions:

(1) What makes you happy and what does happiness mean to you?
(2) Write down ten things (or as many as you can think of) that make you happy. Be as descriptive or imaginative in your answers as you wish.
(3) People sometimes talk about 'the happiest day' of their lives. Do you have a day/time like this? Please give details.
(4) If you could relive a moment in your life again, when would this be and why?
(5) Maybe you feel your happiest day is yet to come, how do you imagine it?
(6) Is there anything that makes you unhappy?

The Mass Observation Panel

The 2013 happiness directive was sent to 592 panel members who constitute a broad range of ages (the minimum age is 16) and live across the UK, with a 55:45 per cent female to male ratio. The panel has been criticized for soliciting accounts from a narrow, predominantly female, older and middle-class segment of the population; therefore, since 2000 the Mass Observation Panel (MOP) has revised its recruitment procedures 'so that its composition gradually becomes more representative of the population as a whole' (Casey et al, 2014: 1).

Despite these efforts, statistical breakdown of the actual respondents to the 2013 happiness directive emphasizes the greater proportion of older and female participants. 45 per cent of respondents were aged over 61 while 65 per cent of respondents were female. The 16–26 age group and respondents living in London are particularly under-represented compared with the UK as a whole (UK Census, 2011). Information provided about employment and education revealed the predominantly middle-class status of the response cohort (Savage, 2015).

Using the archive

One major advantage of the archive for qualitative research is its ability to furnish rich accounts of the everyday, 'revealing the complexities of family, personal and intimate life' (Casey et al, 2014: 9). Therefore, it is well suited to understand how people experience and perceive happiness, what causes it and what it means to them. My data on how happiness is experienced and narrated as a more relational and social process (Cieslik, 2014) contrasts to the more individualistic approaches we see in survey research.

Another noted feature of the archive is the way that it generates unsolicited social commentary from respondents 'speaking about social experience in the context of everyday politics, reflections on public attitudes and beyond' (Pollen, 2013: 223). This was a key attraction as it transcends the traditional numerical self-reports such as those on 'national wellbeing' that neglect the depth of people's concerns, reducing them to self-interested choosers acting within an individualistic framework. A key theme of my research data is how participants expressed concern about social issues in ways that transcended individual self-interest. Such findings imply a more socially embedded human agent than is often depicted in quantitative happiness research (Cieslik, 2014).

While these accounts provided rich, highly personal, biographical and socially engaged interpretations of social phenomena, we should be cautious about reading the responses as direct representations of an authentic, objective reality (Silverman, 2001; Mason, 2002). As May (2008) points out, solicited, open archival documents written for public consumption often convey a fashioned reality or self the author wishes to present. The extent of this performativity in the happiness accounts and the notion of the 'defended self' (Holloway, 2006) is discussed later in the chapter.

The data was subjected to Thematic Analysis, a widely used 'accessible and theoretically flexible approach' (Braun and Clarke, 2006: 77). The themes were developed from initial coding via extensive reading and re-reading of the documents. They were then organized into hierarchies that reflected how respondents ranked their experiences and perceptions of happiness and unhappiness.

Personal happiness, social unhappiness?

Happiness and unhappiness, in the words of one panel respondent, 'intertwine all the time'. The Mass Observation data shows how respondents both experience and expect a range of positive and negative emotions and events to coexist and interact throughout their lives, which echoes findings from recent research (Hyman, 2014; Cieslik, 2017). The respondents offered a critical and sceptical stance about simplistic and popular ideas of happiness as 'pleasure seeking' (Warnock, 2003; Layard, 2011). This is captured by one female respondent's response to Q1 of the directive: 'what does happiness mean to you?'

> Happiness isn't a state, where you just arrive and stay there and never leave – The Happy Ever After Retirement Home. Life is about constant change and uncertainty, so you can have lots of moments of happiness but you will never get one continuous golden chunk.

My research also highlights the interdependence of happiness/wellbeing events, similar to recent qualitative studies (Hyman, 2014; Cieslik, 2017), where many respondents depict happiness as a relational and collaborative activity. Individuals are not only vulnerable to the lack or loss of these relationships but sensitive to the needs of others.

These sensitivities about others broadened to a wider narrative about sociocultural and political practices and their significance for general wellbeing. In their responses to the directive, when individuals explored positive sources of happiness, they did so mostly in terms of their personal life, their relationships, achievements and meaningful engagements and activities. Conversely, when they explored unhappiness, around half the cohort made explicit social commentary a part of their response in addition to these more 'personal' themes. This 'social unhappiness' took three interrelated forms: alienation and dissatisfaction with political structures and ideological practices;

attitudes of 'helpless concern' regarding these; and 'lay normative' (Sayer, 2004) analyses of sociocultural norms and practices.

Political alienation and dissatisfaction

One significant theme of the socially situated character of the responses was how, on the one hand, respondents were often socially and politically engaged as 'concerned citizens' but on the other were disaffected with existing political structures. This chimed with literature about the recent emergence of a 'democratic deficit' defined as a 'crisis of legitimacy in Western democratic states' (Norris, 2012: 2), characterized by growing distrust and disillusionment with political structures and a sense of no longer 'having a voice in the national conversation' (Eatwell and Goodwin, 2018: xxi). This has in turn led to a rise in populism and electoral moments that have 'disrupted the politics of many Western societies' (Norris and Inglehart, 2016: 1) such as the UK EU Referendum and the Trump election in the US. Though written before these seismic events, respondents' dissatisfaction with the political system captures what Norris and Inglehart (2016: 14) see as the phenomenon of citizens becoming 'more critical towards established political institutions and authorities'.

This is reflected in critical commentary about politicians. One respondent, Ellen,[2] 81, a retired shop assistant from Hull, criticizes 'politicians who promise so much and then go back on their word as soon as they are elected' while Jenny, a 51-year-old senior NHS pharmacist, laments politicians who 'don't use their power responsibly'. These are just two examples of how respondents of different ages and occupational backgrounds share feelings of mistrust and disaffection with politicians that mirror research findings suggesting a generalized lack of trust in the UK Parliament (European Commission, 2018; Office for National Statistics, 2018).

This data will come as little surprise to social science researchers and students. Yet, the link between this disenchantment and happiness narratives is underexplored. Although quantitative national and international data sets (Office for National Statistics, 2018; United Nations Sustainable Development Network, 2018) attempt to establish a correlation between social and political structures and individual wellbeing, this methodological approach produces few insights into the way individuals themselves establish these links and why they matter. As Thin (2014: 2) suggests, happiness research needs to shift towards methodologies which constitute individuals 'not only as objects of concern but also as subjective experiencers and evaluators of their own conditions'.

Another reason why happiness research may have missed these social concerns lies in the way these surveys conceptualize happiness as an internal property of a higher or lower quantity of positive emotions and satisfactions that individuals possess and seek to maximize (Thin, 2012; Cieslik, 2017). This neglects an important normative dimension of happiness connected to meaning, values and ideas about what constitutes a good life (Dean, 2009). These could be viewed as abstract matters; indeed, they have been a central preoccupation of Western philosophy for more than two millennia (McMahon, 2006). However, 'as sentient beings whose relationship to the world is one of concern' (Sayer, 2011: 1), these questions about what we should care about, what to choose, what is good and bad about what is happening and what we should aim for are also practical matters embedded in everyday life in the ongoing struggle to flourish (Cieslik, 2017). As socially embedded individuals, sensitive to how others treat us yet also 'alive to their welfare' (Sayer, 2004: 7), everyday normative appraisals 'of what kinds of behaviour are good, how we should treat others and be treated by them ... merge into "conceptions of the good" – how one should live' (Sayer, 2004: 4). As I now go on to show, critical appraisals of policies and politics are directly connected to beliefs and values about the nature of the good life and 'good society' (Edwards, 2005).

Unhappiness, left and right

The respondents also situated their unhappiness with politics on a more ideological and party-political spectrum. Predominantly, this took the form of a 'left' political position, which, according to Curtice (2018: 88) considers 'that society is too unequal and that the government should endeavour to make it less so through, for example, higher taxation, more generous welfare benefits, the provision of public services and tighter regulation of the economy'. Despite almost half of the cohort being over the age of 61, a predictor of voting Conservative (Curtice, 2018), other demographic factors of the panel, education and occupation, are associated with voting Labour (Savage, 2015; Curtice, 2018). These more left-wing views were reflected in how unhappiness took on a more party-political and ideological form in participants writings. For Hannah, 33, a fundraising manager from Leeds, things that makes her unhappy are the 'Tories' and 'People who vote for the

Tories' while Mary, a 39-year-old homemaker from Aberystwyth, declares herself as 'a socialist at heart'.

One contribution that survey research has made into happiness and political beliefs is the paradox that while 'liberal' countries (like the UK) have overall higher than average scores of self-reported Life-Satisfaction, within these societies, individuals who hold 'Conservative' values tend to report higher levels of Life-Satisfaction than liberals (Napier, 2008; Okulicz-Kozaryn and Avery, 2014). One explanation for this (Okulicz-Kozaryn and Avery, 2014) is that conservatives are better able to rationalize the increasing social inequalities in Western democracies whereas liberals experience inequality as a source of unhappiness. Mary illustrates this in declaring that 'inequalities wrangle with me' while Ian, a retired youth and community worker, states that 'injustice, in all its forms, makes me unhappy. Inequality saddens me.'[3]

While the link between inequality and happiness has been explored in a range of studies (Wilkinson and Pickett, 2010; Deeming, 2013; UNSDN, 2018), the causal connections are assumed to impact at the level of individual life satisfaction. However, the comments from Mary and Ian demonstrate a more social conception of happiness and wellbeing that transcend personal circumstances; signifying a thicker depiction of personhood whereby people adopt social roles as public citizens as well as private individuals (MacIntyre, 1981). Survey research neglects this social dimension of happiness, so that on the one hand, attention is focused on self-interested, individualistic pursuit that conceals what people are happy and unhappy about at a societal level, and, on the other, reduces 'national' wellbeing to an aggregate of individual self-reports. This approach obscures how individuals distinguish between what is good for them and what is good for society as a whole. This was noted by the ONS' (2011) own public consultation into measuring national wellbeing in the UK which showed that one priority for increasing national wellbeing was 'the common feeling that there should be a greater sense of fairness and equality'. Other research (Dolan, 2011; Action For Happiness, 2014) also showed evidence of lay perspectives that equated greater equality with general wellbeing.

The social psychologist Jonathan Haidt's (2012) Moral Foundations Theory and its application in public political discourse was useful in understanding these normative appraisals of social wellbeing. According to Haidt, three sets of 'cognitive modules' characterize liberal/left morality: harm to individuals, oppression by powerful groups of the powerless and unfairness in the allocation of social goods. For Nick, a 47-year-old air traffic assistant from Southampton, oppressive, unfair and harmful features of socio-economic structures and inequality takes on an internationalist dimension:

> Day to day I have nothing to complain about, we live in a theme park life – TV, computers, entertainment on tap, a car to travel with, places to see and exercise in. It's the fact that that isn't shared by everyone, and that my life impacts on others in order for me to have the life I live. It pains me that so much that we have in the West is 'cheap'. Everyone loves a bargain. Really? Who pays for that?

Nick's comments show how liberal/left perspectives can be cosmopolitan (Norris and Inglehart, 2016) and global as ideas around Fair Trade and ethical consumerism shape understandings of wellbeing. Nick demonstrates an awareness that the price paid by poorer nations for Western affluence (Hutton, 2003) is often poorer wellbeing – happiness in the West is often gained at the expense of others in developing societies. Additionally, for those within the left/liberal cohort these views were prescient given the context in which they were written, during 2013/14 when the Coalition Government was implementing a range of austerity measures. Their responses stress how these policies were causing harm and suffering. As Louise, a 32-year-old student from Oldham, put it:

> The coalition government and their ideological drive to make the poor poorer and feel completely useless is something I abhor and it makes me unhappy. I can't understand how some people see people from disadvantaged backgrounds as being undeserving, it makes me unhappy to see powerless people being held to account for the social disadvantage they face.

For Louise, the poor experience a double oppression – a combination of material disadvantage through welfare reform and demonization for being 'undeserving'. As Haidt (2012) suggests, a key feature of moral evaluations of unfairness is proportionality – the principle that merit or blame be distributed according to what people deserve. The injustice in this UK case is that welfare recipients are powerless victims of an 'ideological drive' and that they are fundamentally underserving of the contempt they endure (Sayer 2004: 9).

Louise's comments also demonstrate how her own values and social commitments to fairness and equality were being threatened by government policies. Another way that the values of the liberal/ left cohort were threatened was the perceived destruction of cherished institutions. For example, Sandy, a 49-year-old education administrator from Wales, despairs at the Coalition Government's 'destruction of the welfare state and NHS'. Haidt, in his exploration of the moral emotions of wellbeing, has identified a 'psychology of sacredness … people treat objects, places, people and principles as though they were of infinite value' (Haidt 2012: 174). This may explain why attachment to certain public institutions and social goods can be expressed in such forceful emotional language. For Karen, a 48-year-old PhD student from Huddersfield, what constitutes a 'special torment' is 'watching the foundation of social care, education, employment etc being dismantled in my life time'.

This destruction and degradation of cherished values and institutions is significant for understanding how circumstances impact upon personal wellbeing even when they appear to have little direct relationship to individuals because, as Sayer (2011: 1) affirms, 'well-being depends at least in part on how things that people care about – significant others, practices, objects, political causes – are faring, and on how others are treating them'. Consequently, people's evaluation of their own wellbeing depends in part on the flourishing of their commitments (Sayer, 2011; Haidt, 2012). Given the political context in which they were writing, one way of understanding how unhappiness is mediated strongly by social factors for the left/liberal participants is the way in which the dominant political narratives and policies of austerity were at odds with beliefs they hold dear.

Left/liberal perspectives did not completely dominate participants' accounts. A few respondents produced views about unhappiness that seemed to fit 'Conservative, Right' positions in relation to immigration, national identity and welfare (Curtice, 2018). These respondents were older and highlight a generational divide in UK politics (Norris and Inglehart, 2016; Curtice, 2018) between younger libertarians/ social liberals and then other, more authoritarian socially conservative voters who view society as needing 'common moral codes, social mores and linguistic practices as a way of promoting social cohesion' (Curtice, 2018: 89). For example, Michael, at 94 the oldest respondent of the panel, a retired civil servant from Surrey, was concerned 'at the deterioration of our country', and illustrates Curtice's model of 'authoritarian /socially conservative' individuals and their anxieties about the breakdown of traditional moral codes,

> the dreadful obscenity in so called comedy on television,
> the endless emphasis on sex in so many news items, the

breakdown of so many marriages, the loose sexual morality of so many children and young people and the deterioration of the Christian faith in the UK.

Haidt (2012) notes that conservative morality, like liberal morality, is also invested in sacralizing goods and practices, but is expressed through authoritarian and communitarian ideals regarding obligations and loyalties of individuals to traditional moral codes and social institutions including, as expressed earlier by Michael, sexual practices, religious teaching, marriage and language. Alison, a 70-year-old retired bookkeeper from Milton Keynes, also says she gets 'very unhappy about the filthy language that has infected our society and the obsession with sex everywhere'. Here, wellbeing appraisals shift from concern about harm to individuals towards an interest in the integrity or community cohesion or solidarity.

Furthermore, Curtice (2018: 89) suggests that social conservatives 'are personally more comfortable living in a relatively homogenous society' which implies a nationalistic and nativist concept of bounded community. As Haidt (2012) acknowledges, this is potentially oppressive in being defined and expressed in opposition to the 'other', particularly foreigners and other outsiders perceived to threaten group solidarities and norms. Michael, for example, is unhappy about 'mass immigration which seems to go unchecked'. While Carol, a 73-year-old retired teacher from Leicester, expresses these nativist sentiments through alienation: 'what has happened to my city – the place I was born in and grew up in, is so different. I'm a stranger in my own city – so many foreigners all living in their own ghettos or enclaves and not mixing'. The implication here is that foreigners are falling short of the communitarian obligations required to produce cohesive moral community (Etzioni, 1998). The fact that the city Carol refers to, Leicester, one of the most ethnically diverse cities in the UK (Census, 2011), shows how wellbeing accounts are further mediated by place, though curiously, none of the respondents from London, a similarly diverse city, expressed similar concerns.

A key aspect of Curtice's (2018) and also Inglehart and Norris' (2016) depiction of a 'cultural cleavage' dividing social liberals and authoritarians is how this not only runs parallel to, but also cuts across, traditional left/right ideological distinctions. This can be seen in my data in the way that none of the three 'conservative' respondents make any political commentary that aligns with 'right' ideology around economic growth, wealth creation and cuts to state expenditure (Curtice, 2018).

Furthermore, some of those within a left/liberal cohort of the panel also adopted authoritarian or at least more communitarian social values regards a variety of moral concerns concerning parental standards, lack of respect, and general moral decline. One respondent was unhappy about 'the Tories in charge of the country' but also 'the way society is today and how the world is changing, a lack of morals' while another is unhappy with high levels of inequality but also with 'parents who think that rude and inconsiderate children are only "expressing themselves" and don't need to take responsibility for their actions'. These responses show individuals holding quite disparate positions on social issues – self-placement on the ideological left can be accompanied by critiques of 'liberal endorsement of self-expression over collective responsibilities' (Calder, 2004: 2).

These accounts were written before the seismic political events of the EU referendum and the Trump election that 'shocked the west' (Eatwell and Goodwin, 2018: ix) and 'disrupted Western elites' (Norris and Inglehart, 2016: 1). But the alienation shown towards political systems, unhappiness at inequality coupled with a declinist moral narrative echo Norris and Inglehart's (2016: 1) claim of populist sentiment cutting across 'left/right ideological self-placement'. In addition, these accounts seem to both predict and reflect an increasingly polarized and fraught political landscape in the UK.

Social critique: selfishness and moral decline

The themes of anti-elitism, anti-capitalism and moral decline also featured in the data as part of a wider critique of social and moral conduct. This is significant for understanding how alienation from one's society is expressed as an 'aspiration gap' (Taylor, 2010) between personal conceptions of the good and what society values and tolerates (Sayer, 2007).

One subject of concern for respondents merged anti-capitalist critique and moral decline and focused on corporate cultures and practices. Nick refers to 'banks unable to control themselves' while Sheila, a 79-year-old acupuncturist, is more specific in her critique of the behaviours and vices of business elites: 'exploitative power, greed, self-interest, dishonesty (of which there is an enormous amount in commerce these days, more than I have ever known)'. Another dimension of this critique was the perceived damage to personal and social virtue due to selfish materialism, with many respondents listing 'consumerism' or the 'consumer society' as causes of unhappiness. Nick viewed this as antithetical to his own conceptions of the happy life, 'our frantic economy, the me-first culture is so undignified and unpleasant. I would rather have less, treat people with respect, live rather than consume. That would make me happy.'

Nick's views are reflected in many responses from Mass Observation participants to Q1 of the directive about meanings of happiness. Although these took in part the quality of 'do-it-yourself' (Hookway, 2018) normative constructions of happiness, they often involved a grounded, social and relational perspective emphasizing friendships, concrete engagements and contentment that speaks to an anti-materialist hedonic tradition first articulated by the classical philosopher Epicurus (2013). There was also a more 'eudaimonic' sense, of a happy life contingent on meaningful pursuits that counter dominant social tropes around materialism. As Nick puts it:

> Two of the most awful words that are combined are 'consumer society'. Consumption, a passive activity that so many claim to enjoy is hollow and flat – we are made to create. It is a wonderful thing to discover and appreciate your own and other people's creativity.

Nick's words, 'we are made to create', reflect eudaimonic happiness in the way Sayer (2011: 116) suggests 'people tend to have a sense of "leading a life"', which often include learning, creating and social commitments. This eudaimonic pursuit, the 'ongoing struggle to flourish' (Sayer, 2011: 3), involves risking failure and accepting difficult and challenging emotions. This is articulated by Sophie, a 28-year-old assistant psychologist:

> My line of work is stressful and likely to throw me in front of some of the worst of humanity like crime, abuse and trauma. So completing my masters doesn't mean I'm going to be happy in the future, it means I'm (hopefully!) going to be able to develop my career in a way that I find meaningful and satisfying ... I strongly doubt that it will make me happy, but I strongly believe that it will help me satisfied, fulfilled and challenged in my future career. But perhaps these are one and the same?

Reflections like these support Cieslik's (2014) research about the ways subjective happiness accounts contain important themes of hard work, sacrifice and commitment. These themes, according to Cieslik, somewhat undermine the pessimistic strain in sociological depictions of happiness from scholars like Bauman (1992) who focus on individualization, narcissism and the creation of identity through consumerism that 'has become the central feature of our existence as we have turned to focusing on possessions as the main means of expressing who we are' (Jones, 2003: 160).

As Cieslik (2014) has suggested, these sociological theories may obscure the creative ways agents grapple with powerful discourses in their desire to live meaningful and fulfilling lives. It seems significant how anti-materialist stances emerging from the data in this directive underscore a complex depiction of human agency in the pursuit of happiness. It suggests an explicit opposition to hegemonic social norms, as one respondent put it, whereby 'happiness has been sold to us, as a kind of perfectionism'. Instead, individual flourishing, for many respondents, is dependent on their social attachments, relationships and sense of belonging. As Tom, a 41-year-old designer, reflects, 'I tend to be happiest when I feel like I am part of a pack and have a function in that pack, and am valued for being part of it'. This more collaborative understanding of happiness signals how 'flourishing entails a sense that one's pursuits serve a larger purpose' (Nakamura and Csikszentmihalyi, 2003: 94).

Narratives about selfishness also encapsulated a broader evaluation of social and moral decline, so accounts of everyday rudeness, inconsiderate behaviour and selfishness such as littering are combined with reflection about the socially patterned nature of these norms. For example, Laura, a 42-year-old library assistant, is unhappy about 'the way society is today ... that we are more concerned with ourselves and not others'.

These sentiments echo communitarian philosophy (eg MacIntyre, 1981; Etzioni, 1998) concerned about the loosening of social and communal ties and the perceived loss of 'trust, mutual understanding and forms of reciprocity' (Calder, 2004: 1). Where some critiques of capitalism explore social selfishness in terms of irresponsible elites, communitarianism is also interested in the social responsibilities of ordinary citizens. For Martin, 42 from Harpenden, 'generally it is a lack of manners and consideration for others that I find makes me unhappy'.

Through these accounts, we get a sense of how unhappiness focused upon wider society can link to more individual and intimate contexts; the vices and blameworthy conduct of political and corporate elites – greed, thoughtlessness, dishonesty – are also those respondents describe making them unhappy in their everyday life, how others behave and also remorse about their own behaviour towards others.

'Helpless' concern?

Respondents' discussions of unhappiness also explored experiences of cruelty and suffering and feelings of helplessness, what one respondent described as 'injustices in the world I can do little about'. These often focused on cruelty towards and suffering of vulnerable groups, particularly children and animals, but encompassed a range of global examples from stories of abuse and violence to wars, refugee crises and natural disasters. This was often combined with what one respondent called 'the sense of hopelessness in the face of such horrors'.

At such a global level, it is unlikely that individuals would feel able to influence these events. What might be as significant is a psychosocial dimension about how individuals seek to establish cognitive order and coherence connecting their own lives with their external environment (Thin, 2012). As Nakamura and Csikszentmihalyi (2003: 94) assert, 'a sense that life has meaning is associated with wellbeing' and Thin (2012) suggests that meaning-in-life is in part pursued through attempts to establish a sense of order and coherence to one's life and also to our external environment: 'worldwide, people are interested in the aesthetic quality of individuals' lives, seeking the sense that someone's life has a good "feel" or "pattern", that it is a good example of a human life, that it is not a "mess"' (Thin, 2012: 3 22).

Significantly, unhappiness can be accommodated into a wider narrative of meaning providing it has a purpose or contains valuable learning or lessons; suffering too, 'can be tamed by being rendered meaningful' (Thin, 2012: 322). Indeed, respondents explored a range of 'meaningful' suffering; one respondent, for example, explored how his son's death in a motorcycle accident strengthened his marriage through a collaborative process of bereavement and mutual care.

By contrast, tragic events that resist explanation and seem senseless can engender feelings of chaos and frustrate the desire for order and meaning. In global terms, suffering, violence and cruelty 'is "meaningless" if it lacks a clear sense of purpose and justice' (Thin, 2012: 322), reflected in the way some respondents wrote about 'innocent' victims and 'senseless' and 'unnecessary' suffering. If the outside world is bewildering and meaningless, and individuals have no sense of control over events, this has implications for happiness as a good life is associated with personal autonomy (Ryan and Deci, 2000; Ryff and Singer, 2008; Layard, 2011).

Although autonomy has been portrayed as an individualistic concept, for Ryan and Deci (2000: 74) autonomy is not 'antagonistic to relatedness ... it refers not to being independent, detached or selfish but rather to the feeling of volition that can accompany any act, whether dependent or independent, collectivist or individualist'. The ways in which respondents narrate a lack of control through social themes, from global suffering to disaffection with political structures, may signify a more relational and socially engaged nature of autonomy and what it means to feel 'in control'.

The lack of 'a sense of choice, volition and freedom' (Ryan and Deci, 2000: 74) emerged from the data as a key factor associated with unhappiness and was evident across personal and social domains. As Karen frames it, 'lack of control is at the heart of everything that makes me unhappy from not being able to get work in my chosen field to watching the foundation of social care, education, employment etc being dismantled in my lifetime'. These connections between personal and social realms is underlined by another respondent who locates unhappiness in 'the inability to change things that make life difficult for me or other people'.

Of course, not all respondents feel helpless in the face of events. Witnessing or learning about others' suffering can also motivate people to act (Sayer, 2011). For Sally, a retired university lecturer from Brighton, the existence of what she terms 'cruelty and injustice, poverty and deprivation' is the reason why she feels 'compelled to remain involved in various political campaigns even when sometimes I despair of ever making a difference'. Sally's comments also suggest that feelings of powerlessness over events is also a sociological issue. Despite the MOP reflecting the demographic of a UK 'civic core' (Lindsay and Bulloch, 2014), the section of the population most likely to vote and volunteer, few discussed active participation in politics. Overlapping with themes of political disaffection explored previously, one feature of 'helpless concern' may be the belief that citizen engagement cannot affect outcomes. As Sally says herself, 'sometimes I despair of ever making a difference'.

Moral sentiments and elevation

'The relational quality of human social being' (Sayer, 2011: 124) and the way it includes a quality of fellow-feeling and sympathy for the suffering of others is placed at the heart of 18th-century philosopher Adam Smith's Theory of Moral Sentiments:

> by the imagination we place ourselves in his situation, we conceive ourselves enduring all the same torments ... this is the source of our fellow-feeling for the misery of others

... by changing places in fancy with the sufferer. (Adam Smith, 2009: 13)

This fellow-feeling is reflected upon by one respondent as something akin to practical wisdom: 'I learnt early on in life visualising walking in other people's shoes made you realise their needs.' This capacity for empathy Nussbaum (1999) suggests is key to compassion and, for Sayer (2011), offers insights into our own vulnerabilities. Adam Smith begins Moral Sentiments with the observation that

> how selfish so ever a man may be supposed, there are evidently some principles in his nature, which interest him in the fortune of others, and render their happiness necessary to him, though he derives nothing from it except the pleasure of seeing it. (Adam Smith, 2013: 13)

In a similar vein, Jonathan Haidt's empirical work on happiness explores 'the power of positive moral emotions to uplift and transform people' (Haidt, 2003: 275) that he calls 'elevation' related to practices, examples, behaviours and characteristics and 'acts of virtue or moral beauty' (Haidt, 2003: 276) that inspire people. Jenny explores her sense of 'elevation' in this way:

> love hearing or reading stories about people helping each other, especially strangers, through kindness or courage. Kindness might include giving time for a lonely person, or giving refuge to someone without a home. Courage would include hiding people from the Nazis during the Second World War. It makes me happy when people are good to each other for the simple reason that they feel it's the right thing to do.

Haidt's (2003: 276) explanation for 'elevation' is that individuals (intuitively) map behaviours onto a vertical social space with 'good' being equivalent to 'noble, pure and godlike' and with bad located lower down as 'degrading, base, animal or demon-like'. These moral sensitivities, Haidt suggests, explain why individuals feel inspired by virtuous or noble acts but equally feel degraded by what they witness on the news or in their everyday encounters and interactions, experiencing this 'as a kind of debasement, or bringing down of a nonphysical, moral component of their selves' (Haidt, 2003: 281). Significantly, for understanding the phenomenon of social unhappiness in the MOP accounts, 'elevation' and 'degradation' could demonstrate how 'we are easily and strongly moved by the altruism of others' (Haidt, 2003: 284) yet also rendered unhappy by cruelty and suffering.

The defended self?

One challenge facing qualitative researchers is how to interpret the complex meanings around the everyday struggles for happiness/living well, avoiding what Holloway (2006: 545) terms the 'disappointingly descriptive tendencies' of qualitative empirical research. She suggests qualitative research may obscure the way 'anxiety and its related defences are part of the human condition' (Holloway, 2006: 545). These defence mechanisms may be problematic for researchers as respondents through a process of personal displacement focus more on the unhappiness of others than their own experiences. Participants may be unable or unwilling to articulate their feelings around their wellbeing as they are involved in defending the self against feelings of anxiety, loss and failure.

There are certainly instances of this 'defended self' in the directive. It might explain why some chose not to respond to Q6 about unhappiness. But it is also made explicit by some of those who do. As one respondent comments, 'lots of things make me unhappy but I do denial quite nicely, so won't go into them here!'. This avoidance of negative feelings, as another respondent states, '(because) I don't want to destroy my good mood!' echoes Furedi's (2004) notion of a Therapeutic Discourse whereby individuals are governed by the desire to accentuate positive feelings.

However, the majority who discussed unhappiness with society also explored their unhappiness in more personal terms of their own inadequacies and failures such as bereavement and loss. This demonstrates that, as 'normative beings whose fundamental relation to the world is one of concern and care for ourselves and others' (Hookway, 2018: 109), appraisals of happiness at a social level can also be constitutive of personal wellbeing instead of deflecting from it.

Conclusions: implications for happiness and wellbeing research

Qualitative methodologies are key to understanding how personal and social 'conceptions of the good' interact (Sayer, 2004: 4). This research, in line with other recent qualitative projects are examples of what Thin (2014) terms the 'happiness lens', an empathic interest in how individuals themselves construct meanings of happiness and why and how happiness matters. This is especially the case when the themes emerging from these endeavours appear to demonstrate a more socially situated, interdependent self where, as one Mass Observation respondent put it, 'I don't think that the state of happiness can be entirely internal, or self-centred'. This means that 'any account of human social beings which attempts to cast people as overwhelmingly self-interested ... is inadequate, for it ignores our social, relational character and our dependence' (Sayer, 2011: 121). Yet the key trend in happiness research is still to employ quantitative methodologies that produce 'limited, thin-sliced data' (Thin, 2012: 324) that assume individuals pursue hedonic satisfactions and emotions for themselves.

Another implication for happiness and wellbeing research is around the operationalizing of 'national happiness and wellbeing' as the sum of individual satisfactions. How could we say, for example, that national wellbeing levels are 'good' just because enough personal self-reports are 'good', if perceptions of national and social conditions are so disaffected and alienated? Another dimension to Thin's 'happiness lens' is to create positive sociological accounts to draw attention to the 'desirable qualities of a really good society' (Thin, 2014: 2). Through the social critiques explored in this piece, respondents were also constructing implicit conceptions of this good society. Further research that explicitly solicits these accounts would provide a much sounder methodological grounding for debates about increasing social and national happiness and wellbeing. This could include a range of methods including interviews and diaries and draw from a more representative cohort than the MOP, particularly a less middle-class and younger demographic.

Notes

[1] The 2013 Winter Directive comprised three parts: 'Serial Killers', 'The Countryside' and 'What Makes You Happy?' It is not clear whether participants write responses to all three parts at the same time. Only a couple of respondents make explicit reference to the preceding topics. There are no deadlines for returning the responses to each directive, and participants are not compelled to complete all three (or at all). It is possible that the preceding topics (in particular 'Serial Killers'!) may shape and influence the responses they provided to questions about happiness, though the scope of this particular study precluded further investigation of this. Details of all the MOP directives since 1981 can be accessed at http://www.massobs.org.uk/mass-observation-project-directives

[2] Names have been invented.

[3] However, the narratives and responses of this liberal/left group from my data gave no indication that their lives were any unhappier than the cohort as a whole.

References

Action for Happiness (2014) *National Happiness Matters More than National Wealth*, http://www.actionforhappiness.org/news/national-happiness-matters-more-than-national-wealth (accessed 5 August 2015).

Aristotle (2004) *The Nicomachean Ethics*, London: Penguin.

Bauman, Z. (1992) *Intimations of Postmodernity*, London: Routledge.

Braun, V. and Clarke, V. (2006) 'Using thematic analysis in psychology', *Qualitative Research in Psychology*, 3: 77–101.

Calder, G. (2004) *Communitarianism and New Labour*, available at http://www.whb.co.uk/socialissues/vol2gc.htm (accessed 24 December 2018).

Casey, E., Courage, F. and Hubble, N. (2014) Special Section Introduction: Mass Observation as Method, *Sociological Research Online*, 19(3), http://www.socresonline.org.uk/19/3/22.html

Cieslik, M. (2014) '" Not Smiling but frowning": sociology and the problem of happiness', *Sociology*, first published 1 September 2014, DOI: 10.1177/0038038514543297

Cieslik, M. (2017) *The Happiness Riddle and the Quest for a Good Life*, Basingstoke: Palgrave Macmillan.

Curtice, J. (2018) 'New Divides in British Politics?', in D. Phillips, J. Curtice, M. Phillips and J. Perry (eds) *British Social Attitudes: The 35th Report*, London: The National Centre for Social Research, pp 86–114.

Dale, A., Arber, S. and Proctor, M. (1988) *Doing Secondary Analysis*, London: Allen and Unwin.

Dean, H. (2009) *Understanding Human Need*, Bristol: Policy Press.

Deeming, C. (2013) 'Addressing the social determinants of wellbeing: the latest challenge for social policy', *Journal of Social Policy*, 42(3): 541–65.

Dolan, P. (2011) 'Happiness questions and government responses: what the public makes of it all', *Revue d'Economie Politique*, 121: 3–15.

Eatwell, R. and Goodwin, M. (2018) *National Populism: The Revolt Against Liberal Democracy*, London: Penguin.

Edwards, M. (2005) *Civil Society*, Bristol: Polity Press.

Epicurus (2013) *The Art of Happiness*, London: Penguin.

European Commission (2018) *Standard Eurobarometer 89. EuroBarometer Surveys*, available at http://data.europa.eu/88u/dataset/S2180_89_1_STD89_ENG (accessed 29 September 2020).

Etzioni, A. (1998) 'A moral reawakening without puritanism', in A. Etzioni (ed) *The Essential Communitarianism Reader*, Oxford: Rowman & Littlefield, pp 41–7.

Furedi, F. (2004) *Therapy Culture: Cultivating Uncertainty in an Uncertain Age*, London: Routledge.

Haidt, J. (2003) 'Elevation and the Positive Psychology of Morality', in C.L.M. Keyes and J. Haidt (eds) *Flourishing: Positive Psychology and the life Well-Lived*, Washington, DC: American Psychological Association, pp 275–89.

Haidt, J. (2012) *The Righteous Mind*, London: Penguin.

Holloway, W. (2006) 'Psychoanalysis in Qualitative Social Research', *The Psychologist*, 19: 544–55.

Hookway, N. (2018) 'The moral self: class, narcissism and the problem of do-it-yourself moralities', *The Sociological Review*, 66(1): 107–21, https://www.ipsos.com/sites/default/files/ct/news/documents/2017-11/trust-in-professions-veracity-index-2017-slides.pdf (accessed 30 November 2018).

Hutton, W. (2003) *The World We're In*, London: Abacus.

Hyman, L. (2014) *Happiness: Understandings, Narratives and Discourses*, Basingstoke: Palgrave Macmillan.

Jones, P. (2003) *Introducing Social Theory*, Cambridge: Polity Press.

Layard, R. (2011) *Happiness: Lessons from a New Science* (2nd edn), London: Penguin.

Lindsey, R. and Bulloch, S. (2014) 'A sociologist's field notes to the Mass Observation Archive: a consideration of the challenges of "re-using" mass observation data in a longitudinal mixed-methods study', *Sociological Research Online*, 19(3), http://www.socresonline.org.uk/19/3/8.html

MacIntyre, A. (1981) *Beyond Virtue: A Study in Moral Theory*, London: Duckworth.

Mason, J. (2002) *Qualitative Researching* (2nd edn), London: Sage.

Mass Observation Project (2013) *Respondents A–Z Winter 2013: what makes you happy?*, The Keep, University of Sussex, Ref No: SxMOA2/1/98/3/1.

May, T. (2008) *Social Research* (5th edn), Buckingham: Open University Press.

McMahon, D. (2006) *The Pursuit of Happiness: A Hstory from the Greeks to the Present*, London: Penguin.

Nakamura, J., and Csikzentmihalyi, M. (2003) 'The construction of meaning through vital engagement', in C.L.M. Keyes and J. Haidt (eds) *Flourishing: Positive Psychology and the Life Well-Lived*, Washington, DC: American Psychological Association, pp 83–104, DOI: 10.1037/10594-004

Napier, J.L. (2008) 'Why Are Conservatives Happier Than Liberals?', *Psychological Science*, 19(6): 565–72.

Norris, P. (2012) *Democratic Deficit: Critical Citizens Revisited*, Cambridge: Cambridge University Press.

Norris, P. and Inglehart, R. (2016) *Trump, Brexit, and the Rise of Populism: Economic Have-Nots and Cultural Backlash*, HKS Faculty Research Working Paper, Series 16–026, Harvard University, MA, https://research.hks.harvard.edu/publications/workingpapers/Index.aspx (accessed 24 December 2018).

Nussbaum, M. (1999) *In Defence of Universal Values*, Women and Human Development, the Fifth Annual Hesburgh Lectures on Ethics and Public Policy, http://philosophy.uchicago.edu/faculty/files/nussbaum/In%20Defense%20of%20Universal%20Values.pdf (accessed 30 August 2015).

Office of National Statistics (2011) *Supplementary Paper: Findings from the National Wellbeing Debate*, http://www.ons.gov.uk/ons/guide-method/user-guidance/well-being/publications/previous-publications/index.html (accessed 31 August 2018).

Office for National Statistics (2018) *Measuring National Wellbeing: Quality of Life in the UK, 2018*, available at https://www.ons.gov.uk/peoplepopulationandcommunity/wellbeing/articles/measuringnationalwellbeing/qualityoflifeintheuk2018 (accessed 29 September 2020).

Okulicz-Kozaryn, A. and Avery, D.R. (2014) 'The subjective well-being political paradox: happy welfare states and unhappy liberals', *Journal of Applied Psychology*, DOI: 10.1037/a0037654

Pavot, W. and Diener, E. (2013) 'Happiness experienced: the science of subjective well-being', in S. David, S. Boniwell and A. Conley Ayres (eds) *Oxford Handbook of Happiness*, Oxford: Blackwell, pp 134–54.

Pollen, A. (2013) 'Research methodology in Mass Observation past and present: "Scientifically, about as valuable as a chimpanzee's tea party at the zoo"?', *History Workshop Journal*, 75(1): 213–35.

Ryan. R.M. and Deci, E.L. (2000) 'Self-determination theory and the facilitation of intrinsic motivation, social development and wellbeing', *American Psychologist*, 55(1): 68–78.

Ryff, C.D. and Singer, B.H. (2008) 'Know thyself and become what you are: a Eudemonic approach to psychological wellbeing', *Journal of Happiness Studies*, 9: 13–39.

Savage, M. (2015) *Social Class in the 21st Century*, London: Penguin.

Sayer, A. (2004) 'Restoring the moral dimension: acknowledging lay normativity', published by the Department of Sociology, Lancaster University, Lancaster LA1 4YN, at http://www.comp.lancs.ac.uk/sociology/papers/SayerRestoring-the-Moral-Dimension.pdf (accessed 30 August 2018).

Sayer, A. (2007) 'Class, moral worth and recognition', in T. Lovell (ed) *(Mis)recognition, Social Inequality and Social Injustice*, London: Routledge, pp 88–103.

Sayer, A. (2011) *Why Things Matter to People*, Cambridge: Cambridge University Press.

Silverman, D. (2001) *Interpreting Qualitative Data: Methods for Analysing Talk, Text and Interaction* (2nd edn), London: Sage.

Smith, A. (2009) *The Theory of Moral Sentiments*, London: Penguin.

Taylor, M. (2010) *21st Century Enlightenment*, RSA, available at https://www.thersa.org/globalassets/pdfs/reports/rsa_21centuryenlightenment_essay1_matthewtaylor.pdf (accessed 29 September 2020).

Thin, N. (2012) 'Counting and recounting happiness and culture: on happiness surveys and prudential ethnobiography', *International Journal of Wellbeing*, 2(4): 313–32.

Thin, N. (2014) 'Positive sociology and appreciative empathy: history and prospects', *Sociological Research Online*, 19(2): 5, http://www.socresonline.org.uk/19/2/5.html, 10.5153/sro.3230

Tiberius, V. (2013) 'Philosophical methods in happiness research', in S. David, I. Boniwell and A. Conley Ayres (eds) *The Oxford Handbook of Happiness*, Oxford: Oxford University Press, pp 260–72.

UK Census Data (2011) http://webarchive.nationalarchives.gov.uk/20160105160709/http://www.ons.gov.uk/ons/rel/census/2011-census/population-and-household-estimates-for-the-united-kingdom/stb-2011-census--population-estimates-for-the-united-kingdom.html (accessed 28 March 2018).

United Nations Sustainable Development Network (2018) *World Happiness Report*, Chicago: UNSDN.

Warnock, M. (2003) *Utilitarianism and On Liberty*, Oxford: Blackwell.

Wilkinson, R. and Pickett, K. (2010) *The Spirit Level*, London: Penguin.

PART II

Qualitative Research into Happiness/Wellbeing: Communities, Biographies and Identities

5

Developing a Biographical Approach to Happiness and Wellbeing

Mark Cieslik

Introduction

I became interested in happiness studies in the early years of this century as much of the sociological research I had undertaken up to then had been concerned with the many problems people experience in modern societies – educational failure, unemployment, poverty, drug use and offending. I was keen to develop a more balanced account of everyday life as even the most troubled and disadvantaged subjects I researched spoke of their interests, hobbies and small moments of joy in their lives. Thus began an interest in researching the wellbeing of ordinary people – documenting these challenges of life that sociology traditionally explores but with a greater focus on more positive and nurturing experiences that makes life worth living. Approaching middle age, my friends were struggling with demanding careers, teenage children, health problems, failing marriages and bereavement. We were all curious about the strengths, resources and skills needed to live well during these times. We were intrigued by how much of life seems beyond our control, structured by wider social forces yet wished to understand how best to adapt to, resist and manage these influences. Can sociological research into wellbeing offer us insights into the different ways of managing life's challenges? Reviewing the research at the time suggested there were few projects that addressed these questions as many studies offered broad surveys of life satisfaction or critiqued the happiness industry and its commodification of wellbeing. I was interested to hear the voices and stories of ordinary people talking about a good life; how their differing relationships, rituals, communities and shared histories informed their wellbeing. How as people aged their wellbeing evolved with their changing relationships across their biographies creating new challenges and opportunities for a good life.

This chapter discusses some aspects of the qualitative research project I developed to study the biographies of wellbeing: the definition of happiness/wellbeing that I employed reflecting the idea of wellbeing as a collaborative practice and the methods I used to generate data by mapping the life histories of interviewees and their webs of relationships. I then discuss using concepts from Bourdieu to analyse how wellbeing is structured because of unequal opportunities and resources creating classed and gendered patterns of wellbeing. I investigated how people made sense of the influences on their wellbeing and how their interpretations and actions informed the quality of their lives – hence I drew on ideas around reflexivity and agency to complement the Bourdieusian analytical framework. I illustrate these aspects of the research design and some key findings through discussion of some case studies. I draw on two biographies of women, Mary and Jill, who shared their life stories with me and their accounts of trying to live well despite the many challenges they faced. Their narratives suggest patterns of wellbeing emerging from their social networks structured through class and gender relationships. Early life events and the women's creativity and resourcefulness point to the significance of biographies for an understanding of wellbeing in later life.

Reviewing the literature: what is happiness and how to study it?

The definition of happiness/wellbeing that one uses will shape the nature of the research project. My sense from the literature was how many contemporary researchers defined wellbeing quite narrowly reflecting the quantitative methods they employed (Popple et al, 2015) or the political points they wished to make about the happiness industry (Furedi, 2004; Cederström and Spicer, 2015). In contrast I was intrigued by a wide range of other writers that suggested many different dimensions to wellbeing/happiness – as a bodily experience, emerging through relationships, evolving as we age, as a deeply personal psychological phenomenon that is also culturally situated and a shared practice.

The research project I developed, therefore (see Cieslik, 2017), was influenced by many studies such as classic works on happiness (see McMahon, 2006) as well as recent theorizing around identity/self and structure/agency (Archer, 1988; Craib, 2001; Sayer, 2010). I was also interested in psychological research that posits wellbeing as inherently subjective and emotional, and which analyses the everyday balancing of positive/negative affect/emotions (Diener, 1984) as well as some sociologists who have explored the role of values and commitments to living well (Sayer, 2010). These emotional experiences are seen to vary over time as some are fleeting (such as joy) and others more enduring (such as contentment) which echo classical writings around the distinctions between Hedonia/Eudaimonia (Aristotle, 2009). To conceptualize 'wellbeing as a process' implies reflexivity and cognition whereby memories, imagination, internal conversations and creativity all influence everyday practices that constitute our efforts at happiness (Goffman, 1956; Archer, 2003; Sayer, 2011). My studies also mapped the structural or objective features of everyday life such as employment, income, housing, and community relationships and how these influence personal wellbeing (see Layard, 2005: 55–76).

Despite the complexity of happiness the use of quantitative methods by many researchers focuses attention more on the measurable indicators of wellbeing than a subjectively complex, interpretively subtle formulation of wellbeing. Veenhoven (1999), a key proponent of quantitative studies, claims that humans can accurately reflect on their circumstances and make subtle judgements about the quality of their life. Hence, the widely used technique of self-report questionnaires into life satisfaction that forms the basis of much research in happiness studies. Although these offer valuable insights, self-reflection can be flawed producing biases and lacunae in what people know about their wellbeing, its sources, meanings and how we pursue it (Gilbert, 2006; Holthus and Manzenreiter, 2017: 9). Quantitative methodologies, therefore, benefit from being complemented with narrative and qualitative techniques that sensitize us to the consequences of human fallibilities and the place of meaning/interpretation in happiness/ wellbeing. Insights into wellbeing can be achieved if we acknowledge how people's habits and routines often obscure how wellbeing emerges through social networks, interpretative frameworks and complex decisions across multiple domains.[1]

I used a mainly qualitative, biographical approach (that utilizes other secondary data sources) that reflects the notion of happiness as a subjective and social phenomenon – something that we often experience together, share or co-produce (Cieslik, 2017: 67). This idea of 'social happiness' (Thin, 2012; White, 2017; Holmes and McKenzie, 2018) encourages us to explore the cognitive functions that inform everyday social, practical activity such as deliberation, trade-offs, interpretation and reasoning. If wellbeing is something we often 'do' with people rather than existing as something that individuals 'have' then these relational properties imply struggle and conflict as people mobilize resources (involving access to power and opportunities) in their efforts to live well.[2] This relational wellbeing also implies a sensitivity to issues such as structure/agency, objective/ subjective and macro/micro (Archer, 2003; Gilbert, 2006; Mouzelis, 2008; Sayer, 2011). If wellbeing is inherently social it draws attention to its embeddedness in concrete yet changing sociocultural milieu that vary historically and spatially, conditioning the evolving biographies of people as they age (Mathews, 1996).

Theories and methods for researching biographies of happiness/wellbeing

The basic components of my research design were borrowed from an earlier qualitative/narrative study into literacy and learning where the narratives people constructed in interviews were complemented with various maps created by interviewees to describe their changing identities and social networks as they aged (Cieslik and Simpson, 2015). Using this project as a template I asked interviewees to map (on large rolls of paper) their biographical timelines and routes through education, family relationships, intimacy, employment, friends and so on investigating their changing significance for wellbeing. In follow-up interviews we then created a cross-sectional happiness map of recent key events and experiences detailing how wellbeing was influenced by interviewees' social networks and experiences in institutional domains (such as employment, family, leisure and neighbourhood). I usually conducted two interviews with respondents (lasting one to two hours), 6–12 months apart in order to generate the interview narratives and construct these different 'happiness/wellbeing maps'.

In earlier biographical projects (Cieslik and Simpson, 2015) I had used Bourdieu's concepts (habitus, practice, capitals, field, hysteresis and symbolic violence) (Bourdieu, 1990) and so I employed this framework again to investigate 'social happiness' that is socially structured, evolving over the life course as people age. As people grow up they can internalize certain ways of understanding happiness – expectations of what a good life might be. The concept of habitus directs us to how people slowly, habitually acquire these ways of thinking, feeling, talking, choosing, as they age – sometimes embodied, tacit, hidden sense of how to live well – 'a feel for the game' (Bourdieu, 1990: 66). As I illustrate later in the case studies the more affluent may internalize ambitious ideas for their happiness – consumerist and materialistic goals that may prove unobtainable and a source of unhappiness in later life. Whereas others have more modest conceptions of living well that are easier to attain and less threatening for wellbeing.

Bourdieu famously focused on class inequalities and how the family backgrounds of the lower classes offered less resources for children to do well in life compared with their more affluent peers (Bourdieu et al, 1999). The concept of habitus (Bourdieu, 1977: 78) is useful for wellbeing research as it helps explore how different resources and opportunities flow through family backgrounds framing how people's wellbeing develops as they age. The employment of individuals and the income this generates is significant for wellbeing as is the web of social relationships and cultural practices that go with them. Bourdieu's concepts of capitals (economic, cultural, symbolic and social) (Bourdieu, 2004) allows us to analyse how convertible resources flow from different habitus influencing experiences, life chances and wellbeing. As the case studies demonstrate, higher incomes can enable a greater range of cultural experiences and more extensive social networks that cumulatively influence wellbeing.

In studying happiness/wellbeing as a social, collective phenomenon I analysed the connections people have with others, how lives are embedded in customs, rituals, routines and institutions. Bourdieu's concept of 'field' (Bourdieu, 1984: 110) was one way of thinking critically about the nature of these social relationships – how people are situated with others spatially that implies power relationships, struggle and conflict that can shape identities and how we judge the quality of our lives. I illustrate this process later on, showing how learning experiences and peer relationships can be emotionally disturbing involving 'symbolic violence' (such as bullying or labelling that can become routinized) and which have enduring consequences for personal wellbeing (Bourdieu and Wacquant, 1992: 167). These sorts of disappointing moments in life where there is a mismatch between expectations and lived experiences Bourdieu referred to as 'hysteresis' (Bourdieu, 1984: 142). These surprising events, that often had lasting effects on the lives of participants, were a common feature of the biographical narratives constructed by interviewees. Failing examinations at school, redundancy, divorce, and a sudden illness were examples where individuals were caught unawares and unprepared for events that shaped their wellbeing. Very often interviewees spoke of the embarrassment and shame they felt at key moments in their life and I was keen to explore the complex interdependencies people have with others – the need for affirmation and recognition and its role in wellbeing. Again, research points to the classed and gendered patterning of these moral dimensions of life (Sennett and Cobb, 1977; Skeggs, 1997; Reay, 2005; McKenzie, 2015) and their emotional intensity and enduring consequences suggests their significance for wellbeing.

Bourdieu is often criticized for stressing the lasting effects of social background (of habitus in particular) on the life chances of individuals neglecting somewhat the role of practice and agency in people's lives (see King, 2000). Hence, I have drawn on ideas from Andrew Sayer (2010) who suggests combining Bourdieu with other thinkers such as Margaret Archer (2003) and her concepts such as internal conversations, ethical choices and 'trade-offs' in order to research wellbeing. Sayer, therefore, suggests a useful approach to wellbeing using a framework of agency, emotions and Bourdieusian concepts sensitive to the interweaving of structures and agency across the life course (Sayer, 2011).

Jill and Mary: ageing and happiness across the life course

The following case studies illuminate how good wellbeing frequently relies on economic resources, as some studies suggest (Veenhoven, 1999; Layard, 2005), yet there are also variations in subjective experiences of happiness that complicates these relationships. It seems (at the biographical level at least) the quality of social relationships (in families, friendships and communities) mediate the way that structural processes such as income/employment influence wellbeing. Such findings pose questions about the relative significance of economic security and caring relationships for happiness. Hence, these life stories make us ponder the importance of meaning, expectations and affluence for a good life. When considering the role of class and gender relationships, for example, we also need to be open to the variation and diversity of subjectivities and the agency of individuals in the patterning of wellbeing across the life course.[3]

Jill (aged 78 at interview) and Mary (aged 90) lived in South Wales, UK, Mary living in an affluent middle-class community, and Jill residing in a small house on a disadvantaged estate of a former industrial town. I interviewed both women in their homes exploring the habits and routines that structured their daily lives. Mary was usually well dressed in expensive designer clothing, her home was tidy with much china and ornaments. Jill's home was more poorly furnished with basic chairs, TV and carpets. She dressed in an apron and more comfortable blouse and trousers, often cooking in her small kitchen when I called. The different demeanours of the two women suggested that affluence and a middle-class upbringing did not guarantee good wellbeing. Despite her material standing and 'successful' consumerist lifestyle (she spoke, for example, of only using 'high end' retailers in the local town), Mary was more withdrawn than Jill who had a greater zest for life and was more energized than Mary.[4] Both women completed a questionnaire (see Hoggard, 2005: 23–8) and these suggested differences in their subjective wellbeing. Jill responded she felt happy 80 per cent of the time and unhappy 18 per cent whereas Mary said she felt happy 40 per cent of the time and unhappy 50 per cent of the time. Mary said she often 'lacked enthusiasm and energy' and felt 'stuck in a rut' and 'often depressed'. Whereas Jill suggested that 'life was interesting', felt 'enthusiastic about things' and was 'rarely depressed'.

I go onto suggest a number of reasons why a more affluent middle-class woman tends to be less happy than a more economically disadvantaged woman from a working-class background. In particular, there were differences in the size of social networks of these two women as well as the nature and quality of these social connections and sociability.

Social networks, sociability and wellbeing

How do we explain these curious findings from Mary and Jill (that reflect many of the biographies in my research) that suggest good wellbeing does not necessarily flow from the lifestyles often associated with affluence and economic resources? What is it about social relationships and social connections that make them significant for happiness? To answer these questions I initially mapped the women's social networks and activities and identified how these related to different experiences of wellbeing.

The interviews with the two women generated data about their social routines in recent years, identifying the people the women met, places they visited and activities they undertook in an average week. Jill attended church, volunteered at the community centre, visited neighbours, her children and grandchildren and had coffee with friends. She cooked meals (which she shared with neighbours) and baked cakes that were sold at the community centre for charitable causes. Mary in comparison had much smaller networks and less activities, walking her dog, visits to neighbours, lunches with her sister and shopping trips with friends.

> 'I do the bookings for the (community) centre so I know what's going on and we've got something going on every day over there … I play with the kids … If they have any problems I very often sort their problems out … Some of the old ladies will say, "can you make some pasties", or "can you make some Welsh cakes". If it's helping them, I'm happy … I'm just doing things for other people … I always think that you get more back in the long run than you give.' (Jill)

Jill spoke of the satisfaction she felt helping other people and she enjoyed meeting local residents, particularly if they had young children. She felt a sense of "being needed" which was important for her self-esteem. Jill talked animatedly about the many people she met and the activities she did each week, joking that, "I am busier now, retired, than when I was younger and working full-time". She also spoke about "keeping oneself busy" as important for happiness as one has less time to dwell on negative thoughts – one is distracted from the aches and pains of aging bodies and the sadness that comes from losing partners, friends and family. Jill's complex relationships implied social capital and opportunities to meet different people and try out different pursuits which all supported good wellbeing. The differences in capitals influenced the demeanours or embodied characteristics of the women. In contrast, Mary spoke of having too much time to mull over the difficulties of old age, often returning to the same topics in interviews:

Mary: The bad things keep popping up all the time … my husband is not around anymore. My family (sisters and brothers) are not around anymore … I've lost all my loved ones haven't I?

MC: How do you cheer yourself up?

Mary: I've got a bottle of whisky out there. And I put my music on, I love classical music … I always have my down days … I do say to God, "Why did you make me like I am?" I didn't want to be brilliant. I didn't ask for that. I just want to be average. But he won't answer me.

Overall, it appeared that Mary had become much more pessimistic in later life than Jill, regularly speaking of her regrets about her life as well as her aching back, inability to drive, the deaths of friends and siblings and dissatisfaction with being home alone watching TV. Although less happy than Jill, there were distinct contours to Mary's wellbeing in recent years that illustrated some of the positive features of her life – she had good relationships with neighbours, enjoyed coffee with some local friends and walks with her small dog around the local community. By contrast, Jill's life and wellbeing had much more complex roots as she met and talked with different people each day, enjoyed satisfying activities that created a sense of achievement similar to that she experienced when younger and in waged work. Running the local community centre brought her into contact with residents of different ages, like the children's and youth groups and coffee mornings, bingo and quiz sessions for older residents. She was passionate about baking, learning new recipes and was proud about the money she raised for good causes.

Reviewing the data on Mary and Jill it appears the differences in their wellbeing stems partly from the differences in their social networks and activities. Which reflects suggestions that we conceptualize wellbeing as a relational phenomenon, something people do together (Thin, 2012). The more extensive ones relationships and activities are the more opportunities one has to flourish and live well. Researchers such as Coleman (1988) and Putnam (2000) have suggested that complex social relationships and sociability influence other symbolic and cultural resources or capitals promoting a sense of belonging and good wellbeing – that some suggest is important for 'successful ageing' (Ward et al, 2012). The psychologist Csikszentmihalyi (2002) would recognize in Jill's life examples of 'optimal flow' – types of activities significant for good wellbeing. Where, for example, Jill talks of losing herself in her cooking and the achievement she feels creating something new and tasteful for others to enjoy. These social activities, using skills and being creative are essential, life-affirming moments where we are reminded of the wonder and awe of 'being human' (Schiller, 2004). Mary's interview accounts in contrast suggest fewer experiences of 'flow' and less opportunities for achievement and fulfilment – lengthy spells watching TV alone, for example, is noted by Csikszentmihalyi as the sort of unfulfilling activity that can often be corrosive of good wellbeing. Mary's narrative, however, is an increasingly common one in aging societies that see growing numbers of elderly citizens experiencing social isolation and poor wellbeing (Scambler et al, 2002; Age UK, 2018).

Biographies and wellbeing: how social networks evolve over the life course to influence happiness

After my initial discussions with Mary and Jill I was curious about the origins of these differences in their social networks and their wellbeing. And how as a result of these variations it seemed that affluence was no guarantee of contentment in later life whereas cultivating relationships might help sustain a good life. Jill's example suggested that more extensive social networks and rewarding activities offered a more meaningful life and a sense of belonging that supported happiness far more than an affluent lifestyle. But how did these differences emerge – what can we learn from Mary and Jill's life stories about the development of happiness as we age? By examining the women's life histories I uncovered class and gender processes shaping their habitus, social identities and wellbeing. We also see the enduring influence of family relationships, faith and spirituality on Mary and Jill's wellbeing.

In follow-up discussions with Mary and Jill we mapped out their biographical timelines that identified the key events and their influences on their happiness. Jill had modest ambitions and horizons, inculcated from her parents – certificates at school, a job in a local shop, a husband, motherhood and part-time work. Jill spoke about the importance of 'doing ones best', working hard at school and work and contributing to the local community. These are respectable working-class notions (a key feature of her habitus) informing how to live well and involving values and expectations inculcated by her religious parents about the importance of hard work, faith and community – the Christian ethos of 'good works', self-sacrifice and compassion.

> 'My mam always took care of us and I was lucky to have parents like what I had ... my parents were the backbone of us ... I went to church from the time I was little. I mean we had to go because our mam made sure we went. But as I grew up, I still went and I feel it gives me strength to keep going ... My mother used to go out on a Tuesday night for the Tuesday Club which is what I am still running now ... we've been going 60 odd years.' (Jill)

Throughout her interview Jill spoke of her mother's influence on how she has lived her own life, particularly the importance of a loving family, church and community for living well. Her mother ran the local community centre and helped neighbours with their many issues and problems that confront people in disadvantaged working-class communities. When growing up Jill could see her mother's good wellbeing emerging from the dense complex of relationships she had across the community underpinned by her faith and loving family. Jill grew up to follow her mother's example becoming a pillar of the local community, moving just a few streets from her parent's home when she married and taking over much of the community activities that her mother had begun. Her mother's example and her religious faith influenced Jill's values and the ethos that framed much of her life.

> 'If you live according to your means and don't greed for everything you can (be happy). I've never got any money to spare ... not to want all the time. Make do with what you've got and be happy and say, "thank God, I'm alive".' (Jill)

The dense social networks we see in Jill's later life, what we might refer to as bonding social capital (Putnam, 2000: 22) that enabled her good wellbeing, were made possible by the earlier experiences, values and ethos growing up in a working-class community.[5] Mary, in contrast, spoke of growing up with a much more individualistic and materialistic ethos than Jill (an integral feature of her middle-class habitus), was far less religious and had family relationships that were more distant than the supportive environment Jill enjoyed. Her father was a shopkeeper and she spoke of growing up with an acute awareness of the material and cultural differences between the classes. She internalized a lower middle-class habitus, sensitive to her position caught between the poorer working classes below and affluent high-status professional middle classes above.

> 'My father came from Cornwall, his father was a shoemaker ... and he taught my father and my brothers. We rented a shop ... we only rented a house, people in those days didn't (buy houses), unless you were a doctor, a dentist, a solicitor, a headmaster maybe. All those houses up there, that's where the rich people used to live ... We weren't a rough family, my mother taught us manners. I know that you lived in a council estate ... my father wouldn't live on a council estate, he'd rather rent a house than live there, so we lived in a rented house.' (Mary)

Mary commented on the different dress, lifestyles and housing of the poorer working-class families compared with her more comfortable lower middle-class lifestyle. Yet Mary was also conscious their home was not as large or comfortable as the more respectable professional middle classes. This structural location (or field) that framed Mary's life is important as it suggests an economic and cultural insecurity – a family caught in a liminal space between the working classes below and the secure middle class above. Mary internalized a sensitivity about her status and these insecurities influenced her wellbeing when she was young. She spoke of periods of anxiety and unease as a child and young teenager. Mary's parents encouraged their children to do well at school viewing education as a route to a more secure, higher-status professional life. These early influences encouraged Mary to study hard and aim for a university place and a traditional profession for a middle-class woman as a teacher or nurse. However, unlike her nine siblings who all achieved at school and went on to middle-class careers, Mary found school very challenging, which had a significant effect on her wellbeing.

> 'I left school at 14 ... didn't pass anything. Well I wasn't a scholar. I had a learning difficulty but so far as the teacher was concerned, I was just not very bright at all. They had never heard of (dyslexia) then. They just said that you were backward ... I just didn't have very good memory ... I couldn't see the words. I was able to read things but not write things down ... I felt dreadful, I used to suffer with what mother called depressions. I used to just sit for ages and ages ... I would have loved to have been a nurse and I would have a made a good nurse but when it came to the theory I would have been lost. This is where I think education is wrong. They put you to one side, "You are no good".' (Mary)

The undiagnosed dyslexia and painful labelling she experienced at school meant Mary did not enjoy school and did badly in examinations, denying her a university place and middle-class career. This failure to live up to the cultural expectations of her class and gender and the troublesome psychic effects this generates is an example of what Bourdieu refers to as 'hysteresis' (Bourdieu, 1977: 77). Bourdieu shows (Bourdieu et al, 1999) how a mismatch between culturally prescribed expectations/ambitions and opportunities can have a significant effect on wellbeing. Mary too spoke of the profound disappointment she felt at this time watching her older brothers and sisters attend university and start their middle-class adult lives, noting the lasting corrosive effects these events had on her self-image and wellbeing (see also Sennett and Cobb, 1977; Reay, 2005).

> 'That was dreadful my school days, well I suppose if I've been able to commit suicide I'd have done it ... I could never be anybody special because I hadn't the brains for it ... I couldn't do an office job, I want to do things, I'm artistic, if you want to put it (that way) ... when I got to know my husband at first (at 37 years of age), because he was very intelligent I told him straight away, "you're not marrying anyone with brains", he said, "I don't want anyone with brains, I want a good housewife".' (Mary)

Mary often spoke about herself in interviews as a failure, even as an adult when it appeared she had lived a rich and varied life. She felt that her parents were disappointed in her and these self-judgements and powerful negative emotions she carried with her throughout life were a consequence of the symbolic violence she had experienced when young. These problematic early life events and how they were internalized helps us understand how Mary may have come to have poorer wellbeing later on in life.

However, the patterning of wellbeing across biographies is rarely straightforward and so in Mary's life there were periods she described as very happy ones, despite her earlier troubles. Mary was 18 years of age at the start of World War Two in 1939 and though this was a period of much privation, anxiety and uncertainty for many people, for Mary it was a much more positive enjoyable time. She joined the Women's Air Auxiliary Force (WAAF), spending the war years at an air base repairing aircraft, working as a seamstress mending seats and parachutes.

> 'Joining the services was the best thing I did in my life, the happiest time of my life. I like company, I like people, I liked the girls, we all slept in these huts and we went out, to the dances and we had lots of fun ... I was a good seamstress, I like sewing.'

Being a Waaf offered Mary an opportunity to leave home, make new friends and learn new skills as a seamstress. The war offered Mary a far more positive sense of self after the disappointments of childhood. Although at interview I was curious that the war years were seen as the happiest years for Mary rather than the period she was married – for wellbeing research usually identifies falling in love and marriage as the happiest moments of life (Clark et al, 2018: 79). As we discuss later on, this period in her life may have also offered her an insight into her identity and sexuality which helps us understand why Mary often felt disappointed with her later life and which impacted on her wellbeing.

At the end of the war Mary returned to the family home, living with her parents who were running a small village shop in Middlesex and again she spoke of her wellbeing being relatively poor during these years at home. She was consciousness of her siblings marrying and establishing their own homes as she increasingly felt like the unmarried, unwanted spinster in the family. Although Mary eventually did marry.

> 'I met my husband when I was working in the shop (owned by her parents) and we married when I was 37 ... I had known him for two years before he asked me to marry him. I thought now or never, I'm always telling people, you won't get another chance ... I married him because I was 37, he was nice, he came from a nice family and had a nice mother and father and we got on quite well. (My husband), well he should have gone places, he was going into engineering ... after he had been in the army he couldn't settle down. He travelled a lot, working on window displays for those big shops. We could only afford a maisonette ... to get our foot on the ladder. He said that we'll live there for three years and be able to move on ... Then we moved to a detached house ... He had a company car, we went to Spain and Portugal on holiday ... David was always buying me things.' (Mary)

We can see in Mary's account of her marriage the importance she placed on living a materialistic, respectable, middle-class life – values and lifestyle that emerged when she was much younger. Also significantly how this key moment in her life and for her wellbeing emerged from time reflecting on her options and choices – whether to remain single at home or choose an independent life as a married women. Once married Mary worked part-time and her husband's career afforded them the consumerist trappings of a middle-class life – expensive cars, clothes, foreign holidays and larger and larger homes as her husband's career progressed. Although marriage appeared as a solution to the insecurities and disappointments of Mary's early life, she spoke of her disappointments with this life and how she came to regret much of how she lived at this time which shaped her wellbeing in later life. On the one hand their 'successful' middle-class life involved her being a 'stay at home wife' which proved to be very lonely as they moved house several times and she missed her colleagues from work. Mary spoke of having few local supportive relationships so although she may have enjoyed what Putnam calls 'bridging social capital' (Putnam, 2000: 22) and a materially successful life she did not experience that sense of embeddedness and belonging that comes from bonding capital enjoyed by Jill. With the premature death of her husband in 1986 after 26 years of marriage Mary became very aware of this lack of support and disconnection from the community where she lived. Her marriage however was also problematic for her wellbeing in other respects, suggesting it was more a marriage of convenience than one founded on love and intimacy.

> 'My mother always used to say to me, "you might think you are in love, but it's not that, it's the chemistry between two people … Well I said, "what do you mean the chemistry?" Well she said, "if you have never had it, you don't know" … I never got that you see … You are disappointed because you haven't got that something that she is telling you about … Yes I did get the chemistry but not through my husband … If the chemistry is there you would die for that person … I can't explain it to you. It's a part of my life that is private, a private thing for myself.' (Mary)

Mary's experiences seem contradictory and difficult to understand as on the one hand she was living what appeared a happy, affluent married life, conforming to the norms of the time, yet also felt this was not quite the life she had hoped for. There were hints in the transcripts about the nature of her wellbeing and how her identity and emotional needs were more complex than they appeared. How, for example, 'the happiest years of her life' were those war years surrounded by other women, enjoying their camaraderie rather than the years of marriage in a conventional heterosexual relationship. I have read and reread these transcripts many times and the reader like myself can come to their own conclusions about the reasons why Mary was disappointed about her marriage which cast a long shadow over her wellbeing in later life. Researchers like Neil Thin (2012) and ethnographers such as Lisa McKenzie (2015) document the centrality of intimacy, affection and love for happiness and so perhaps these were missing from her married life? And this it appears was confirmed to her after her husband died and she found a new love – another man or perhaps another women that she wished to keep secret, from me at least, for some reason? When married she felt unable to be true to herself and this was a source of regret and unhappiness. But in later life she did find this authentic love and with it hopefully a deeper more meaningful happiness that was missing when young.

In summary, I noted earlier how the more affluent Mary appeared less happy than the working-class Jill. I suggested that these counter-intuitive differences in wellbeing may be attributed to the very different social networks of these two women. Mary having a smaller number of friends and more restricted range of activities. Whereas Jill enjoyed a complex set of relationships across her working-class community that supported a diverse array of pursuits and interests. One advantage of qualitative wellbeing research therefore is how, over months and years, we can investigate the way that daily habits and routines construct social networks that come to influence happiness. I then suggested that we could have a greater understanding of these women' socials networks and wellbeing by also exploring their biographies. Their very different life stories and particularly formative experiences when young helped us understand how they came to develop rather different approaches to life that framed their relationships and in turn their happiness. Jill's more supportive family- and community-focused ethos led to a life centred around one small working-class community in South Wales but a set of relationships that nourished a deep meaningful wellbeing. Mary's life was marked more by insecurities, about her class position and her academic abilities that informed some of her life choices (such as her marriage) and a materialistic ethos that had led to an apparently 'successful' life yet limited the scope and quality of her social networks and in turn provided a poorer wellbeing in later life.

Conclusions

I have illustrated how we might use qualitative biographical research into happiness/wellbeing and how this differs from existing survey approaches concerned with measurable conceptions of wellbeing or political critiques of the happiness industry. We do need new perspectives that research wellbeing as a social practice something that we experience and share with friends, colleagues, neighbours and loved ones. I drew on Bourdieu and qualitative biographical methods to illustrate how happiness flows from the places we live and evolves as we grow. This embeddedness and biographical contours suggests the need for a host of concepts to discern the shifts in wellbeing as we age – such as habitus, capitals, practice, field, reflexivity, fallibility and so on. By interviewing people about their social networks and life stories we can show there are indeed patterns to wellbeing as existing studies suggest, that reflect the social divisions and differential resources and opportunities that colour societies. But qualitative research also documents the lived experiences behind these power relationships and the efforts of ordinary people to manage these structures. Thus, qualitative biographical research illustrates the interweaving of structures and agency across the life course and their influence on wellbeing. Although I utilize the survey data and the political polemics from mainstream research, a critical, qualitative approach to wellbeing also details the narratives, images and language of trade-offs, dilemmas, choices and surprises that flow from people's efforts to live well. As we witnessed with Jill and Mary there are often predictable structured patterns to wellbeing but when we map their networks and biographies exploring their complex meanings around living well we also discern the subtle ebb and flow of happiness that makes up their lives. It is these stories and contours that are at the heart of happiness research and deserve our attention.

Notes

[1] One challenge for qualitative research is how people construct narratives about their lives and how much of these are rooted in actual events – 'differences between narrating a life and living a life'.

[2] Though this may not be a conscious effort to live well but rather the product in part of pursuing other life goals/activities.

[3] Although I only draw on two case studies here the arguments I present are reflective of more general trends and findings across the overall sample.

[4] I did initially suspect that these differences in wellbeing might be due to Mary's older years but both women at initial interview spoke of being in good physical health.

[5] We see here the role of religious beliefs and principles that inform notions of living well, ideas explored by Weber in his discussion of theodicy in 'Social psychology of world religions' (Gerth and Mills, 1982).

References

Age UK (2018) *All The Lonely People: Loneliness in Later Life*, Age UK, https://www.ageuk.org.uk/our-impact/policy-research/loneliness-research-and-resources/

Archer, M.S. (1988) *Culture and Agency: The Place of Culture in Social Theory*, Cambridge: Cambridge University Press.

Archer, M.S. (2003) *Structure, Agency and the Internal Conversation*, Cambridge: Cambridge University Press.

Argyle, M. (2001) *The Psychology of Happiness*, London: Routledge.

Aristotle (2009) *Nicomachean Ethics*, Oxford: Oxford University Press.

Bourdieu, P. (1984) *Distinction: A Social Critique of the Judgement of Taste*, London: Routledge.

Bourdieu, P. (1990) *The Logic of Practice*, Cambridge: Cambridge University Press.

Bourdieu, P. (2004) 'The forms of capital', in S.J. Ball (ed) *The Routledge Falmer Reader in the Sociology of Education*, London: Routledge Falmer, pp 15–29.

Bourdieu, P. (1977) *Outline of a Theory of Practice*, Cambridge: Cambridge University Press.

Bourdieu, P. et al (1999) *The Weight of the World: Social Suffering in Contemporary Society*, Stanford: Stanford University Press.

Bourdieu, P. and Wacquant, L. (1992) *Invitation to Reflexive Sociology*, Cambridge: Polity Press.

Cederström, C. and Spicer, A. (2015) *The Wellness Syndrome*, Cambridge: Polity.

Cieslik, M. (2015) 'Not smiling but frowning: sociology and the problem of happiness', *Sociology*, 49(3), 422–37, DOI: 10.1177/0038038514543297

Cieslik, M. (2017) *The Happiness Riddle and the Quest for a Good Life*, London: Palgrave.

Cieslik, M. and Simpson, D. (2015) 'Basic skills, literacy practices and the hidden injuries of class', *Sociological Research Online*, 20(1), http://www:socresonline.org.uk/20/1/7.html

Clark, A., Fleche, S., Layard, R., Powdthavee, N. and Ward, G. (2018) *The Origins of Happiness: The Science of Wellbeing Over the Life Course*, Oxfordshire: Princeton.

Coleman, J.S. (1988) 'Social capital in the creation of human capital', *American Journal of Sociology*, 94 Supplement, S95–120.

Craib, I. (2001), *Psychoanalysis: A Critical Introduction*, Cambridge: Polity Press.

Csikszentmihalyi, M. (2002) *Flow: The Classic Work on How to Achieve Happiness*, London: Harper and Row.

Davies, W. (2015) *The Happiness Industry: How the Government and Big Business Sold Us Wellbeing*, London: Verso.

Diener, E. (1984) 'Subjective wellbeing', *Psychological Bulletin*, 95: 542–75.

Furedi, F. (2004) *Therapy Culture: Cultivating Vulnerability in an Uncertain Age*, London: Routledge.

Gerth, H.H. and Mills, C. Wright (1982) *From Max Weber: Essays in Sociology*, London: Routledge Kegan Paul.

Gilbert, D. (2006) *Stumbling on Happiness*, London: Harper Perennial.

Goffman, E. (1956) *The Presentation of Self in Everyday Life*, Edinburgh: Edinburgh University Press.

Hoggard, L. (2005) *How to be Happy*, London: BBC Books.

Holmes, M. and McKenzie, J. (2018) 'Relational happiness through recognition and distribution: emotion and inequality', *European Journal of Social Theory*, 25 September: 1–19, DOI: org/10.1177/1368431018799257

Holthus, B. and Manzenreiter, W. (eds) (2017) *Life Course, Happiness and Well-being in Japan*, London: Routledge.

King, A. (2000) 'Thinking with Bourdieu against Bourdieu: a practical critique of the habitus', *Sociological Theory*, 18(3): 417–33.

Layard, R. (2005). *Happiness: Lessons from a New Science*, London: Penguin.

Manzenreiter, W. and Holthus, B. (eds) (2017) *Happiness and the Good Life in Japan*, London: Routledge.

Mathews, G. (1996) *What Makes Life Worth Living: How Japanese and Americans Make Sense of their Worlds*, London: University of California Press.

McKenzie, L. (2015) *Getting By: Estates, Class and Culture in Austerity Britain*, Bristol: Policy Press.

McMahon, D. (2006) *Happiness: a History*, New York: Grove Press.

Morgan, A. (2014) 'The happiness turn: Axel Honneth, self-reification and sickness unto health', *Subjectivity*, 7(3): 219–33.

Mouzelis, N. (2008) *Modern and Postmodern Social Theorizing*, Cambridge: Cambridge University Press.

Pople, L., Rees, G., Main, G. and Bradshaw, J. (2015) *The Good Childhood Report 2015*, London: Children's Society.

Putnam, R. (2000) *Bowling Alone: the Collapse and Revival of American Community*, London: Simon and Schuster.

Reay, D. (2005) 'Beyond consciousness: the psychic landscapes of social class', *Sociology*, 39(5): 911–28.

Sayer, A. (2010) 'Reflexivity and habitus' in M.S. Archer (ed) *Conversations About Reflexivity*, London: Routledge, pp 108–22.

Sayer, A. (2011) *Why Things Matter to People: Social Science, Values and Ethical Life*, Cambridge: Cambridge University Press.

Scambler, S., Victor, C., Bond, J. and Bowling, A. (2002) 'Promoting quality of life: preventing loneliness among older people', Paper presented to the XV World Congress of Sociology, 7–13 July, Brisbane, Australia.

Schiller, F. (2004) *Letters on the Aesthetical Education of Man*, New York: Dover Publications.

Sennett, R. and Cobb, J. (1977) *The Hidden Injuries of Class*, Cambridge: Cambridge University Press.

Skeggs B. (1997) *Formations of Class and Gender*, London: Sage.

Thatcher, J., Ingram, N., Burke, C. and Abrahams, J. (eds) (2016) *Bourdieu: The Next Generation*, London: Routledge.

Thin, N. (2012) *Social Happiness: Theory into Policy and Practice*, Bristol: Policy Press.

Veenhoven, R. (1999) 'Quality of life in individualistic societies: a comparisons of 43 nations in the early 1990s', *Social Indicators Research*, 48: 157–86.

Veenhoven, R. (2008) 'Sociological theories of subjective wellbeing', in M. Eid and R. Larsen (eds) *The Science of Subjective Wellbeing: A Tribute to Ed Diener*, New York: Guildford Publications, pp 44–61.

Ward, L., Barnes, M. and Gahagan, B. (2012) *Wellbeing in Old Age: Findings from Participatory Research*, Brighton: University of Brighton.

White, S.C. (2017) 'Relational wellbeing: re-centering the politics of happiness, policy and the self', *Policy and Politics*, 45(2): 121–36.

6

Considering the Body in Happiness Research

Richard Gibbons

Introduction

The core aim of this chapter is to present an argument for a greater focus on the body in happiness research. I will explore what this might look like using my own work and insight from the last four years, which has mainly been focused on the significance of the body in people's lives across different age ranges, and how we see this translate into embodied practice. But why is it important to specifically consider the body in our research? How does the body and wellbeing actually relate? It is quite easy to think of bodies simply as functional, or indeed, to not think of bodies particularly much at all. The body does not naturally resonate with our lay understandings about happiness. We tend to acknowledge happiness more often as a cerebral concept, and think of ourselves as reasoned, feeling beings. However, I will go on to argue that we are also embodied beings too, and that this corporeal aspect of our presence in the world has ultimately been neglected in happiness research, but is an important and nuanced facet of our wellbeing. Researching wellbeing is already a complex endeavour and factoring the body into this can, of course, make those waters even murkier. This chapter, therefore, aims to demonstrate why it is still a worthwhile pursuit, and one that can lead us to a better understanding about the approaches that people adopt to live both fulfilling and meaningful lives.

The simplest argument I could present that endorses this claim is the overwhelming presence the body has in our everyday lives. A presence that, as researchers, we are often arguably guilty of overlooking, despite it actually being rather easy to see evidence of the body's significance all around us. We can gauge this visibility straight away in our own immediate reality; in our endeavours, actions, movements and experiences. Something as simple as the groan of a knee as we get up in the morning, or the warmth of a hug from a partner at the end of a difficult day can resonate with us in meaningful ways. Even when it is often quite difficult for us to articulate exactly why this is the case. We also see evidence of the body more generally in life and in the world around us, and we take stock of its value usually without much in the way of specific acknowledgement. We will take the measure of a person without even knowing anything about them, simply by how they carry themselves. We will make snap judgements on the health of others based only on how they look. Surface-level observations such as these are commonplace, but it is also just as natural for us to take readings of the world around us pre-reflectively, by way of the body's tendency to form an intentional equilibrium with the world around us (Merleau-Ponty, 1962). As example, we may register the familiar struggles of those toiling in the next lane at the swimming baths, and find solace in their shared plight. We might gain a sense that the person we are engaged with in conversation is on our wavelength, even without much being said. Ultimately, our research needs to consider the body because it is integral to our understanding of the social world at this level through the underlying somatic awareness that bodies bring into our lives.

On a wider scale, tracing back throughout history bodies have regularly been a site of interest, both as vessels for ritual, symbolism and traditional practice, as well as vehicles for identity, agency and individual or collective expression. Our health, fitness and vitality are highly commodified resources fought over by huge industries. Online spaces such as Instagram, Twitter, Facebook and Reddit promote a more visual culture than ever before, one where we have the option to present an image of ourselves that is distinct from our everyday lives. Nowadays, we all have or at least know someone with one or more form of body modification, and, in some cases, even a form of surgical alteration. At the very least, most of us subscribe to the fluid whims of fashion and cosmetics, reacting to trends and lifestyle advice that is often shaped on a global scale. Even our film and TV industries tap heavily into our fascination with the body. They depict Marvel and DC superheroes with empowered physiques, bodies that are hollowed, empty and zombified husks in shows like *The Walking Dead*, or flesh that is warped and moulded in popular cult media such as *Frankenstein* or *Stranger Things*. Many of our sweetest fantasies and deepest nightmares play out in the world around us using the body as the canvas.

Bodies are literally everywhere, and should arguably have a place in happiness studies and be acknowledged as a facet of life that is integral to our wellbeing. Yet, as alluded to already, this is not currently the case within happiness literature, which largely overlooks the body, only ever really highlighting ways the body can negatively impact our wellbeing (see as examples Keery et al, 2004; Mond et al, 2011; and Swami et al, 2015, which accumulatively scratch the surface of the literature covering 'Body Image'). There are undoubtedly numerous reasons for this limited focus on bodies in wellbeing research. After all, the West has a rich history of objectifying the body, viewing it as physical matter subject to external regimes and rules that frame bodies as object, abject, and subject (Cregan, 2006). We have a tendency to acknowledge that our mind, our very consciousness, represents that core essence that *is* us, relegating the body to an 'it', or often at best something we refer to as a possession (Reeve, 2011). It is actually a linguistically tricky exercise trying to avoid writing or talking about the body in an objectifying manner, by referring to 'it' as 'my body', essentially a vessel that's main purpose is simply to hold our true self (Crossley, 2006). From an ideological standpoint, Western society also rests upon a strong philosophical foundation that separates mind from body (see Descartes, 1974, 1983; and Kant, 1985 [1797]). This translates into many of our key societal infrastructures; health/medical, religious, and academic institutions, the places we pursue leisure, or workplace organizations, all of which promote in one way or another a distinction between mind and body (Reeve, 2011). This way of understanding the world and our presence within it is deeply entrenched, and naturally affects our world view.

My own research does at least on the surface echo these commonplace understandings. It highlights how despite living in a world that is ever more body conscious, people frequently seem to let the body recede into the background of their lives in an almost absent-minded manner. It is somewhat of a paradox that even though we are granted a deeply corporeal awareness of life and the world around us – who and what we are is made up of our physicality after all – the body is still generally hidden from us, as if it is an 'absent presence' (Leder, 1990) as we move through our everyday biography. Yet despite this regularly being the case for my respondents, they all did recognize the importance of their body in many different ways, and the body became a defining focus for many of them over long periods of time. At the same time they bestowed both great power and fragility on their bodies, often giving accounts that blurred the lines between nourishing, unsettling, or more ambiguous experiences which centred around their body. This dissonance arguably problematizes the societal understandings I have already outlined. It is therefore important to note that just thinking about the body and wellbeing together can make for a challenging research focus, because it is something that simply does not come naturally to us. For instance, I found that during the interviews, respondents would often try to directly relate their body to their wellbeing but struggled to make intuitive links that adequately summed up what they felt. This presents an issue for quantitative research approaches, because they essentially ask participants to attempt exactly that. However, as we will go on to demonstrate, the way the body and wellbeing are experienced is full of ambiguity and nuanced meaning for an individual. Qualitative approaches are therefore needed to tease out these more complex understandings.

Background to the study

Whenever conducting research, it is, of course, always recommended to focus on things we are passionate about. Tattoos were the catalyst for my own interest in the body. I am what most people might describe as heavily tattooed, which originally stems from my long-standing love of music and the local music scene that I was an active part of, both in bands and social groups. However, it was not until I began studying sociology that I really started to think critically about what being tattooed meant to me. Then as I started researching the body, this gradually transitioned into an understanding about how I orientate to the world around me, aided in tacit, felt ways through my body. I began to take note of how key aspects of my identity and performance (quite literally, by way of musical performance) are facilitated by my body, and how this changed over time as my experience deepened. I started to notice how people respond to the symbolism inscribed into how I look and carry myself; how there is a certain power in the way we embody our interests and the aspects of our lives that mean the most to us. Of course, this is interesting because it connects to some of the key debates in sociology around power, identity, and the self. Identity and power are also two of the cornerstones of the sociological imagination (Mills, 1959), and sociology has so much that it can bring to an analysis of the body in this regard. For instance, sociological theory has a rich tradition of exploring class (Bourdieu, 1984, 1986; Marx, 2013 [1867]), gender (Butler, 1990; Bordo, 2003), performance (Goffman, 1959), sexuality (Foucault, 1981), and many other facets of life that are useful guides when thinking about the body and wellbeing.

I believe sociology enriches happiness research in this way and helps us to find and ask meaningful questions.

But despite these strengths, I have found in my own work that we cannot look to sociology alone to create an analytical framework. In the realm of body studies, the literature provides a great deal of compelling, thought-provoking theory. This ranges from classical theorists who focus on the technical aspects of performance (Mauss, 1973 [1934]) or transmission of meaning via symbols (Elias, 2000 [1939]). To current theories that look to synergize different perspectives to create a framework for examining the body and society (Crossley, 2006; Shilling, 2012). It makes body studies literature highly useful when building a methodological framework, because there is a great deal of thought and insight to draw on. However, actual empirical research seems comparatively under-represented. Sociological literature on wellbeing does a better job here, but as highlighted fails to consider the body adequately, often frames happiness around separate, wider debates of interest (Cieslik, 2015), and also leans heavily towards a quantitative analysis of happiness (Bartram, 2012; Cieslik, 2017). Beyond these evident issues, the task of where to turn to for academic inspiration hides within it a deeper problem. While conducting research on the body and wellbeing, it became increasingly apparent from a personal perspective that my approach to living life is heavily impacted by life's many ups and downs. I think generally we need to be more transparent about how our own lives can filter into our research, and researching wellbeing actually forced me to acknowledge this as a reality.[1] However, it can be problematic to articulate and unpack tacitly felt understandings such as these in a sociological way. This in many ways illuminates the difficulty inherent in researching the body and wellbeing more generally, because what we are aiming to explore actually starts to blend into the notion of what it is to be human. It also highlights the limits inherent in how sociologists traditionally study these things.

As an example, sociologists tend to understand power in terms of patterns, and the patterns they often depict centre around issues of structured experience, class, age, gender and so forth. My research demonstrates how the body does fit within this frame of reference. It uses sociological tools which illuminate how the body functions in people's lives to either empower or restrict their wellbeing, sometimes concurrently. This means that the body is at one and the same time both a resource for wellbeing, and a potential barrier to it, and we can see these patterns unfold sociologically (for instance by exploring experiences of aging). However, this does not adequately express the range of ways we experience our body and wellbeing on a day-to-day basis. What we might refer to as the granular detail of life, such as the more fleeting, ephemeral moments of internal struggle or weariness from a difficult day, or the sedimentation of a series of smaller life events that gradually impact us over a prolonged period of our biography. We need to therefore cast our analytical net wider. While partially abandoning our sociological roots may feel challenging, my own experience highlights how researching the body and wellbeing can be an interesting endeavour. We are forced to think outside the box to draw upon other subjects and their ways of doing things, further enriching our perspective and research scope.

Contours of the research

To this point my intention has been to briefly furnish a rationale for considering the body in your work, as well as to provide some insight into why doing so adds both an interesting and enriching facet to researching wellbeing. I have also highlighted how researching the body in tandem to wellbeing can be challenging, and tried to convey the general messiness inherent in this as a research focus. However, this of course needs to coalesce into something more structured for the purposes of this chapter, so I will now briefly cover the main contours of the research and qualitative approach used to obtain data. I adopted a 'phenomenological' position, which allows one to understand how people experience something in their lives (Crotty, 1998), and it has a robust and relevant philosophical and theoretical platform from which to build (Husserl, 1931; Merleau-Ponty, 1962, 1963; Crossley, 2006, 2013). After conducting two pilot interviews to test the primary research instrument, the empirical work was guided by some key questions that focused on how people understand and experience their bodies, and how this works across a biography as bodies age and change. Another aim was to explore the key moments in respondents' lives, as these are often drivers for change (Cieslik, 2017), and I was interested to examine how people coped and adjusted during these periods. Finally, I wanted to tap into the more mundane facets of everyday life; work, routine, hobbies/play, caring for others, and so forth, to explore the role of the body more generally in the day-to-day lives of participants.

Already having a sense of the challenges that lay ahead to access qualitative data about fluid, ambiguous phenomenon such as happiness, experience and embodiment, a 'purposive sampling' approach was deemed the best fit (Patton, 2015). This allowed me to identify people that represent information-rich cases, whom were ideal candidates to talk about how they understand their body and the significance it holds in their lives. In addition to the two participants in the pilot, a further 15 respondents were interviewed, with as even a spread of men and women from both working-class and middle-class backgrounds as possible, ranging in age across six decades. Two interviews were conducted with each of the 15 primary research respondents, for a total of 32 interviews. Another feature of the sample was that each participant engaged with at least one Reformative Embodied Technique (RET), which is the umbrella term I use for a range of disciplines such as different martial arts, yoga, tai chi or meditative-type practices. The argument for this was that I would be able to engage respondents already well positioned for the research due to their commitment to activities that factor prominently in bodily expression.

In hindsight, I could have just as effectively chosen another criterion, such as cycling or another sporting activity, parenthood, people that walk dogs, or really any engaging practice that could be used at times to frame discussion in the interviews around that topic. This is because for the semi-structured interview method chosen (and I would argue for qualitative happiness research more broadly) it was desirable to not always lead with the main research concerns so as to not focus the interview narrative too linearly. It is also for this reason that the topics of happiness and the body were used sparingly when building interview questions. I instead pursued insight about these topics through a deeper understanding of a respondent's biography and their engagement with their practice, which is a beneficial approach that anyone can apply to research. As highlighted earlier, two separate interviews were conducted with each participant. The first explored their biography to gain a sense of their lives, key events, and what was important to them, and the second asked questions that had emerged from a review of relevant literature as well as an analysis of their first biographical interview. I would especially recommend this dual-interview approach for any hermeneutically grounded exploration of wellbeing. This is because what we are essentially asking people to do is open up insightfully about the complex self, which is a very intricate task full of grey areas, pitfalls, and misunderstandings for both the researcher and participant. Having as broad a picture as possible of a respondent's biography certainly benefits this process, particularly when it comes to the eventual task of analysing data and drawing out findings. We will come back to some of these challenges presented by researching happiness and the body, but will first explore a small selection of findings from my own research.

Some themes and findings – understandings about the body

My thesis unpacks the complex intersection of numerous forms of experience respondents bring to the social world. It does this by delving into the mindful, embodied, and temporal dimensions of this experience, explored across three separate analysis chapters that highlight the contribution an embodied focus brings to qualitative research in happiness studies. The confines of this single chapter do not afford us the luxury of covering these findings comprehensively, and I will instead focus on answering some of the key questions posed in the Introduction, regarding how the body and wellbeing relate to one another and what this might look like when applied to research. What is important to note is that the findings discussed later represent only a fraction of the many complex situated/embodied meanings that emerged from the research. These themes could only be accessed through a qualitative analysis of the body and wellbeing, which reveals the granular details that are missing from the large data sets generated by quantitative research approaches (Greener, 2011). It also illustrates the importance of life-course narratives as a means to access such understandings, as well as highlighting the significance of biography generally as a conduit that people draw upon to facilitate better wellbeing.

Using the research instrument outlined in the previous section, many different narratives organically emerged that illustrated how respondents acknowledge and interpret the importance of the body in separate domains of life. This data was then used to develop eight broad categories of understandings in relation to the body. These categories are useful to demonstrate how the body is orientated in people's lives towards their wellbeing. They serve as a framework for thinking about the embodied dimension of wellbeing in happiness research that other projects can draw from. They also highlight to those considering the body in their research that when they begin conducting interviews, these are the types of things their respondents might talk about. People will, of course, understand their body in slightly different ways, but there tends to be patterns to this which we can draw on sociologically, and it is always useful to build from similar work in the field.

The structured body, impacted by social forces

For the purposes of this chapter, we will focus on just two of the eight categories of understanding the body, and we will concentrate mainly on the perspectives of two of my respondents; Karate Guy, a 56-year-old man from a middle-class background, and Nancy, a 40-year-old woman from a working-class background. They make for an interesting comparison because both were in the middle period of the normal lifespan, and were in a good place at the time of interview, with rich and rewarding lives. However, both also encountered difficulties due to their bodies, which challenged aspects of their identities. Each then drew from their biographies to help reconcile this through embodied practice. The body, therefore, functioned both as a barrier to and resource for wellbeing. The first category that will explore this is 'the structured body', which relates to the body as it is impacted by wider social forces. Before the categories were even in place in the research, this had emerged as a theme from my review of the body studies literature (some prominent examples are, Foucault, 1979; Bourdieu, 1984; Butler, 1993; Elias, 2000 [1939]; and Turner, 2008 [1984]). I was therefore interested to see if respondents might allude to any potential structuring or control of their bodies. Perhaps unsurprisingly, female participants did recognize more explicitly that social forces and the widely shared assumptions held by society had an influence on the understandings they themselves had about their own bodies. Most female respondents spoke about this issue directly, without any prompting, and could link this to personal experiences. Nancy was originally a midwife working in maternity wards, but had over time climbed up the management hierarchy to a support/research position.

> 'I feel like I have to try twice as hard (as men). So, I've got a colleague who's a man and who's on the same level as me; we do the same job just in different divisions. There's an assumption that whenever we go to meetings that he's in charge, and it just pisses me off. I'm actually better at my job than he is and I know a lot more about what it is we're trying to do than he does. It really gets on my nerves. Equally, when the bosses are away, their phones that people contact them on are just kind of automatically given to him.' (Nancy, 2017)

We can draw an obvious link to the structured body here, with regard to how social understandings about authority and power can be more favourable to men, which in Nancy's case leads to a disempowering gendered experience in the workplace. Additionally, trying "twice as hard" did not only mean with regard to application of work, because Nancy went on to link this to putting extra effort into looking "glamorous", and like "this young, smiley and happy woman" (Nancy, 2017). She resented doing this, but also thought it necessary to maintain a degree of her own power, using her body. In a similar fashion, the majority of my female respondents highlighted that they felt compelled to cover up supposed imperfections with make-up, or attempt to appear younger, more beautiful, slimmer, and a range of other desires linked to social ideals. The feminist philosopher, Sandra Bartky (1990), would highlight such understandings as a 'fashion-beauty complex', and a range of empirical research also highlights that commonplace societal understandings affect women's experience of their own bodies more forcefully than they do for men (Bordo, 2003; Cash and Smolak, 2011).

Of course, men also do struggle with body image issues rooted in social understandings about what it is to be masculine. Longitudinal studies highlight that feeling negatively about our body image, regardless of sex, can lead to a marginalization of potential life outcomes (Gupta et al, 2016). However, my findings in this area upheld that women are more likely to experience this negatively over prolonged periods of their biography than men are. Men seem to have a greater number of viable options open to them as alternative routes into an embodied masculine identity, one in which the tropes of masculinity are more forgiving, even as men age and their bodies change. Karate Guy illustrates this when giving his account of getting older as a man. During his biographical interview, he described a schoolyard brawl that he was involved in when he was younger. He spoke at length about how powerless and useless he felt during this event, and how he froze, helpless to defend himself. It proved to be the catalyst for his pursuit of martial arts, and over the course of many years the deepening of this practice instilled meanings around his body, linking its wellness and functionality to his overarching wellbeing.

> 'I feel like I want to feel capable of functioning as an animal in terms of self-defence. Not that it's something that I ever anticipate occurring, but just on general principle being a viable animal. That I can physically have a sense of taking care of myself, you know, physical survival. That at the basic level of fight or flight, those would both be options. Yeah, so like I feel that on some level I maintain the idea

that I'm not going to be useless and that I'm going to be able to make a respectable stand.' (Karate Guy, 2016)

Exploring the nuances of Karate Guy's biography helped to unpack how he has bolstered traditional understandings about the aging body, especially in ways that are nourishing and harmonious with his core identity as a martial artist. The quote is taken from a point much later in the interview process than his earlier account of the schoolyard brawl, as Karate Guy was now talking about how he deals with growing older. It highlights the strength of conducting biographical interviews as part of a qualitative approach to researching wellbeing, because they allow us to see links between more complex and layered life events (Bryman, 2016). This in turn helps us to unpack broader themes across a respondent sample, such as the different ways that men and women adapt to the shifting parameters of age.

As we age there is an inevitability about the fading of looks. We sag all over our body, we may lose hair, go grey, our skin wrinkles and mottles, and beyond all of these realities there is also a societal understanding associated with a 'lessening' of ourselves as we get older (Shilling, 2012). Even if we come to terms with it for ourselves as a reality within the aging process, how do we uphold or combat the tropes of masculinity and femininity? Being able to position himself as maintaining his physical prowess and viability, Karate Guy does arguably meet this masculine standard. This is also a route into a genuinely embodied masculine identity even as age can strip men of other features of masculinity, such as hair loss or muscle degradation. However, as we have already discussed, a core aspect of the social construction of femininity links it to understandings about the maintenance of beauty and grace. Considering the inevitability of these things fading with time, it is arguably more difficult for women to practice an equally validating experience of an embodied feminine identity. This is not to say that women cannot be feminine in other ways, or that it is even a necessary or required pursuit to begin with. Nevertheless, several women in the sample felt a level of injustice about this facet of femininity. We can argue that there is an inherent inequality embodied within the current social incarnation of femininity simply due to the reality of aging, and that this is not quite as evident within the current social incarnation of masculinity and how men can express being masculine, especially as they age. Therefore, the body can be related to wellbeing in gendered ways based on how an individual understands or interprets socially held beliefs/values about their body.

The negotiated body, 'mindfully embodied philosophies to live by'

The second category of understanding about the body we will explore is 'the negotiated body'. This links to the ways that respondents mindfully embody philosophies to live by and how important these were as foundations to their wellbeing and ability to lead a good life. The body, as the fulcrum of social action and cornerstone of embodied knowledge, is integral to this process (Shusterman, 2008, 2012). The negotiated body explores how respondents orientate themselves to the world through a complex set of understandings, embodied practices, and ways of being. Throughout the interview process it became apparent that while the messiness of life often poses challenges, respondents tended to have core principles and approaches to living that served to guide them through these on a day-to-day level. These ranged from simple morning routines aimed at gearing oneself for a day at work, to more complex, multifaceted approaches as we will explore with Nancy's redefining of guilt. These negotiations can, of course, change, or even come and go over time, but many are also incredibly solid frameworks that respondents live by, both explicitly and implicitly, and are especially evident in older respondents who have had more time to develop them and tend to have a greater range of life experience to draw from. This is admittedly a complex category, and due to space, I can only briefly address it here in terms of how Karate Guy and Nancy understood their different circumstances, and then framed them within mindfully embodied philosophies to live by. These were negotiated between practical needs, personal desires and understandings, and wider life parameters.

We will start by examining the particular circumstances and mindfully embodied philosophies to live by of Karate Guy, as way of example. He and his partner started their relationship when he was 37 years old, and almost 20 years later at the time of interview, they have two young children aged 5 and 7. He was keenly aware that since he was 56 years old, he would be in his seventies by the time both his children exited their teenage years. He spoke about this being a factor in how he approaches life and the reality of being an older father. He had a contract of sorts with his body that was not a straightforward desire to maintain health and vitality for his own needs. It instead was negotiated on both practical and symbolic levels; "I had kids quite late in my life, so if I'm going to see them grow up, I need to live a nice long time ... I got to give those shoulder rides and play the bouncy games!" (Karate Guy, 2016). Bourdieu (1984), in his theory of physical capital, highlights the body as integral to accumulating resources.

Most sociologists read this as it applies to accessing forms of social, cultural, and economic capitals (Shilling, 2012). However, as we see with Karate Guy's circumstances, the physical capital of the body is also deeply rooted in symbolic forms of commitment that are, in this example, integral to fatherhood. What is interesting is these forms of commitment operate externally to the usual forms of self-interested bodily upkeep. My interviews with Karate Guy highlighted numerous life philosophies connecting to this understanding, such as approaches he used to prevent getting side-tracked or distracted by peripheral enticements, or quite long and involving philosophies about dying without having regrets. All of these helped to facilitate an approach to life that underpinned his core values and goals with his family. It is often worth reminding ourselves when discussing happiness or wellbeing in relation to the body that it is not always simply relating to that individual. The body is social, and wellbeing in relation to the body often has tacit social impact.

Nancy also demonstrates the negotiated body, but for her it was not age but inability that called into question what she understood to be key aspects of womanhood. She faced an array of challenges throughout her upbringing, with a violent father and distant mother who was herself experiencing abuse. Then in her early twenties her younger brother committed suicide in the flat they both shared, with Nancy herself finding his body. This underpinned a period of several years of poor choices and decision-making, in which she developed an unhealthy approach to drinking, going out, and sleeping around. These choices, which were the product of youth and an emotionally scarred biography, led to future fertility issues, with Nancy now being unable to have children. She was racked by guilt about this for a number of years, and directed anger towards the choices she had made and the body that had failed her. Nancy came to resent her periods, seeing them as serving no purpose other than as a reminder of her inability to conceive a child. She even rather drastically considered getting a hysterectomy and "just whipping it out" (Nancy, 2017). Then progressively over time her evolving practice of yoga began to shift her understanding around the body, particularly with regard to how she sees her body as harbouring emotions. She began to make small subtle changes to her approach to life, to deepen her connection with her body, which completely changed her psychology about what had happened to her.

'Gradually I have grown more compassionate towards my body, and towards that bit in particular that didn't function, and that's taken some kind of natural things that have helped to stabilise that side of thing. I do things like I take notice of what the moons doing at certain times of the month in correlation with my cycle, and as a woman that's really important to know things like that. I tried to escape it for so long because it was just too painful to think, "What's the bloody point; why is my body going through these cycles cause it's not functioning properly", you know?' (Nancy, 2017)

In a similar fashion to how Karate Guy faced the issues inherent in being an older father, Nancy negotiated complex challenges by creating a new way to live that worked for her. By implementing small changes in her day-to-day life, such as those discussed, she found nourishing ways to show commitment to her body that ultimately underpinned better wellbeing. Her perspective has shifted from wanting to physically cut parts of herself away, to being able to not only overcome the anger she once felt, but importantly also look back and show compassion for her younger self. Discovering links between the past and present self was something that often happened during interviews, in almost eureka-like moments of realization for respondents. This not only again demonstrates the hidden nature of the body, even to ourselves, but also highlights how embedded these moments of discovery are within the qualitative interviewee experience.

Nancy's biography is an example of how people can transition from unhealthy ways of coping with the path their life has taken, to approaches that underpin better wellbeing. This raises questions about the choices we make when we are younger, particularly around key moments of our biographies and how they might impact us in the future (see Gilbert, 2006, Dolan, 2015, and Cieslik, 2017 for further discussion on the issue of fallibility). Importantly, we are only able to uncover and explain these kinds of narratives through a qualitative, biographical approach to researching wellbeing. However, as is already widely covered, choosing to pursue a qualitative-research approach comes with a range of challenges (Crotty, 1998; Mason, 2013; Bryman, 2016). While I do not feel it necessary to rehearse all of this here, there are some issues I feel need to be covered if you wish to consider the body in your work. The following two sections will therefore explore some less obvious research demands that emerged due to my focus on wellbeing and the body. I will also make some suggestions regarding how you might avoid these pitfalls in your own qualitative work.

Tackling fluid, intangible concepts

One of the most challenging aspects of conducting this research has been how difficult it can be to express in words what we know on an embodied or felt level. For example, how exactly does a respondent convey the nuances of a routine or habit they have? After all, they perhaps do not even know they have it. This conundrum refers to all parties in the work, both researcher and respondent. It is challenging because any type of research always has to take into account the very reductive filtering process that goes on when we put something that is known, in a non-verbal way, into a verbal way for ourselves, or for others. We need to attempt to express something in a verbal way for somebody else, who then attaches to that verbal expression and tries to re-create that understanding inside, but that is then subject to all his or her cultural, social, personal and embodied frameworks of reference. An immense amount can be therefore lost in translation during the interview setting. It can trip us up in many ways when we are talking about something that has a physical, objective reality, but when talking about complex concepts, we also have no third-party reality to which we can both refer. This means that you and your respondents will not necessarily understand each other when talking about terms such as happiness, the body, or embodiment.

My best advice is to just be aware of these challenges from the outset, so that you can be as open and flexible as possible during your interviews. This might include conducting interviews in a setting that respondents are most comfortable, such as their own home. Taking note of body language during interviews, which can often open up layers of hidden meaning. Conducting more than one interview with each respondent, especially incorporating a biographical interview, and then frame the discussion around wider topics so respondents can use their own words, rather than being led by our primary research interests. This point focuses on the inherent strengths of qualitative research, which afford us the luxury of really getting to know respondents and map out a more comprehensive picture of their lives. Finally, take care when developing research questions so that they are clear and do not require you to extrapolate on what you mean, as this can be an issue when dealing with ambiguous subject material. It can also be problematic if we rely too heavily on a purely sociological language, because we have a tendency to pathologize the discourse on happiness (Cieslik, 2015). It is therefore advisable to explore other literatures when developing questions,[2] as well as simply spending time acknowledging a range of positive words and phrases that could be incorporated. These are all practical solutions to the challenge of tackling fluid, intangible concepts. However, it is also important to note that sometimes things outside your control can impact your research, which is something I feel has not had enough discussion from wellbeing researchers.

How I changed doing wellbeing research – a health warning

The final point I would like to make comes as somewhat of a health warning for those serious about immersing themselves into qualitative happiness research. The irony inherent in conducting research about wellbeing is that it develops in us a sensitivity to and self-awareness about having good wellbeing ourselves. The process itself therefore changes you, and as a research topic sensitizes you to a set of issues that can potentially make you more vulnerable *because* of your investment in happiness research. It forces you to confront the characteristics of your own life which can manifest in a range of ways depending on how your life is unfolding. I will reflect on my own PhD journey and recent past to illustrate this point. I have been experiencing a very difficult period in my biography, and have at the same time seen a number of people close to me struggle to manage issues that have made their own lives challenging. My father was diagnosed with stage four stomach cancer, and passed away shortly afterwards. Additionally, my partner has a serious form of epilepsy after experiencing a brain injury, which has complicated her life and means she often requires some further caring needs. Of course, one of life's more reliable facets is that we all go through difficult periods at times, and these key moments will often lead to some fundamental life adjustments (Cieslik, 2017). For me, these changes, in tandem with my focus on wellbeing research, have made apparent that aspects of my recent experience have led to new embodied discourses and ways of doing things. The events of my recent past have ultimately changed me as a person.

It took a long time for me to come back to the research after my father passed away, and I know that if the research focus was in a field other than wellbeing, I would have been able to get back to it sooner. There have been a number of times that I have considered moving away from it all together, and therein lies the paradox of researching happiness. The very act of immersing ourselves in the research opens our eyes to aspects of our own wellbeing, which can erode and impede our capacity and willingness to keep going with it. This is the challenge that you might be faced with; just like the people we are writing about, we will grapple with life's struggles, and strive to continue in a way that is healthy. It is important that you find a balance between the different facets of your life, especially when researching wellbeing. However, I believe we ultimately emerge from these challenges as more complex and nuanced individuals. Therefore, rather than backing away from these challenges, we can draw on our experiences to improve not only our future work, but also our own lives, relationships, and work/life balance.

Conclusion

This chapter has discussed the insights that can be brought to happiness research when the body is considered as an important aspect of people's wellbeing. It has also argued that we can only pursue the more complex understandings people have about their body (and wellbeing more generally) by using qualitative research approaches. I have discussed a range of examples using my own research on the body and wellbeing, and have demonstrated how biographical methods open up a world of nuance and richness about our respondents that quantitative approaches could never uncover. The aim has ultimately been to give some practical advice throughout the chapter so that you are now in a position to embed an embodied perspective into your own work.

Notes

[1] This transformative aspect of researching wellbeing will be reflected on towards the end of the chapter.
[2] I engaged heavily with dance and movement academic literatures, and also used Merleau-Ponty's (1962) 'essences of experience' as a framework to develop questions, because he suggests these can assist in the interpretation of our lived experience.

References

Bartky, S. (1990) *Femininity and Domination: Studies in the Phenomenology of Oppression*, New York: Routledge.

Bartram, D. (2012) 'Elements of a sociological contribution to happiness studies', *Sociology Compass*, 6(8): 644–56.

Bordo, S. (2003) *Unbearable Weight: Feminism, Western Culture and the Body* (2nd edn), Berkeley: University of California Press.

Bourdieu, P. (1984) *Distinction: A Social Critique of the Judgement of Taste*, London: Routledge.

Bourdieu, P. (1986) 'Forms of Capital', in J. Richardson (ed) *Handbook of Theory and Research in the Sociology of Education*, New York: Greenwood Press, pp 241–58.

Bryman, A. (2016) *Social Research Methods* (5th edn), Oxford: University Oxford Press.

Butler, J. (1990) *Gender Trouble*, London: Routledge.

Butler, J. (1993) *Bodies That Matter*, London: Routledge.

Cash, T. and Smolak, L. (eds) (2011) *Body Image: A Handbook of Science, Practice, and Prevention* (2nd edn), New York: Guilford Press.

Cieslik, M. (2015) '"Not smiling but frowning": sociology and the "problem of happiness"', *Sociology*, 49(3): 422–37.

Cieslik, M. (2017) *The Happiness Riddle and the Quest for a Good Life*, London: Palgrave Macmillan.

Cregan, K. (2006) *The Sociology of the Body*, London: Sage Publications.

Crossley, N. (2006) *Reflexive Embodiment in Contemporary Society*, Berkshire: Open University Press.

Crossley, N. (2013) 'Habit and habitus', *Body and Society*, 19(2–3): 136–61.

Crotty, M. (1998) *The Foundations of Social Research: Meaning and Perspective in the Research Process*, London: Sage Publications.

Descartes, R. (1974) *The Philosophical Works of Descartes*, translated by E. Haldene and G. Ross, Cambridge: Cambridge University Press.

Descartes, R. (1983) *Principles of Philosophy*, translated by V.R. Miller and R.P. Miller, New York: Springer-Verlag.

Dolan, P. (2015) *Happiness by Design: Finding Pleasure and Purpose in Everyday Life*, London: Penguin.

Elias, N. (2000 [1939]) *The Civilizing Process* (revised edn), Oxford: Blackwell.

Foucault, M. (1979) *Discipline and Punish: The Birth of a Prison*, Harmondsworth: Penguin.

Foucault, M. (1981) *The History of Sexuality, Vol 1: An Introduction*, Harmondsworth: Penguin.

Gilbert, D. (2006) *Stumbling on Happiness*, London: Harper Perennial.

Goffman, E. (1959) *The Presentation of Self in Everyday Life*, Harmondsworth: Penguin.

Greener, I. (2011) *Designing Social Research: A Guide of the Bewildered*, London: Sage Publications.

Gupta, N., Etcoff, N. and Jaeger, M. (2016) 'Beauty in mind: the effects of physical attractiveness on psychological well-being and distress', *Journal of Happiness Studies*, 17: 1313–25.

Husserl, E. (1931) *Ideas: General Introduction to Pure Phenomenology*, London: Allen and Unwin.

Kant, I. (1985 [1797]) *Foundations of the Physics of Morals*, London: Macmillan.

Keery, H., van den Berg, P. and Thompson, J. (2004) 'An evaluation of the tripartite influence model of body dissatisfaction and eating disturbance with adolescent girls', *Body Image*, 1: 237–51.

Leder, D. (1990) *The Absent Body*, Chicago, IL: University of Chicago Press.

Marx, K. (2013 [1867]) *Capital: Volumes One and Two*, London: Wordsworth Editions.

Mason, J. (2013) *Qualitative Researching* (2nd edn), London: Sage Publications.

Mauss, M. (1973 [1934]) 'Techniques of the body', *Economy and Society*, 2: 70–88.

Merleau-Ponty, M. (1962) *The Phenomenology of Perception*, London: Routledge and Kegan Paul.

Merleau-Ponty, M. (1963) *The Structure of Behaviour*, Boston: Beacon Press.

Mills, C.W. (1959) *The Sociological Imagination*, London: Oxford University Press.

Mond, J., van den Berg, P., Boutelle, K., Hannan, P. and Neumark-Sztainer, D. (2011) 'Obesity, body dissatisfaction, and emotional well-being in early and late adolescence: findings from the Project EAT study', *Journal of Adolescent Health*, 48: 373–8.

Patton, M. (2015) *Qualitative Research and Evaluation Methods* (4th edn), London: Sage Publications.

Reeve, S. (2011) *Nine Ways of Seeing a Body*, Devon: Triarchy Press.

Shilling, C. (2012) *The Body and Social Theory* (3rd edn), London: Sage Publications.

Shusterman, R. (2008) *Body Consciousness: A Philosophy of Mindfulness and Somaesthetics*, Cambridge: Cambridge University Press.

Shusterman, R. (2012) *Thinking Through the Body*, Cambridge: Cambridge University Press.

Swami, V., Tran, U., Stieger, S. and Voracek, M. (2015) 'Associations between women's body image and happiness: results of the YouBeauty. com Body Image Survey (YBIS)', *Journal of Happiness Studies*, 16: 705–18.

Turner, B. (2008 [1984]) *The Body and Society*, Oxford: Blackwell.

7

How Cultural Heritage can Contribute to Community Development and Wellbeing

Claire Wallace and David Beel

Introduction

Community wellbeing as an element of happiness research is a rather nebulous concept because first of all it is not clear how collective wellbeing amounts to more than the individual wellbeing of its members and second because it is not clear at what level 'community' takes place (see Phillips and Wong, 2017). While usually referring implicitly to a geographical location, community can also refer to the kinds of networks of affective connection and social ties that constitute people's lives – and in a globalized and digitally connected social world these can be increasingly complex and manifold (Rainie and Wellman, 2012). Elsewhere we have described the ways in which information technology impacts on these local affiliations (Wallace and Vincent, 2017). Here we look more explicitly at one aspect of community wellbeing – that of cultural heritage. In doing so we argue that wellbeing is a property of communities rather than only of individuals. This therefore goes beyond the conventional view of happiness as an individual phenomenon.

One way of understanding wellbeing as a collective property is to consider the interactions of cultural and social capital and the way in which these convert into economic capital. Cultural heritage can be seen as an aspect of collective cultural capital and here we draw upon Bourdieu's discussion of these issues. Bourdieu defines cultural capital as the set of attributes, dispositions and 'taste' that is valued in a given society (Bourdieu, 1984) and reproduces elite positions through the artefacts and knowledge that embody cultural goods. While Bourdieu was concerned with society as a whole, we can also consider the generation of cultural capital within specific locations where the valuing of particular artefacts, expertise or knowledge has more specific meanings. Bourdieu was concerned with cultural capital mainly as a form of inclusion/exclusion in hierarchal social relations. We argue that we need to look at how cultural capital is generated at a community level from the bottom up. In other words, we stand Bourdieu's concept of cultural capital on its head to show how this is generated by locational communities from below rather than by hegemonic authority from above (Beel and Wallace, 2018). In order for heritage from below to be generated and shared, it relies upon social capital – or participation in associational life and the mobilization of resources at a community level – that represent a collective rather than just an individual asset (Putnam, 2000). While Bourdieu sees social capital as the property of networks, Putnam sees it as the property of communities – something which adds an intangible value to community membership. Hence, when considering both social and cultural capital from a community perspective they can be seen as a collective rather than an individual resource.

Here we show how cultural heritage can help to develop rural communities, generating community wellbeing at a collective level and making them better places in which to live. This can happen in many different ways, reflecting different kinds of grassroots movements. Cultural heritage can take many forms including intangible cultural heritage such as songs, music, and skills, and tangible cultural heritage in the form of buildings, monuments and landscape. Rural communities can be home to both types. Far from being just about the past, cultural heritage is about how this develops into networks, activities and resources, which are rooted in the present and can help shape positive trajectories into the future, enabling community 'resilience' (Beel et al, 2016).

In this chapter we consider two case studies from Scotland – Portsoy, near Aberdeen and the Islands of the Outer Hebrides – and we argue that cultural heritage can add real value to communities by helping to build a sense of place, generate social capital and mobilize community participation. The two case studies that follow illustrate how cultural heritage can be an important element of community wellbeing with significant economic ramifications. In this way we consider the conversion of different types of capitals – economic, social and cultural – in particular settings (Bourdieu, 1983). After describing two case studies we shall consider the implications and the challenges that the community approach brings to happiness studies.

The two case studies were chosen because they formed part of a study of the implications of digital communications for rural development.[1] The role of cultural heritage emerged in these discussions with communities as a key concern of communities themselves – it was something local people cared about. While we looked at a number of different communities in the context of these funded projects, the two used here were good examples of successful cultural heritage projects. The reasons for this success and threats to it are discussed at the end of this chapter. The projects enabled us to do extensive fieldwork in these communities and to interview different participants over a period of time. They were more recently (2018) followed up for the purposes of this chapter.

Case Study 1: Portsoy

Portsoy is a small former fishing community on the north coast of Aberdeenshire with a resident population of around 2,000. Created as a 'Burgh of Barony', or independent town, by Mary Queen of Scots in 1550, it opened for trade in 1693 to become an important international trading harbour. The old warehouses still dominate the harbourside. At the beginning of the 19th century it transformed into a fishing port and was soon witnessing the catching of salmon in nets from the sea for transportation to the rest of the UK. Like many of these peripheral coastal communities, it had latterly suffered decline especially after the Second World War, as the economic basis for much of the prosperity vanished with the demise of this kind of salmon fishing and the movement of other fishing to larger deep-water ports. It became instead more of a dormitory town with an ageing population as young people moved out in search of education and jobs and older people moved in to retire to a seaside location where property prices were relatively low. Many who grew up there moved back to retire. The oil industry boom since the mid-1970s touched Portsoy by providing lucrative employment for some people 50 miles away in Aberdeen. By the 1990s it had a collection of historic but collapsing old buildings – more evidence of a neglected past than a happy future.

Portsoy was always a picturesque town with a thriving civil society. However, one transformative and significant initiative was the creation of the Portsoy Traditional Boat Festival. Established in 1993 to mark the 300th Anniversary of the 'New' Harbour (built in 1825) and celebrating its restoration, it originally took the form of a small sailing regatta. However, it has since grown to include boat racing, displays of boat building, traditional music and dancing, traditional food and crafts and attracts upwards of 16,000 people over a weekend in June.

The revival of cultural heritage helped to boost the prosperity of the town and encouraged the further restoration of old buildings. The many activities spawned by these heritage activities led to the creation of 'Portsoy Community Enterprise', an umbrella organization for managing some of them. Hence, when the Aberdeenshire Council decided to relinquish control of the Portsoy campsite, this organization stepped in to take it over and this has provided an important income stream for Portsoy Community Enterprise. It further restored some ruined buildings at the far end of the campsite, which had been used for sail making in the 19th century, to become a Bunk House for visitors in 2017.

A community leader who was one of the key people involved in developing the Boat Festival and CEO of the Portsoy Community Enterprise (a collection of projects including the Boat Festival) explained to us how the Boat Festival transformed into various other projects, including restoration of local buildings, opening of a local museum, taking over a campsite and creating a bunkhouse out of some ruined buildings:

> 'Yes, it started off as boats ... it was very much about boats and round the harbour there were stalls which included community organisations, the RNLI [Royal National Lifeboats Institution] and others ... Music was also there, but incidentally ... the music developed steadily ... I am not sure when food first appeared ... so it kind of, yeah, grew like Topsy, I can't think of any other way to describe it. But I think, wittingly or unwittingly, the intention was always for it to be a celebration of the cultural heritage of the area. I think it's taken a while for that to be put down on paper but I think it had naturally become that and the music was always focused more on traditional music and of course the area is very rich in traditional music. And the food was always local. What I term 'artisan' companies demonstrating and selling their products. So it kind of grew by chance and then again, probably more unwittingly than wittingly, it began to evolve into this encapsulation of the cultural heritage of the North East [of Scotland].'

The Boat Festival concentrated on traditional sailing craft, both restored and newly constructed. Consequently, an interest in intangible cultural heritage was generated through the revival of boat building skills and activities that take place throughout the year and have educational outreach to young people.

> 'Yes, basically, it was difficult to practically give something to the community [from the Boat Festival] other than the commercial opportunity that it provides for local traders. So we thought: well, what could we do? And we thought, "let's focus on youth" and that started with the music and we got Youth Music, YMI funding, and started a programme which has run for seven years. We bring in tutors, go into primary schools and work with them on traditional music … and that culminates in a concert which is held at the festival. And that has grown in stature and proved very, very, popular … The next stage was that we did the same thing for sailing. So we provided opportunities again, for primary school children to learn about sailing and we must have had, over the years, in excess of a thousand children. And it went through a sort of metamorphosis in that it went from just learning how to sail, to learning how to build a boat.'

This in turn had an impact on tangible cultural heritage through the restoration of many of the old buildings.[2] The first building to be restored was the Salmon Bothy (restored in 2009), the storage warehouse for salmon at the time of the fishing industry. It consists of a large stone building, originally constructed in 1834, where the temperature could be kept constant for salmon stored prior to transportation by train to other parts of Great Britain. The Salmon Bothy is now a museum housing a range of traditional fishing implements and information. The restoration of the Bothy enabled a meeting hall to be built at the top of the building and it is famed for its knitted mural spanning one wall. Local women knitted a harbour scene of Portsoy – much like a locally produced version of the Bayeux Tapestry – and is an example of the use of traditional skills as well as being a work of art, in its own right. The meeting hall is used to house a lively folk club and other community events including storytelling, sea shanty singing, film screenings and so on.

> '[The Salmon Bothy meeting room] has spawned a number of groups which didn't exist before, which is interesting – like

the knitting group, the painting group, the craft group …
the upstairs facility seemed to be the catalyst that got those
groups going and that's been hugely encouraging and very
exciting to see. The other thing is that the acoustics are
good, so it has become a centre for traditional music and
in fact … the Bothy group was created that meets monthly
and has its own festival in May of each year.'

The success of this enterprise was followed by the opening of another
community museum in the old bakery when the individual who
inherited this property opened it to the public and housed some local
artefacts and materials. It is the home of 'Portsoy Past and Present'
which collects stories, poems in the local Doric dialect and hosts a
lively Facebook page where photos are posted and discussed as well as
a website where articles and stories are published.

Volunteering has had a strong tradition in Portsoy, but these
activities reinforced it. Other community activities emerged involving
volunteers, including a thrift shop opened in empty retail premises,
which annually donates up to £2,000 to the town. Another retail
outlet was opened for the local crafting community to rent space and
sell their goods. Volunteers likewise maintain the local clifftop walk
and other foot and cycle paths around the town and there are plans to
develop more. These activities have helped to harness local volunteer
effort, engage local people, improve the local area and create a sense of
pride and progress that have improved the town in many different ways.

The benefits of these activities were reflected in the money raised
for community improvements, sponsorship for different activities and
making Portsoy an attractive and vibrant place to live. This in turn
encouraged people to move in and restore some of the old buildings
for residential use. The two hotels, ice cream parlour, fish and chip
shop, various cafés and bakeries and an antique shop were all helped to
thrive by the resulting influx of visitors. The high levels of participation
are reflected in the vibrant and active Community Council (the lowest
tier of elected governance in Scotland and staffed by volunteers).
Nevertheless, several issues that need tackling have been identified
by the Community Council, including the lack of transport facilities
as well as health and social care coverage associated with an aging
population in a rural area. Wellbeing research helps us to identify and
appreciate the local embeddedness of these kinds of activities.

Thus, it is clear that both social and cultural capital play a role in
the development of Portsoy as a community and that the two capitals
interact economically as well. Hence, wellbeing needs to be seen in

terms of the interplay of participation and social networks and the way in which cultural heritage acts as a spur to this. In the case of Portsoy, the cultural heritage was 'discovered' and even invented by the local activists in the form of the Boat Festival and subsequent activities.

Case Study 2: the Comainn Eachdraidh in the Outer Hebrides

The Outer Hebrides consists of a string of Islands on the westernmost fringe of Scotland. Their scattered and remote populations, numbering 27,000 altogether, include a strong Gaelic-speaking element. Cultural heritage plays a very important part in these small settlements. This is borne out by the fact that most villages host a Comainn Eachdraidh (CE) or Historical Association and nearly all residents are members of it.

The CE Movement began in the 1970s with a very specific political and cultural purpose: the collection and preservation of highland and island cultures, with reference to Gaelic. The first phase of the project took place from 1976 to 1982, beginning in Ness where the first CE started. It began with the key aim to create 'an awareness of the cultural identity and community history as a means to boosting morale and promoting a discriminating understanding of the past and of its influence on the present' (Mackay, 1996). It is from this position that over the subsequent years new CE groups began in different areas of the Hebrides.

Today, 20 CEs are currently active in the Outer Hebrides, all of which are entirely independent of each other. Each group has its own members, committee and collections, and are dedicated to researching their own localities. The different groups collect a wide variety of materials relating to both their tangible and intangible heritage. In this case the intangible heritage consists of knowledge of oral histories, songs, genealogies of people in the area, Gaelic place names, poetry and song. Tangible heritage might include school log books, diaries, fishing boat records, recipe books, 'rolls of honour' for those lost in the War, crofts, gravestones and archaeological artefacts. The history of the area is often traced through the changing ownership of crofts, some of which is documented and some is based upon tacit local knowledge of families and locations.

Some CEs have opened museums, and these are often housed in the old school houses – the need for the school houses having changed with the centralization of the school system. Elsewhere they are housed in people's private houses or other buildings that can be communally accessed (Tait et al, 2011). Where the school house has been repurposed, this often includes a café and meeting rooms (staffed by volunteers) as well as a display of artefacts that might have little interest in themselves but whose relevance is determined by their location in the local community. For example, spinning wheels were passed down through the female line of the family, while shepherds' crooks were passed down the male line. Hence, these artefacts have a meaning according to how they are embedded in local community relationships.

Some of the museums have developed further functions. For example, the one CE located at Ravenspoint on the Isle of Lewis has developed further activities including Gaelic-language teaching courses, a book publishing enterprise, a local shop and in 2015 established a petrol station for locals who would otherwise have to travel many miles to fill their tanks. As in Portsoy, cultural heritage encourages many ancillary activities that are valued by the local community and which arise from their needs.

The CE involves volunteers who meet on a regular basis to sort through photographs and other documentation and to exchange information about them. This is cross-checked against an index of information about people living in the area, school records and so on, representing a mixing of volunteers' 'living knowledge' with what has been recorded. This is a highly social activity as volunteers reminisce and tell stories about the documents.

This also highlights something else about the process of maintaining and producing archives: the sense of self-worth that members gain from their participation in the process of producing the archives. Despite it being slow and highly time consuming, many still took great pleasure from these activities. For the volunteers, the contribution of their own knowledge and remembering people, places, and events together with others, gave them great satisfaction. Furthermore, the desire to comprehend personal and community histories and genealogies often acts as the 'spark' that draws people into being involved with CE. As one of the contributors told us:

> 'I just, again, came to Comann Eachdraidh, I don't know how, it's so long ago I can't remember! I suppose I was always interested in my roots and I had an uncle who was very interested in genealogy and I suppose I just got into it that way and here I am, decades later and that's it: once you are in, you are in, you are hooked! Decades later and that's it.'

Some of the CEs are linked through an electronic database organized by an organization called Hebridean Connections (https://www.hebrideanconnections.com). This organization originally contacted us for help in setting up digital archives that would enable the data to be linked across the Islands and is searchable by people external to the community – for example, people researching their ancestry. With a long history of emigration to the New World, this is an important source of information about both real and virtual visitors. However, some CEs are fiercely protective of their collections and will not allow them to go online (Beel and Wallace, 2018).

Hence, while cultural heritage plays an important part in the life of people in the Outer Hebrides, this takes a different form to Portsoy. It is related to the Gaelic language, to a local sense of independence and opposition to mainstream historical narratives and is anchored in the remote life of islanders, many of whom have personal connections to their history. Cultural heritage is defined as something oppositional and involves the local state and mainstream organizations only when necessary. Portsoy, by contrast, draws upon more mainstream narratives of cultural heritage, working together with Historic Scotland, Museums Scotland and other organizations. However, Portsoy has likewise invented an important connection with the past through the traditional boat-building festival and related activities, while the Portsoy Past and Present also connects individuals to events, families and friends in living memory.

Both are examples of rural cultural heritage, its relation to the generation and circulation of social, cultural and economic capital and how this leads community development. These are all foundations for community wellbeing. In the next section we look at some of these connections in more detail.

Cultural heritage and cultural capital

Rural cultural heritage can include a range of things identified by UNESCO as being worthy of recognition and preservation. However, local communities create their own cultural heritage informally, irrespective of these official definitions. This can include tangible cultural heritage such as buildings, monuments and landscapes. It can also include intangible cultural heritage in the form of songs, stories, skills, music and so on. Each suggests a different form of recognition and preservation (Giglitto, 2017). In the case of the former it can mean the restoration and protection of important physical features. In the Outer Hebrides this was old school houses (most of the school houses dated from the 1960s), some crofts (dating from the end of the 19th century but mostly later) and the artefacts they contained.

The tangible cultural heritage reflects the tradition of hard scrabble subsistence croft farming and the culture that it sustained. In Portsoy tangible cultural heritage is mainly focused on the rich collection of traditional buildings in the area from a much earlier period – from the 17th century onwards – reflecting its rise and fall as a Burgh town. In the case of the intangible cultural heritage, it might mean the creation or recreation and transmission of recognized crafts, knowledge and activities. This suggests that such activities are rooted in local knowledge and culture which is ongoing and living tradition rather than part of an extinct legacy. In the case of Portsoy this was focused on the revival of the tradition of boat building as well as knitting, while in the Outer Hebrides the ongoing knowledge of landscape and people as well as the Gaelic language was the most important element of this activity.

An important aspect of this recognition is the ownership by local communities and the engagement of community members through 'heritage from below' – without this interest the knowledge will disappear and the buildings decay (Robertson, 2012). Cultural heritage is therefore as much about the current creative activities of local communities who help to create heritage as it is about any 'objective' classification by international organizations such as UNESCO. The relevance associated with both types of cultural heritage depends upon their meaning in everyday life and they are therefore not mummified museum objects but rather activities and collections that gain their recognition from the interactions of communities around them. Since they are embedded in communities with different kinds of social and economic characteristics, cultural heritage can take very different forms and can be shaped in very different ways, as our two case studies make clear.

The key to these initiatives is that they were *local*. This was not about mainstream 'high' cultural heritage in the same way, as say, a stately home and less formal than an officially recognized UNESCO designation. Rather, it arose organically from remembering and celebrating the life and work of people in a particular locality and it was embedded in the present-day lives of people within that locality. Cultural heritage remembers both the economic (fishing, crofting) and the cultural (Gaelic language, Doric dialect, traditional music) legacy of the past but recreates it in the present. These were geographically and economically marginalized people whose lives would otherwise be forgotten. Cultural heritage is thus meaningful only insofar as it has meaning for local people. In this sense rural cultural heritage represents an alternative to mainstream historical discourses and the values they represent.

Cultural heritage and social capital

Social capital as a set of connections (Bourdieu, 1983; Lin, 2001) and as a potential for political change (Putnam, 2000) is generated by voluntary work and participation. Communities rich in social capital have many volunteers and this makes them better places in which to live. We have already described the prevalence of this but the sense of connection to the community and to others in the community is in this way reinforced. In Portsoy, this was achieved through the volunteering activities at the museum and elsewhere and this was also the case in the Western Isles, where the CE provides a vehicle and a focus for participation. In both communities a variety of organizations for volunteering provided a spread of activities (Beel et al, 2016).

In both communities it was pointed out that while it was often the same people who became involved in multiple organizations and were important nodes for social capital and provided community leadership (Wallace et al, 2015), this was nevertheless a way of providing access for others who might not have been quite so involved. Previously we have argued that community leadership works best where it is spread around several people and organizations rather than relying on one or two people who might die or move away (Wallace et al, 2015).

Strong social capital has long been associated with wellbeing both as a collective and an individual good (Pichler and Wallace, 2009). The reinforcement of connections and collective purpose provides a collective form of social capital, or social cohesion, while the individual ties to the organizations and to one another provide individual inclusion. At a national level, collective social capital is more sustainable and has more impact than individual social advantages (Pichler and Wallace, 2009). Hence, collective social capital is more than the sum of its individual parts. Social capital has also been shown to be related to individual wellbeing at a national level – people feel good because everybody feels good. The fact that cultural heritage of the kinds we describe here is organized in a bottom-up fashion means that it is stronger and more sustainable than top-down efforts by local authorities or other projects to mobilize communities.

We have explored elsewhere the role of cultural heritage and cultural capital. Cultural heritage provides the opportunity to generate locally produced cultural capital 'from below' which has a value and a currency in local communities (Robertson, 2012; Beel and Wallace, 2018). Hence, local knowledge is an important part of local community identity.

However, social capital generated in this way still depends upon having appropriate community leadership with the ability to raise money, write grants and make connections with external organizations. In Portsoy, for example, this involved contacting grant-awarding organizations to raise many different sources of funding and making personal connections with companies who were prepared to offer sponsorship (for some years the Boat Festival was sponsored by Aberdeen Asset Management). The role of community leaders such as the CEO of Portsoy Community Enterprises can be crucial in this respect, making connections between public authorities, funding bodies and private sponsors. Inevitably there is disappointment where companies or organizations are not interested or withdraw their sponsorship for whatever reason. Although millions of pounds were raised, this is an ongoing and continuous activity so social capital can also break down with discontinuities of funding.

Both case studies illustrate the role of community mobilization to raise funds, to buy land, to build boats and to restore buildings. These activities create collective enterprise that enables engaged communities. Even if not everyone was involved in each of these case studies a large part of the population were involved in one or other activity.

The large numbers of volunteers in each case study is a testament to the force of community mobilization. While other things can also mobilize communities (for example, protests against the siting of windfarms), cultural heritage provides a strong incentive to get involved. The aging population (especially large in the countryside as people retire there) provides a readily available pool of volunteers and the relatively affluent character of incomers means that they are keen to explore local history. Community mobilization around cultural heritage encourages the empowerment of local residents which helps to ensure more mobilization around this or other activities. Rather than dividing incomers from natives it provides a common activity and source of pride for both groups.

In the Outer Hebrides, the shared experience of participating, collecting and listening with others; the sense of producing something of worth for the community and its ability to bring people together, contributed to a sense of wellbeing and cohesiveness. As one member of the CE on Lewis put it:

> 'I think the word in itself says that: "community"; because it is bringing something together which is common to us all. We don't get together that much, as a community, as people here – as they used to in the past. And if you've got

something like this and it will drag people together, then it's a good thing. We need something in our communities actually to keep the people coming together as a community and if we didn't do it, it would be just another bit that was lost.'

Hence, key to the process of understanding how cultural value is constructed by different CEs is understanding how, in a very 'on-the-ground' way, it is embedded into the everyday lives of many Islanders. Ingold (2000) would label this the *taskscape*, and it is useful to think of community heritage in relation to this term, especially when thinking through how cultural value in this setting relates to notions of dwelling and place identity. The following quotations are from two different CE members on Lewis:

'I think it's very much an island thing as well, I'm not sure they have the same commitment on the mainland to recording the local history, I don't know if it's the same anywhere else but certainly in the Islands it's always been the case; they've always held on to their oral history.

Perhaps because people didn't move much in the old days so ... we're all related to each other just about in here so there's not the same turnover of people, well until fairly recently, people coming in and out didn't happen so there's more of a sense of identity.'

The value of community mobilization is that it then leads to other things. In the Outer Hebrides, shops, cafes, land purchase and so on grew out of the CE. In Portsoy the campsite, Bothy, museum and boat-building sheds grew out of the Boat Festival.

'I mean, come the Boat Festival, there must be circa 300 people involved in the community and that's fantastic ... We're just very lucky – we've got a lot of people who are prepared to put in a lot of very hard work. People who are very competent as well ... I think it's involvement, I think it's because it is something that people can involve themselves in and truly contribute to.' (Community Councillor, Portsoy)

Yet with these kinds of community initiatives, there is the danger of a disproportionate amount of the work falling on the shoulders of a few people, mainly volunteers, leading to burnout (Woolvin, 2012). There is also the danger of disconnected activities reflecting different community factions. All communities have social and political divisions which can lead to animosity and undermine social capital. Where there is good community leadership it can help to bridge these differences but elsewhere it can be divisive (Wallace et al, 2017). Respondents in Portsoy insisted that interest was spread across the community with some volunteers being involved in some activities and others in other activities, while there were also people were involved in all or most of them. In the Outer Hebrides an interest in cultural heritage helped to bring together the potentially divisive fractures between incomers and locals as well as between Gaelic- and non-Gaelic-speaking communities.

Cultural heritage and a sense of place

A sense of place suggests a rootedness in a landscape rather than just a place where you happen to live. Here, agency lies with the community to present and articulate their historical sense of place for their own purposes. In the Outer Hebrides this is reinforced through the archival work undertaken by the CE volunteers and the ways in which members of different historical societies reflect upon their desire to represent their histories and to tell the everyday stories about their communities.

In the Outer Hebrides, where there is reference to a previous era of clearances, dispossessions and subjection to (and often oppression by) landlords, the historical narratives of place take on a political dimension. In the present day, it is also an assertion of identification with locality against the more sweeping local state or nationalistic heritage claims that miss out the finer-grained and everyday social histories of place (Mason and Baveystock, 2008). For Creswell, such community archives represent spaces of 'marginalised memory' that draw 'attention to the things people push to one side and ignore, the things that do not make it into official places of memory' (Cresswell, 2011). Furthering this point, MacKenzie argues that cultural heritage projects in North West Sutherland are a method of rehabilitation in collective psyches for dealing with past grievances:

> Part of that bold, collective, effort to turn around centuries of dispossessions, defined not just through the Clearances, but also through more contemporary loss – of people, of jobs, for example, in the fishing and forestry sectors and of the houses which have been turned into holiday homes. These collective projects are about re-mapping the

land in ways that suggest an alternative imaginary to that
aligned with processes of dispossession and the practices of
privatisation and enclosure that have underpinned them.
(MacKenzie, 2013: 163–4)

Hence, in this context cultural initiatives are part and parcel of '*a culture
of resistance*', in that they chart cultural territory – the 'reclaim[ing],
renam[ing], and reinhabit[ing] [of] land' that precedes 'the recovery of
geographical territory' (Said, 1994: 209–26). The process of collecting
these marginalized memories is one that seeks to disrupt conventional
knowledge-power asymmetries, especially those associated with official
histories, by creating their own places of memories and documenting
them through archives. For each of the CE groups there is a micro-
politics that 'can affect [shared] heritages and through which attempts
can be made to reorganise time and space as memory is mined,
refigured and re-presented' (Crouch and Parker, 2003). Articulations
of (historical) place, space and hierarchy drives their activity to collect,
research, preserve and present own place histories and heritages. As
one member of the CE put it:

'Not people looking in and telling you what you should be
doing or exploring your differences and making out that
you are freaks because of what you believe in, what you
do, way of life and so on. So I think that's the strength of
a Comann Eachdraidh – showcasing ourselves.'

Robertson (2012) discusses this in the context of a '*heritage from below*'
whereby it 'is both a means to and manifestation of counter hegemonic
practises' (Robertson, 2012). The very purpose is hence to articulate
a position that does not conform to a top-down narrative but aims to
represent those more 'ordinary' lives and incumbent practices that go
along with their history. Central to these arguments is place, identity
and a notion of dwelling (Ingold, 2000) that builds over time and
reinforces each in relation to the heritage the communities wish to
create. This reflects on the types of materials that are collected in these
communities. In the context of the Western Isles this further builds
upon a relationship in the Gaelic communities between sense of place,
identity and possession whereby 'attachments to place are intrinsic
to identity, rather than to buildings or monuments' (Robertson,
2012: 154). It is the history of dispossession and the 'colonial' legacy
this has created that greatly shapes the rationale and need for such
community-level collecting.

As local history groups, CEs aim to present a historical sense of place, which is tied to the land (crofts) and the people who lived on those crofts, who are often connected genealogically to current members. This link between land, people and place is probably unique to cultural heritage in comparison with elsewhere in the UK; few places can represent such a lineage. It is also a strong political statement with regards to land tenure – an exceptionally contentious issue in the Islands (Hunter, 1976). In this respect the archive represents a form of historical continuity. The archive is therefore a testament to these continuing connections showing that while landlords might have come and gone, many of the tenants remained. The connection to Gaelic place names reinforces this connection.

Nevertheless, many who lived there did not have these historical roots and did not speak Gaelic either. But moving to such a remote location is already testimony of a commitment to a particular way of life. The remoteness of the places meant that people had to depend upon one another no matter where they came from and newcomers were just as active in the historical associations and in preserving cultural heritage as local people. Indeed, CE activities helped to bridge the differences between incomers and locals.

At the time of the research there was a community buy-out of land around Ravenspoint, something made possible by legislation in Scotland (Mackenzie, 2013) but requiring the mobilization of collective resources and raising substantial financing. This gives communities real control over their physical spaces and can provide power sources and other financial advantages – for instance, through erection of wind turbines or setting up hydroelectric plants.

For Portsoy this kind of visceral connection to the landscape was less obvious, as was the political dimension of reclaiming rights. However, many of the community were descended from the fisher folk of the past or were involved in this activity (crab lobster creels, line fishing) in the present day so the connection between sea, harbour and livelihood was maintained. The Salmon Bothy and the Sail Bunk House reinforced these maritime connections, as does the Traditional Boat Festival, and this was the rather unique aspect of cultural heritage in Portsoy. Furthermore, the village museum located in the bakery was owned by a descendant of the baker. Therefore, cultural heritage was built around the social and economic relationships between people and landscape in the past, continuing into the present.

Despite the significant influx of new residents, people identified with the place through 'elective affinity' if they had moved there (Savage et al, 2005), reinforced by ties of social capital and volunteering.

Great pride was expressed in the town and its achievements as it became famous locally and regionally for the traditional boat festival. While some felt overwhelmed by the large influx of visitors even they acknowledged that this had helped to create a strong outward-facing image for the town.

> 'But there is an awful lot of people who are and there's pride in it – people who like to say "Yeah, I'm from Portsoy". To see how often almost across the country now and increasingly overseas people say "Portsoy – yes the boat festival". I think all those things mean that there is an energy and it's self-driving.' (Community Councillor, Portsoy)

In terms of the more recent past, the photos displayed at 'Portsoy Past and Present' helped local people to identify school friends and relatives as well as events and places in the recent past. We have demonstrated elsewhere that a virtual community can be important for reinforcing a real one (Wallace and Vincent, 2017). In this respect the websites for the different festivals helped to create a sense of place in the virtual world as well (Hampton and Wellman, 2003).

Hence, in different ways, cultural heritage had helped to reinforce and create a sense of place in both regions, albeit in different ways. By accessing cultural heritage, even those who had moved to the regions recognized the distinctive identities that had been created and felt a pride in the achievements of their community. Indeed, it was one of the factors that made these communities attractive ones to which to move. Therefore, these communities were more than just residential areas. Pride in a place and strong sense of identity is associated with wellbeing in the sense that it creates a sense of inclusion, empowerment and connection (Abbott et al, 2016).

Cultural heritage and community

We have mentioned previously that one of the problems of defining community wellbeing is the lack of clarity about what 'community' is. It is seen as a target of public policies, but often in the sense of making up for some deficiency or social problems. Community can merely mean a residential area, but it traditionally implies a more collective identity and set of relationships that go beyond this (Delanty, 2003). Hence, while communities usually imply a residential area, not all of these form communities. Indeed, communities can increasingly become virtual. Wellman and others have argued for new forms of community constructed online, rather than being location based (Rainie and Wellman, 2012). However, the virtual community as an extension of the residential community through Facebook groups, WhatsApp, email lists, websites and so on is an increasingly important aspect of local social relationships (Hampton and Wellman, 2003; Wallace et al, 2017).

In contemporary Europe, communities are no longer a set of ascribed relationships that arise out of a place of birth as was set out in the classical literature (Tonnies, 2002 [1887]). The increasingly mobile populations of the 20th and 21st centuries mean that communities are places where people might choose to live, and they may likewise choose to engage or not to engage in local social relationships. They may even be virtual rather than geographical and the virtual set of community relations can help to reinforce the geographical ones. Rural communities are often ones of choice as people move to rural areas precisely in search of a 'community' and an imaginary set of 'cosy' social relationships and interactions (Pahl, 1965). Although Pahl was critical of this 'community in the mind' created by incomers, we can also see this as a way in which community is positively constructed and acted upon, much in the same way as the nation state described by Benedict Anderson was based on an 'imagined community' (Anderson, 1983). Although residents might not know everybody in the area and may or may not be constrained by their social relationships with them, they might feel themselves to be part of community nevertheless.

Cultural heritage helps to create a sense of place and a community as people engage with aspects of their history and recreate different kinds of tangible and intangible heritage. The community thus created may or may not correspond with local authority boundaries but do create the 'community in the mind' which has real implications for the activities and actions of people on the ground.[3]

Conclusions

In this chapter we have looked at the role of cultural heritage in community development and wellbeing through the example of two rural communities in Scotland: Portsoy and the Outer Hebrides. We have argued that community heritage can be an impetus to the circulation of cultural, social and economic capital within communities. In this way it was stimulus to both community development and community wellbeing. Cultural heritage reinforces a sense of place and encourages community mobilization.

Our contribution to knowledge through this work is to look at community wellbeing as an important aspect of 'happiness' research and to try to understand the collective as well as individual connotations.

Second, we have emphasized the importance of qualitative research, including both fieldwork and interviews in understanding how community wellbeing and cultural heritage are connected.

Third, we would argue that cultural heritage and wellbeing should be key components of community development, thus extending that paradigm in a way that begins with how communities themselves define their needs. In this way, cultural heritage can be a form of community empowerment through mobilization of resources. But the local ownership of heritage is an important factor.

A limitation of this research is that by collecting the story that communities want to tell of themselves, we tend to emphasize the positive rather than the negative aspects of community development. Likewise, we have focused on two 'success stories' or well-functioning communities rather than problematic ones, which are more commonly the focus of community development programmes.

Notes

1   This emerged from the dot.rural Digital Economy Hub funded by the Research Councils UK between 2009 and 2015 EP/GO6651/1 and Culture and Communities Network+ EP/KOO3585/1, 2012–16 and EVIDANCE 'Exploring Value in Digital Archives and Commainn Eiachdriadh', AH/L006006/1, 2012–14.

2   Tangible cultural heritage is drawn from the UNESCO definition referring to landscapes, buildings and monuments, while intangible cultural heritage refers to such things as songs, crafts, traditions, drama and so on, and was first codified in 2003.

3   Our case studies illustrate successful heritage projects; there are, of course, many examples where other schemes failed, often in part through lack of community involvement.

References

Abbott, P., Wallace, C., and Sapsford, R. (2016) *The Decent Society*, London and New York: Routledge.

Anderson, B. (1983) *Imagined Communities: Reflections on the Origin and Spread of Nationalism*, London: Verso.

Beel, D.E. and Wallace, C. (2018) 'Gathering together: social capital, cultural capital, the value of cultural heritage in the digital age', *Social and Cultural Geography*, DOI: 10.1080/14649365.2018.1500632

Beel, D.E., Wallace, C., Webster, G., Nyugen, H., Tait, E., MacLeod, M., and Mellish, C. (2016) 'Cultural resilience: the production of rural community heritage, digital archives and the role of volunteers', *Journal of Rural Studies*, 54: 459–68, DOI: 10.1016/j.jrurstud.2015.05.002

Bourdieu, P. (1983) 'Forms of capital', in J. Richardson (ed) *Handbook of Theory and Research in the Sociology of Education*, New York: Greenwood Press, p. 241–58.

Bourdieu, P. (1984) *Distinction*, London: Routledge and Kegan Paul.

Cresswell, T. (2011) 'Value, gleaning and the archive in Maxwell Street, Chicago', *Transactions of the Institute of British Geographers*, 37(1): 1–13.

Crouch, D. and Parker, G. (2003) 'Digging up utopia? Space, practice and land use heritage', *Geoforum*, 34: 395–408.

Delanty, G. (2003) *Community*, London and New York: Routledge.

Giglitto, D. (2017) *Using Wikis for Intangible Cultural Heritage in Scotland: Suitability and Empowerment*, PhD Thesis, University of Aberdeen.

Hampton, K.N. and Wellman, B. (2003) 'Neighbouring netville: how the internet supports community and social capital in a wired suburb', *City and Community*, 2(4): 277–311.

Hunter, J. (1976) *The Making of the Crofting Community*, Edinburgh: John Donald.

Ingold, T. (2000) *The Perception of the Environment: Essays on Livelihood, Dwelling and Skill*, London and New York: Routledge.

Lin, N. (2001) 'Building a network theory of social capital', in N. Lin, K. Cook and R. Burt (eds) *Social Capital: Theory and Research*, New York: Walter de Gruyter.

Mackay, D. (1996). 'We did it ourselves: an account of the Western Isles community education project *sinn fhein a rinn e: Proisect muinntir nan eilean* 1977–1992', Bernard van Leer Foundation.

Mackenzie, A.F.D. (2013) *Places of Possibility: Property, Nature and Community Land Ownership*, Oxford: Wiley-Blackwell.

Mason, R. and Baveystock, Z. (2008) 'What role can digital heritage play in the re-imagining of national identities: England and its icons', in M. Anico, and E. Peralta (eds) *Heritage and Identity: Engagement and Demission in the Contemporary World*, London: Routledge.

Pahl, R.E. (1965) 'Class and community in English commuter villages', *Sociologica Ruralis*, 5(1): 5–23.

Phillips, R. and Wong, C. (eds) (2017) *Handbook of Community Well-Being Research*, Dordrecht: Springer.

Pichler, F. and Wallace, C. (2009) 'More participation, happier society? A comparative study of civil society and the quality of life', *Social Indicators Research*, 93(2): 255–74.

Putnam, R.D. (2000) *Bowling Alone: the Collapse and Revival of American Community*, New York: Simon and Schuster.

Rainie, L. and Wellman, B. (2012) *Networked: the Mew Social Operating System*, Massachusetts: MIT Press.

Robertson, I.J.M. (ed) (2012) *Heritage from Below*, Farnham: Ashgate.

Said, E.W. (1994) *Culture and Imperialism*, New York: Knopf.

Savage, M., Bagnall, G., and Longhurst, B. (2005) *Globalization and Belonging*, London: Sage.

Tait, E.J., Wallace, C., Mellish, C.S., McLeod, M. and Hunter, C.J. (2011) 'Creating and sustaining rural digital heritage resources using online databases', Paper presented at the Conference, *Supporting Digital Humanities. Answering the Unaskable*, Copenhagen, Denmark.

Tonnies, F. (2002 [1887]) *Community and Society*, Mineola, New York: Dover Publications.

Wallace, C. and Vincent, K. (2017) 'Community well-being and information technology', in R. Phillips and C. Wong (eds) *Handbook of Community Well-Being Research*, Dordrecht: Springer, pp 169–88.

Wallace, C., Vincent, K., Luguzan, C. and Talbot, H. (2015) 'Community broadband initiatives: what makes them successful and why?', *Proceedings of the 7th International Conference on Communities and Technologies*, New York, pp 109–17.

Wallace, C., Vincent, K., Luguzan, C., Townsend, L. and Beel, D.E. (2017) 'Information technology and social cohesion: a tale of two villages', *Journal of Rural Studies*, 54: 426–34.

Woolvin, M. (2012) *Mapping the Third Sector in Rural Scotland: An Initial Review of the Literature*, Edinburgh: Scottish Government Social Research.

8

On Post-traumatic Growth and 'Choosing' to be Happy: Stories of Positive Change from African Refugees and Asylum Seekers

Brianne Wenning

Introduction

Sandra, an energetic woman in her early thirties, sat facing me. We were in one of the support offices of the West End Refugee Service (WERS), located in Newcastle-upon-Tyne, UK. Posters offering various services and phone numbers were pinned on boards on the wall, while an old desktop computer sat neglected in the back corner. Sandra gesticulated wildly as she talked, occasionally dropping her hands to the white table top and stretching them out before her. She seemed comfortable here, impervious to the impersonal nature of the office. It was not like the other offices which housed permanent members of staff; those were cluttered with knickknacks, personal photos and hand-scrawled notes. Instead, this 'desk' was a table, and all it contained was my open notebook, a recorder and occasionally Sandra's hands.

She was discussing her life and some of her experiences thus far. I laughed with her as she related her most ridiculous moments – my eyes filled with tears as she related her sorrows. As she told her story, I sensed that it was coming to the present day where her situation remained unresolved. She was a refused asylum seeker in the UK, at the mercy of friends and acquaintances (as well as a few charities) to meet her basic needs: food, shelter, clothing. She explained how she was given accommodation in Newcastle as an asylum seeker, only to be evicted when her application was refused. Now she lived with an older British woman who attended her church. I expected a rather bleak conclusion, given the difficulties she had faced and continued to face for the foreseeable future. She surprised me, however, when she glanced out of the window at the overcast autumn sky and turned back to me with a smile tugging at the corners of her mouth. "I'll tell you the truth," she began thoughtfully. "This journey is one of the most weirdest things I've ever – I don't know when it's gonna end, how it's gonna end, but – it's like most of the days is really, really good," she declared. I stared at her, taken aback. "It's by the grace of God that I have managed to still kind of like, have a smile although all of this crazy crazy things are happening, ya know?" She paused a minute, reflecting. "It's – I didn't know that I could go through something like this and still be okay. Not okay, but positive," she emphasized.

After our conversation ended and we had gone our separate ways, her words swirled through my head as I left the converted two-story house that was the office of WERS. As I walked past the Afro-Caribbean barber shop and carefully picked my way down the uneven pavement near the patch of grass generously called a park, I tried to tease apart why I was so surprised. I was studying wellbeing and happiness; why was I taken aback? Isn't it intuitive that the good experiences exist along with the bad, and that's why people keep going, physically, mentally and spiritually? The confident, self-assured voice ran through my head, repeating *most of the days is really, really good*. I mulled this phrase over as I rode the metro back to my house.

The 'goodness' in life

My initial surprise from Sandra's interview stems from the fact that much of the research on wellbeing in refugee studies tends to be pathological in nature – that is, it focuses on the negative effects and experiences that forced migration can have on people and communities. As Tribe (2002: 245) notes, one of the dominant themes in the literature assumes refugees must be 'damaged' or 'traumatised'. Summerfield (in Tribe, 2002) echoes this, noting that refugees are often portrayed in terms of suffering and vulnerability to the neglect of other characteristics such as resilience and agency, while Siriwardhana et al (2015) concede that forced migrants face increased risks of mental disorders.

Rather than reiterate the pathological focus, my research focuses on what makes life "really, really good" – to paraphrase Sandra – in spite of, or alongside, the macro and micro traumas and hardships that accompany life as a forced migrant. This chapter draws on findings from my doctoral research (Wenning, 2019). I worked with African refugees living in two urban areas in two vastly different countries: Newcastle-upon-Tyne in the UK and the greater Serrekunda area of the Gambia. I focused on refugees and asylum seekers (including those whose applications for asylum have been refused) and how they create and find this 'good' in their lives, both personally and interpersonally.

The research on the 'goodness' of life is becoming increasingly prominent within anthropology. Joel Robbins (2013: 457) highlights the change from an anthropology focused on a 'suffering subject' to 'a new focus on how people living in different societies strive to create the good in their lives'. This 'goodness' in life is divided into three areas: (1) how people understand the good and its pursuit; (2) how people create the good in social relationships; and (3) how people envisage they can create a good beyond that which is found in their present lives. While elements of all three areas emerged in the narratives of my informants, I will focus primarily on the first one by elucidating the concept of post-traumatic growth.

Post-traumatic growth

Post-traumatic growth (PTG) goes beyond the discussion of resilience and coping that typifies wellbeing studies on refugees. As Peter Gatrell (2013: 251) notes, 'the "bland language" of humanitarian intervention, with its talk of "survival" and "coping", does scant justice to the depth of [refugees] cultural imagination and practices, or the intensity of the adventures during their trek across difficult terrain'. Instead some refugees he spoke with 'mobilise[d] images of being adventurous, tough and independent, rather than marginalised, displaced and helpless' (Gatrell, 2015: 251). While my informants did not use these terms, many did frame their experiences of forced migration and resettlement as a journey, much like Sandra in the opening vignette. This way of framing experiences allowed them to make sense of hardships endured and incorporate the personal changes they experienced into their sense of self.

While resilience denotes a return to the baseline functioning one was at previously, PTG recognizes a surpassing of this baseline. Bensimon (2012: 783) differentiates resilience from PTG, asserting that resilience is a personality trait, while PTG is a mode of adjustment to traumatic events. Typically, this adjustment involves a recognition of the ways in which one has somehow personally benefitted from surviving the trauma experienced. The definition of PTG describes it as 'the experience of positive change that the individual experiences as a result of the struggle with a traumatic event' (Calhoun and Tedeschi, 2013: 6). This reflects a 'silver linings' approach to life in which positives emerge from life's trials (Cieslik 2017: 10). Recall Sandra emphasizing that she was not just surviving as an asylum seeker but was able to feel positive throughout. It is this transformative element that makes it distinct from other positive concepts such as coping and resilience (Tedeschi and Calhoun, 2004).

The concept of PTG states that growth occurs in relation to five different factors that relate to three different conceptual categories. The five different factors are 'personal strength', 'relating to others', 'new possibilities in life', 'greater appreciation of life' and 'increased spirituality', which can be subsumed under the three conceptual categories of 'changed sense of self', 'changed sense of relationships with others' and 'changed philosophy of life' (Calhoun and Tedeschi, 2013: 7). To date, there are a multitude of studies and examples to show the existence and importance of this concept, especially in the field of psychology and, most importantly for my research, in the context of working with refugees.

Refugees and PTG

Most relevant for my research was literature that draws upon the experiences of those who have survived various conflicts, ranging from refugees and internally displaced persons to prisoners of war and those who were forcibly relocated. In a study of former refugees and displaced people in Sarajevo, researchers found that even among those exposed to the most extreme traumatic events, growth was still possible and, indeed, reported (Powell et al, 2003).

Another study, conducted with Congolese refugees living in camps in Uganda, corroborated the experience of growth following traumatic experiences (Ssenyonga, Owens and Olema, 2013). Although it mainly examines factors related to PTSD, the authors conclude that resilience and PTG offer protection against PTSD in developing countries (Ssenyonga et al, 2013).

One issue is that many studies are based on quantitative rather than qualitative data. Tedeschi and Calhoun's Post-traumatic Growth Inventory (PTGI), for example, employs a six-point Likert scale. This is surprising given the emphasis the authors place on narrative accounts of PTG, stating 'the development of the individual's personal life narrative and posttraumatic growth may mutually influence one another' (Tedeschi and Calhoun, 2004). Hence, incorporating trauma into life narratives can reframe the experience and facilitate factors associated with growth. While they tout this mutually reinforcing process in a clinical setting (Calhoun and Tedeschi, 2013), few studies utilize qualitative approaches. One study among Tibetan refugees in India confirmed the presence of PTG in narratives among their sample of refugees, remarking the method allowed individuals to discuss openly their understandings of positive self-transformation (Hussain and Bhushan, 2013: 206). Another study on Cambodian refugees resettled in the US noted that, 'the process of meaning-making and trauma reconstruction includes trauma-disclosure and the sharing of narratives, which leads to outcomes of PTG' (Uy and Okubo, 2018: 14). They recognized the importance of personal trauma narratives, suggesting it 'can be vital in the process of becoming empowered in the spirit of healing and overall psychological recovery' (Uy and Okubo, 2018: 14). Clearly, the importance of narratives for not only resilience but growth is crucial, lending support for the importance of qualitative methodology for this topic.

A cautionary note on using PTG

While it remains true that PTG as a concept began in the psychology discipline, its reach has extended more broadly into a plethora of different disciplines, not least the social sciences. Anthropologists and sociologists have engaged with PTG in samples as diverse as children suffering from bereavement in the UK (Brewer and Sparkes, 2011) to those reacting to extreme weather events as a result of climate change (Ramsay and Manderson, 2011). Despite its wide adoption as an object of study, however, it is worth reminding that PTG is very much shaped by Western notions of psychology, trauma and forms of mental illness. As Behrouzan (2015) reminds us, concepts such as depression, PTSD and, by extension, PTG, are very much Western in origin and carry a specific sociocultural history. In her research, Iranians readily adopted Western psychiatric ideas related to mental health, particularly depression, and moulded them to their own experiences in the aftermath of the Iran–Iraq War. The adoption of this new vernacular, immersed in the supposedly neutral, objective and progressive context of psychology, provided a way for people to discuss their distress with the social and political circumstances in a legitimate way. This is not to say, however, that it accurately described the experiences of her interlocutors, but rather that they chose to engage with it in a very particular way within a very particular broader social context.

It still must be said, however, that psychology and psychiatry are steeped in their own socio-historical contexts and cannot, therefore, be seen as objective. Argenti-Pillen (2000: 94) notes that trauma, and specifically PTSD, is a 'discourse' rather than an objective fact, and as such is greatly influenced by history, the organization of society, Euro-American institutions and moral culture. Furthermore, ideas surrounding PTG and PTSD tend to privilege individual notions of trauma while ignoring collective experiences of hardships and healing. Taken together, these ideas do remain a limitation of using this concept. In particular, imposing these categorizations of mental health, illness and psychiatric disorders on non-Western populations may only imperfectly reflect their perceived social world. Of course, the world is becoming increasingly globalized and with it a mixing of cultural ideas is taking place. This perhaps explains why PTG (and even PTSD) are increasingly resonating with governments and populations in non-Western countries. It is for this reason that I have chosen to engage with this topic as a useful framework for understanding my informants' narratives.

The importance of narratives

Research on PTG tends to use quantitative methods. To add a qualitative perspective to this research area, I provided rich narrative examples to further develop themes around PTG. In addition to extensive periods of participant observation, I employed a narrative-inquiry approach. This approach allowed me to use stories to analyse the ways my informants navigated their everyday meaning-making and 'being-in-the-world'. The vignettes I use demonstrate how different areas of PTG were experienced and narrated to me by my informants.

Storytelling orients people towards their lives and provides a useful way for framing experiences. The stories we tell about ourselves provide the basis for a stable concept of identity over time (Farmer and Tsakiris, 2012: 125). 'The success of this storying of experience', White and Epston (1990: 10) remind us, 'provides persons with a sense of continuity and meaning in their lives, and this is relied upon for the ordering of daily lives and for the interpretation of further experiences'. While there is some dissent on the importance of stories (see Strawson, 2004), I agree with those who argue that narrativity and storytelling are part and parcel of the human experience.

In the telling and retelling of stories, 'persons are reauthoring their lives' (White and Epston, 1990: 13). More specifically, 'persons give meaning to their lives and relationships by storying their experience and that, in interacting with others in the performance of these stories, they are active in the shaping of their lives and relationships' (White and Epston, 1990: 13). This action in the form of storytelling can be seen as a 'vital human strategy for sustaining a sense of agency in the face of disempowering circumstances' which is particularly useful for individuals such as refugees and asylum seekers (Jackson, 2002: 15).

In addition to fostering a sense of agency, narratives provide an interesting lens to further engage with refugees and asylum seekers. As Jackson (2002: 79) notes: 'Many anthropologists have been troubled by the inordinate amount of quantification, objectification, and technicism in the field of refugee studies – the apparatus of statistics, graphs, tables, category terms, and authoritative generalization that are brought to bear, in the name of both humanitarianism and the public good, on the so-called "refugee problem".' Borwick et al (2013: 3) find similar discontent with the methods used in refugee studies, noting that the 'voices of refugees are largely absent from the literature on refugee mental health'. Instead, they argue for a language-based approach like in-depth interviewing to more fully understand how people construct meaning about their world, themselves and others. Narratives remain a fruitful yet neglected approach when looking at factors of wellbeing and growth among refugees and asylum seekers.

The setting(s)

My research focused on narratives of happiness and wellbeing among African refugees and asylum seekers. I spent 20 months (between August 2014 and April 2016) in two fieldsites in two vastly different countries and contexts: a charity called the West End Refugee Service (WERS) in Newcastle-upon-Tyne, UK and the implementing partner for the United Nations High Commissioner for Refugees (UNHCR) called the Gambia Food and Nutrition Association (GAFNA) in Bakau, the Gambia. In both contexts I worked with those from a range of sociocultural, economic, political and geographic backgrounds living in an urban area.

The organizations acted as gatekeepers, providing me with access to those they supported. Working in these different contexts allowed me the opportunity to compare and contrast the experience of seeking asylum in two vastly different environments. Many of those in the UK were at some point in the asylum process, including refused. Refused asylum seekers could not access housing or income from the government and were barred from seeking any form of employment.

Though they had reached what many asylum seekers would presume was a safe and, ultimately, desirable country (as narrated to me by those living in the Gambia), their situation did not necessarily reflect this idealized version.

The Gambia offered a very different experience as those seeking asylum had merely to present themselves to the Gambia Refugee Commission in Banjul to receive their refugee card. Refugees are then entitled to seek waged employment and can access the same social amenities available to Gambians (Gambia Refugee Act, 2008: 23). In contrast to the 'Fortress Europe' image of the UK, the Gambia is viewed as 'one of the most "refugee friendly" countries in all of West Africa' (Conway, 2004: 3; EASO, 2017).

Despite the glowing review of the Gambia as a refugee-hosting country, it remains a refugee-generating country as well. Though praised for its treatment of refugees, it still represented a temporary home for many I spoke with who hoped to resettle in Europe, North America or Australia. The two countries thus provided me with vastly different contexts in which to compare the presumably universal concept of PTG.

Methodology

My primary method of data collection was ethnography, particularly participant observation coupled with interviews. My informants were told at the outset that I was interested in hearing their stories, both 'the good and the bad'. Though I focus here mainly around 'the good', I in no way intend to trivialize the 'bad' or imply that it was not a topic of discussion. I include portions of these stories where appropriate to illustrate the complexity of experiences.

Participant observation allowed me to establish myself in the community and build a rapport with members. I conducted 40 interviews in total, evenly split between the UK and the Gambia. While informal ethnographic interviews took place in the hallways, meetings rooms and wider community, I invited participants to sit down in a more private setting to allow them to delve fully into their experiences. These interviews mainly took place in the office of WERS or GAFNA. The lengthy participant observation in the two fieldwork settings helped me generate a sample of interviewees reflective of the wider refugee population in the two sites.

I transcribed all interviews verbatim (which varied in length from 30 minutes to three hours) and coded the topics discussed. I did the same with conversations recorded in field notes. Formal analysis began by grouping topics into themes noting how themes related to one another. Here I noticed the ways these topics could be grouped and connected to broader themes within the wellbeing and happiness literature. While analysis was guided by previous research on wellbeing, I was not restricted to these categories instead letting interviewees narratives inform the analysis.

Findings

Elements from each of the domains outlined by Tedeschi and Calhoun were mentioned by my informants. There is insufficient space to mention them all; instead, I focus on a few of these domains ('spirituality', 'new possibilities' and 'changed relationships') to show how they were embedded in the stories told by informants. This shows how people's stories are rooted in their striving for wellbeing and happiness, despite the difficulties they experienced. I also demonstrate how elements of PTG can coexist with PTSD, describing a more balanced picture of refugees and asylum seekers than we often see, and one that suggests a rich and diverse range of emotions and experiences that includes both positive and negative experiences.

A note on religion and spirituality

Spirituality, as Tedeschi and Calhoun call this category, was the most commonly cited example in the literature relating to growth, coping and resilience. Indeed, in Park's (2006: 288) article comparing several studies on PTG, she found that the strength of the relationship between growth and religion is one of the most consistent findings. In my research I did not meet a single respondent who claimed to be atheist or agnostic. All belong to one of the various branches of Christianity or Islam.

Religion is appealing as it can be accessed by all at any time. Many people turn to religion to provide a meaningful framework to help structure their lives. Religion and specifically a belief in God can play a role in providing context and purpose and seems to be one of the most common resources at one's disposal when it comes to meaning-making. Religion is cited as a source of strength and coping in refugee groups as diverse as Burmese refugees in Australia (Borwick et al, 2013) and Somali and Zimbabwean refugees in the UK (Sherwood and Liebling-Kalifani, 2012). Jackson and Piette (2015: 12) even claim that submitting to a higher power is actually a way of recovering one's agency by creating a relationship with something beyond oneself.

Religious forms of coping allowed an individual to continue with their daily lives while fostering, where possible, a positive sense of wellbeing. Coping successfully can allow people to lead a happy life, and, given the high rates of religiosity around the world, religion has a clear role to play in fostering this happiness. In fact, data on this subject strongly suggests that religious people are happier than non-religious ones (eg Clark and Lelkes, 2009; Graham, 2009).

Religion can aid someone after a trauma in different ways and remains an important aspect in the lives of many people. Eyber (2016: 202) contends that 'to ignore the religious facets of people's personal, social, cultural and political lives excludes a significant element in how people construct their own wellbeing'. Regardless of the specific relationship between religion and happiness, the literature consistently places the two together. My informants did the same, embedding religious aspects (both personal and interpersonal) into their discussions of wellbeing and happiness as I go onto describe.

New possibilities in life

One of the PTG areas narrated to me highlighted how an individual's experiences led to a positive change by adopting a changed philosophy of life, particularly in the domain of new possibilities. Yasir's family moved to Dubai from Somalia before he was born. Though technically born in Dubai, he was not considered a citizen and therefore was listed as a dependent on his father's visa. His mother passed away when he was very young leaving him dependent on his father. When Yasir was 13 years old, his father also died and he was unable to stay in Dubai due to immigration rules. He then went to the Netherlands to live with an uncle. This relationship was one fraught with conflict. He claimed he "couldn't cope" living with him and all they did was "fight, fight, fight after fight". He eventually severed ties with his uncle and, after being denied refugee status in the Netherlands, came to London. He applied to remain in the UK, but this was subsequently denied. He became increasingly worried about his precarious status and found himself homeless, resorting to 'couch surfing' with various friends and acquaintances. He found a church that housed homeless asylum seekers in Sheffield but still lacked access to financial support. To earn some money he agreed to be an 'off the books' tester for new and experimental drugs. After severe reactions to the drugs that led to hospitalization, he was forced to withdraw from the study, leaving him homeless and penniless.

Some friends offered Yasir opportunities to sell drugs, but he declined this to work instead in a take-away restaurant. During this time he drank alcohol excessively. "Me, I was loving it," he explained. "I enjoyed drinking, cause like when you got ... problem, too stressed, maybe you drink to enjoy, to chill, cope at it, but I used to drink ... to go home just like, [drink] a bottle of vodka, a bottle of whisky." Drinking served as his coping mechanism for the harsh realities of life on the streets as a refugee – a feature of others I interviewed. Substance abuse, including alcohol, is frequently cited in the literature as a common coping mechanism following a trauma (Calhoun and Tedeschi, 2013). For Yasir, "I get drunk and go to bed," he said of his former routine. "So I don't feel no pain, no stress, no sadness." Charity workers commented that Yasir would often become violent when drinking. Yasir knew he was on a destructive path, but he felt helpless as to how to change it. "I tell her [charity worker] 'I don't want to drink, but I have to drink. I'm homeless, I'm illegal here, five times they refuse me in the court!' Then, when I come back, they arrest me, the immigration, for working."

The charity working with Yasir enrolled him at a residential facility to help with his alcohol abuse. After this course he felt much better, attending a gym and finding a job as a plasterer and welder. However, he was again arrested by immigration authorities for working illegally and was sentenced to 16 months in a detention facility. Surprisingly, Yasir was very positive about his detention. "God is great, like sometime you think, bad thing happens, but saves [you] from something worse. It was very good for my life. They opened my case." Being detained meant the authorities re-opened his case for asylum and he was entitled to housing and other benefits, representing the 'silver lining' that Cieslik (2017) discusses. Yasir has since won his claim, which the Home Office is appealing. The first two appeals by the Home Office determined that their case was not strong enough, and Yasir's lawyer told him that the final appeal did not look to be any better. Yasir could see a potential end in sight. "My hope's come back," he explained.

In addition to his newfound hope, he acknowledged that becoming sober and then being placed in detention turned his life around. "I'm a changed man now," he said frankly. "Before I went to detention, I would make friends and that, but we're not gonna laugh like that. You will never see me laughing for nothing out of stress. But now, I know that life is good." When encouraged to explain how life was good now, he replied with "I got guaranteed tomorrow is gonna be good for me, I will get my status, get a girlfriend." While he did not enjoy his time in detention, describing it like a prison, it did give him another chance to gain legal status in the UK. He earned educational certificates for courses undertaken while in detention, reigniting his passion for learning. His outlook on life had changed. He was more positive and hopeful about the future and improving his relationships with others, connecting with those around him on a deeper level.

Changed relationships

Narratives involving growth were not limited to those living in the UK. Evette, a refugee from the Democratic Republic of Congo (DRC), discussed personal growth during interviews. Her individual growth changed not only herself but changed her relationships with others. She had experienced a very trying series of hardships which impacted on her wellbeing. She was a university student, studying nutrition, when she was forced to flee from the violence that erupted in the DRC in 2001. She fled by plane landing in Dakar, Senegal, before taking a car to the Gambia.

A short time after this she experienced another loss. After giving birth to a baby girl, the child died. Her daughter had been born at home, so nurses took the baby to hospital for treatment. Sadly, the baby died shortly afterwards. The father was a white British man, and Evette's eyes shined as she told me how her baby had the most beautiful light skin. The tragic loss of her daughter was deepened by the sudden death of her partner to cancer a few months later.

According to Evette, "This make me change." She recalled how she kept thinking about the baby, wondering what she would be doing, how big she would be. She even became so distraught with her poor mental state that she visited several doctors to see about a biological cause for her continuing depression. After catching herself thinking about her daughter again, she finally decided, "No, I must avoid these things, thinking about this baby is no good for me." To keep her mind from ruminating on how her baby would be if she were still alive, Evette returned to her books. "If I thinking [about her] I take one book, take any book, reading reading … when I finish reading that book, the mind for the baby gone," she explained. This focus on the loss of her baby can be seen in another way. According to Becker (1997), babies can serve as powerful metaphors. 'Babies represent life, death, hope, energy, transformation, productivity, and perseverance' (Becker 1997: 179). She notes that the world of Julia, one of her informants, went from ordered to disordered and chaotic with the death of her baby representing not only a physical loss, but also the loss of hope as well (Becker 1997: 63–4). Based on Evette's story, her daughter also represented hope for the future, while her death signalled a spiral into disorder and chaos which included the death of Evette's spouse shortly afterwards.

This chaos, fortunately, did not become a defining feature of the rest of Evette's life. She changed her actions and redeveloped her narrative around this crisis event. As Becker (1997: 166) suggests of a personal narrative, 'it enables the narrator to mend the disruption by weaving it into the fabric of life, to put experience into perspective'. Evette's coping techniques, her conscious striving for wellness and her attempt to make sense of her suffering led to her conclude that for the past five years she has been better. Now, when she sees others who are experiencing difficulties in their lives, she shares her story with them and encourages them. "If I see somebody stressed," she said, "I will talk with that somebody [and say] 'You will see, everything will be okay'." "So, you help others now?" I asked. "I try, me I try. If I see somebody sad like that, I will talk to them. 'Do this, do that.' You see somebody change. I change a lot of people, just talk with them. I say, 'I had this life before, just leave it.' They listen," she concluded. This empathetic focus changed her relationship with others she encountered. Easing the pain of others allowed her to find a sense of meaning in her own loss.

This sentiment was reported by several other interviewees, both in the UK and in the Gambia, echoing the wider literature that 'finding meaning through helping others' is significant in cases of PTG. For example, compassion for others is a significant sub-theme of PTG in recent research with Tibetan refugees (Hussain and Bhushan, 2013). Their informants noted that supporting others in need helped them pursue a more meaningful life, similar to experiences related by Evette.

Multiple domains in one

It is fitting to conclude with Sandra, who opened this chapter. Not only are several different domains of PTG mentioned by her, but she also described how "most of the days is really, really good" and how she changed her mindset to be happier. This happiness shaped her relationships with herself, others and God, feeding back into areas of PTG. She drew on her deeply religious background and values as resources when times became difficult. Sandra was happy in the present and optimistic for the future, particularly as she was able to find meaning through PTG.

Sandra came from Zimbabwe on a student visa and had been in the UK for seven years. Her student years were full of friends and a fierce commitment to her managerial position at a fast-food chain. Despite daily stressors, she recognized that life passes through various stages. "As I look back I see … I know bad things happen, it's difficult, but it is a phase. And I always ask myself, 'What am I learning?'" she explained. She tried to focus on new insights, hidden meanings and opportunities that each hardship brought her.

True to a PTG model, she highlighted how these periods of difficulties allowed her to gain new skills. She had experienced a changed sense of self, particularly in the form of realizing her personal strength. Growth, big and small, was mentioned equally. She amazed herself even with what might be considered mundane tasks. "I didn't know that I can manage to budget!" she exclaimed, highlighting how she learned to adapt to the meagre £15 a week she received in support from WERS. She claimed that before she put in her asylum claim she "loved money". Now, she felt that God was teaching her a lesson, that He was saying to her, "Now you see how life is when you don't have money." These changes in her life were perceived to be for the better.

Though PTG is different to happiness, Sandra did claim that she was happy. When I probed deeper and asked what made her happy, she furrowed her brow thoughtfully and gave me a year: 2012. "2012," she continued when I looked puzzled, "that's when I literally chose. I was like, 'God, I'm choosing to be happy.' And I'm choosing that no one should have my joy. No one should be responsible for my happiness. Happiness – being happy – it is a decision." She paused for a moment before adding, "It's my own responsibility to make myself happy. After that, I started looking at my life in a different way." She narrated her creative solution – and one that drew on a sense of agency – to structure her life personally and interpersonally. She highlighted her difficulties but remarked that it wasn't productive to worry about it because "you will drive yourself crazy". "Sometimes you don't have control over certain things, so you have to accept that you don't have control over that and let it be," she added.

I probed deeper following her declaration that a conscious choice made such a difference in her life, particularly as some commentators (Davies, 2015) have been critical of suggestions by some in the 'Happiness Industry' that improvements in personal wellbeing can be achieved through relatively small changes in lifestyle. She told me that she had been spiralling into a depression which began when her brother passed away from cancer. Her life became wrapped up in working long hours, showing up late, talking back to her manager and consuming too much alcohol (much like Yasir). On New Year's Eve, going into 2012, she realized that she was unhappy with her life. This led to her decision. "You have to choose to be happy," she clarified. "Find a way. Choose, you choose. So I chose to be happy and I choose to do positive things." Sandra described this happiness as peace. She said, "You have to be happy from inside out. I have this peace within me. And even sometimes I don't understand it. But I know I have peace." She was very determined about her positive thinking. "Be positive, start saying positive things about your life and it will come to pass, it will," she told me. "Sometimes it is difficult when you're in the tornado to believe that, but you still have to believe that." This emphasis on choice is echoed even by Viktor Frankl, the psychiatrist who spoke and wrote extensively about his time in a concentration camp in World War II. 'The last of the human freedoms', he explains, is to 'choose one's attitude in a given set of circumstances' (Frankl, 1984: 12). Sandra felt similarly, which is why choosing to be happy seemed a viable option to her. Following this conscious choice, Sandra then went on to create a 'bucket list'. For her, these were inexpensive or free activities that she and her friends could do, such as ice skating or a barbeque in the park.

Her decision to be happy also affected her interpersonal relationships in a way similar to Evette. She reflected on her desire to improve the lives of others, stating "Sometimes that's the reason why we go through these things, so you help other people, you know?" She continued, "I just like to do something positive in people's lives like, that's how I cope as well. I'm going through whatever, but for that time I've escaped that thing and I'm doing something positive instead of me always focusing on my problem." She described a situation in which she offered advice to a colleague in an attempt to give her more confidence. "I wanted her to have that juice I was on," she commented.

Sandra eventually accepted an invitation to live with church members in Newcastle and was now a very active member in their church. "I thank God for those people," she told me, "because also they push me to do things that I would not usually do, like standing in front of people, or even like giving an announcement, I would never do that but she [friend she lives with] just pushes me like, 'Go, do it!'" Through these new relationships fostered by her rejected asylum claim, she finds she is capable of doing things she never previously entertained as well as using her decision to be happy to inspire those close to her.

Future directions

These accounts of growth do not imply that these individuals are more resilient or better adjusted than those who did not discuss PTG. As

Calhoun and Tedeschi (2013: 13) suggest, '*Posttraumatic growth is common, but it is by no means universal*' (emphasis in original). Furthermore, experiencing and narrating PTG does not exclude the possibility of also experiencing and narrating PTSD. Tedeschi and Calhoun (1995) remark that PTG and PTSD remain largely independent of each other and may, in fact, be reported by the same person at the same point in time. Joseph and Linley (2005: 273) note that it is entirely possible that 'growth may leave them sadder, but almost inevitably wiser'. For my informants, then, PTG is not a necessary ingredient of all of their life stories, and the instances of growth do not exclude the possibility of sadness. Absences of PTG in life stories do not mean that a person is less adjusted or less happy than their counterparts who do discuss PTG. Similarly, after so carefully outlining how refugees and asylum seekers are not merely passive victims helpless in their situation, I would not wish to then paint them as individuals who are inevitably traumatized by PTG in their lives. Categories of PTG appeared in several of my informants' narratives and, given the proliferation of studies around this concept, I found it useful to engage with this topic in an area in which it is relatively understudied – namely, among refugees and among those in an African context.

Conclusion

Refugees and asylum seekers frequently manage to find positivity in an otherwise stressful and potentially trauma-laden experience. The attention to positive experiences and interpretations is not to trivialize what people have gone through. This chapter is heavily ethnographic in focus to provide a background to those I discussed in order to talk about growth and resilience not as the whole or underlying experience, but merely as a part of it. Even I must admit to being initially surprised at the level of resilience most exhibited. Clearly, I am not alone as many researchers and even philosophers have pondered over the puzzle of how most people can go on with their lives and 'be okay' despite a severely traumatic experience. True, this resilience took many forms among my informants. Nevertheless, people were managing as best they could, with many even able to comment on the positive changes experienced as a result of their situation. PTG was certainly not rare among those I spoke with, despite the seeming improbability of it all. Thus, given the possibility of finding positive changes or positivity in general among refugees, it seems more pertinent than ever to look at refugees or 'the refugee experience' (if one can even use such a phrase) through a wellbeing lens. Anthropology can add much to this topic by using qualitative data in the form of elicited narratives.

References

Argenti-Pillen, A. (2000) 'The discourse on trauma in non-western cultural contexts', in *International Handbook of Human Response to Trauma*, Boston, MA: Springer, pp 87–102.

Becker, G. (1997) *Disrupted Lives: How People Create Meaning in a Chaotic World*, London: University of California Press.

Behrouzan, O. (2015) 'Writing Prozāk diaries in Tehran: generational anomie and psychiatric subjectivities', *Culture, Medicine, and Psychiatry*, 39(3): 399–426.

Bensimon, M. (2012) 'Elaboration on the association between trauma, PTSD and posttraumatic growth: the role of trait resilience', *Personality and Individual Differences*, 52(7): 782–7.

Borwick, S., Schweitzer, R., Brough, M., Vromans, L. and Shakespeare-Finch, J. (2013) 'Well-being of refugees from Burma: a salutogenic perspective', *International Migration*, 1–15.

Brewer, J. and Sparkes, A.C. (2011) 'Parentally bereaved children and posttraumatic growth: insights from an ethnographic study of a UK childhood bereavement service', *Mortality*, 16(3): 204–22.

Calhoun, L.G. and Tedeschi, R.G. (2013) *Posttraumatic Growth in Clinical Practice*, London: Routledge.

Cieslik, M. (2017) *The Happiness Riddle and the Quest for a Good Life*, London: Palgrave Macmillan.

Clark, A.E. and Orsolya, L. (2009) 'Let us pray: religious interactions in life satisfaction', *PSE Working Papers* n° 2009-01.

Conway, C. (2004) *Refugee Livelihoods: A Case Study of the Gambia*, UNHCR.

Davies, W. (2015) *The Happiness Industry: How the Government and Big Business Sold us Wellbeing*, London: Verso.

European Union: European Asylum Support Office (EASO) (2017) *EASO Country of Origin Information Report: The Gambia Country Focus*, available at http://www.refworld.org/docid/5a338fb54.html

Eyber, C. (2016) 'Tensions in conceptualising psychosocial wellbeing in Angola: the marginalisation of religion and spirituality', in S.C. White and C. Blackmore (eds) *Cultures of Wellbeing*, Hampshire: Palgrave Macmillan, pp 198–218.

Farmer, H. and Tsakiris, M. (2012) 'The bodily social self: a link between phenomenal and narrative selfhood', *Review of Philosophy and Psychology*, 3: 125–44.

Frankl, V. (1984) *Man's Search for Meaning: Revised and Updated*, New York: Washington Square Press.

Gambia Refugee Act (2008) *Gambia: Refugee Act*, 23 October 2008, available at http://www.refworld.org/docid/4a71a8202.html

Gardner, K. (2016). 'The path to happiness? Prosperity, suffering, and transnational migration in Britain and Sylhet', in I. Kavedžija and H. Walker (eds) *Values of Happiness*, Chicago: Hau Books, pp 191–214.

Gatrell, P. (2013) *The Making of the Modern Refugee*, Oxford: Oxford University Press.

Graham, C. (2009) *Happiness around the World: The Paradox of Happy Peasants and Miserable Millionaires*, Oxford: Oxford University Press.

Hussain, D. and Bhushan, B. (2013) 'Posttraumatic growth experience among Tibetan refugees: a qualitative investigation', *Qualitative Research in Psychology*, 10(2): 204–16.

Jackson, M. (2002) *The Politics of Storytelling: Violence, Transgression, and Intersubjectivity*, Copenhagen: Museum Tusculanum Press.

Jackson, M. and Piette, A. (2015). 'Anthropology and the existential turn', in M. Jackson and A. Piette (eds) *What is Existential Anthropology?*, New York: Berghahn Books, pp 1–29.

Joseph, S. and Linley, P.A. (2005) 'Positive adjustment to threatening events: an organismic valuing theory of growth through adversity', *Review of General Psychology*, 9(3): 262–80.

McAdams, D. (1993) *The Stories We Live By: Personal Myths and the Making of the Self*, New York: Guilford Press.

Park, C.L. (2006) 'Religiousness and religious coping as determinants of stress-related growth', *Archive for the Psychology of Religion*, 28(1): 287–302.

Powell, S., Rosner, R., Butollo, W., Tedeschi, R.G. and Calhoun, L.G. (2003) 'Posttraumatic growth after war: a study with former refugees and displaced people in Sarajevo', *Journal of Clinical Psychology*, 59(1): 71–83.

Ramsay, T. and Manderson, L. (2011) 'Resilience, spirituality and posttraumatic growth: reshaping the effects of climate change', in *Climate Change and Human Well-being*, New York: Springer, pp 165–84).

Robbins, J. (2013) 'Beyond the suffering subject: toward an anthropology of the good', *Journal of the Royal Anthropological Institute*, 19(3): 447–62.

Sherwood, K. and Liebling-Kalifani, H. (2012) 'A grounded theory investigation into the experiences of African women refugees: effects on resilience and identity and implications for service provision', *Journal of International Women's Studies*, 13(1): 86–108.

Siriwardhana, C., Abas, M., Siribaddana, S., Sumathipala, A. and Stewart, R. (2015) 'Dynamics of resilience in a forced migration: a 1-year follow-up study of longitudinal associations with mental health in a conflict-affected, ethnic Muslim population', *BMJ Open*, 5(2): 1–10.

Ssenyonga, J., Owens, V. and Kani Olema, D. (2013) 'Posttraumatic growth, resilience, and posttraumatic stress disorder (PTSD) among refugees', *Procedia-Social and Behavioral Sciences*, 82: 144–8.

Strawson, G. (2004) 'Against narrativity', *Ratio*, 17(4): 428–52.

Tedeschi, R. and Calhoun, L.G. (1995) *Trauma and Transformation: Growing in the Aftermath of Suffering*, London: Sage Publications.

Tedeschi, R G. and Calhoun, L.G. (2004) 'Posttraumatic growth: conceptual foundations and empirical evidence', *Psychological Inquiry*, 15(1): 1–18.

Tribe, R. (2002) 'Mental health of refugees and asylum-seekers', *Advances in Psychiatric Treatment*, 8: 240–7.

Uy, K.K. and Okubo, Y. (2018) 'Re-storying the trauma narrative: fostering posttraumatic growth in Cambodian refugee women', *Women & Therapy*, 1–18.

Wenning, B. (2019) '"Most of the days is really, really good": narratives of well-being and happiness s among asylum seekers and refugees in the UK and the Gambia', PhD thesis, University of Edinburgh.

White, M. and Epstom, D. (1990) *Narrative Means to Therapeutic Ends*, New York: W.W. Norton & Company.

9

Using Social Wellbeing to Inform Regeneration Strategies in a Former Colliery Town in Northern England

Kelly Johnson and Sarah Coulthard

Introduction

There is now an established argument that public policy should focus on conditions necessary for people's wellbeing as well as those for economic growth (McGregor, 2007; Bache and Reardon, 2013). In 2009, the Commission on the Measurement of Economic Performance (Stiglitz et al, 2009) published an influential report which argued that to achieve sustainable and inclusive development necessitates a clear shift from measuring societal progress in terms of production and consumption, to measures of human wellbeing. The last decade has seen an explosion of initiatives to conceptualize and measure human wellbeing and to put it into practice in academia and policy (OECD, 2011; Helliwell et al, 2017; Bache, 2018). The concept of wellbeing now appears at the heart of many UK public policies from the 2014 Care Act, to the current 25-year plan for the Environment (DEFRA). The UK Office of National Statistics created its National Wellbeing Programme, which aims to 'produce accepted and trusted measures of the well-being of the nation' and has incorporated subjective wellbeing questions into the Annual Population Survey since April 2011. This is viewed, by some, as a long-term process of transformative change, which could lead to a refocusing of government policy and agenda across many public policy sectors (Kroll, 2011).

To realize the full potential of wellbeing-orientated policy, beyond just the measurement of wellbeing, will require greater understanding about how wellbeing can be creatively employed in policy and practice, and the difference it can actually make to people's lives. Very often wellbeing is used narrowly as an output following an intervention or is used as an indicator of social change over time. It can also be used more ambitiously as an 'input' – a framing concept in the design phase of policy and practice. We can use it to understand the different wellbeing strategies people deploy, and the values which underpin these, illuminating new forms of social policy interventions. In their review of wellbeing and public policy in the UK, Bache et al (2016) distinguish two aspects to the wellbeing agenda: 'measurement' and 'policy application' arguing that while the former is well advanced, the latter remains 'somewhat embryonic', illustrating a clear gap in understanding how wellbeing influences research, policy and practice. At the same time, recent critiques of wellbeing-orientated public policy stress that poor engagement with wellbeing as a concept, means that wellbeing data may be used to simply promote those existing policies instead of informing new policy directions and wellbeing initiatives (NEF, 2012). Of particular relevance to readers of this volume, Scott (2012) critiques the dominance of certain types of quantitative wellbeing research calling for further use of in-depth qualitative, participatory and context-dependent studies to help inform debate, policy and practice.

This chapter is based on a recent PhD on *social wellbeing* drawing on data from residents of a coastal community called Seaham, a former colliery town in County Durham, Northern England. The foundations of Seaham as we know it today were laid in 1828 formed from three collieries, Seaham Colliery, known locally as 'the Nack', Dawdon Colliery, and Vane Tempest. Working 'down the pit' gave many local men employment until the pit closures in 1987. In 1951 when all three mines were operational 70 per cent of the economically active males worked in mining (Vision Through Time, 2017). This report also shows that unemployment was also very low during this period at 2 per cent. As in many mining towns, the collieries had enormous influence on social life, directly through provision of secure employment which often transcended generations, but also shaping social activities such as holidays, a common 'pay day' and subsequent shopping days that created a platform for social exchange and togetherness (Bulmer, 1978; Williamson, 1982). The town of Seaham has witnessed many social, economic and environmental changes over the past 50 years, and after efforts to save the local pits, Seaham Colliery shut in 1987 followed by Dawdon Colliery in 1991. The last mine, Vane Tempest, saw its last working shift in 1992 and officially closed in 1993 marking the end of the mining industry in Seaham leaving many families unemployed. Today the town's unemployment rate is high with 18 per cent of economically active people out of work. Over the last 20 years, Seaham has experienced many regeneration and investment initiatives, such as industrial clean-up programmes aimed at improving employment prospects in the community. Despite this, the most recent Index of Multiple Deprivation (IMD) indicates that two out of the nine neighbourhoods within the region remain in the 10 per cent most deprived neighbourhoods in the country.

The chapter begins with an overview of the social wellbeing framework adopted in this research, and then reflects on the methods applied in the Seaham case study, with illustrative data from the PhD. We then discuss how the findings can be useful for regeneration strategies in Seaham town and the wider region and consider the value of a multidimensional approach to wellbeing research.

A three-dimensional approach to social wellbeing

There is an emergent consensus in the relevant literature that the concept of wellbeing should be multidimensional (Stiglitz et al, 2009; OECD, 2016). Consequently, this PhD research is informed by a social wellbeing framework (also known as 3D wellbeing) (Gough and McGregor, 2007), which structures wellbeing around three interdependent dimensions: a *material* dimension (tangible things that people have access to, and the resources they can employ), a *relational* dimension (the social interactions people engage in and are affected by), and a *psychological* dimension (people's values, ideologies and beliefs, and their own subjective assessment of their lives) (McGregor et al, 2015). The conceptual foundations of the 3D framework are embedded in a eudaimonic concept of wellbeing (Coulthard, 2012). For example, 'wellbeing as the fulfilment of human potential' rather than as a sensory pleasure (Wiseman and Brasher, 2008: 354).

Each of the three aspects is important and wellbeing depends on all of them being satisfied to a reasonable extent, which will be different to different people dependent upon their cultural and personal experiences (Sayer, 2011). The framework's incorporation of a *relational* dimension is particularly innovative and responds to critiques calling for much greater acknowledgement of the dynamic nature of wellbeing as shaped by everyday relations through which wellbeing is negotiated (White, 2015; Bache et al, 2016). This *social* concept of wellbeing explicitly recognizes that the wellbeing of one person is heavily determined by social relations, in both terms of what people can have, and achieve, and also how well they perceive themselves as being, compared with others. It was considered that relational dimensions of wellbeing may be particularly relevant in a post-industrial context, where society has lost many of the networks and opportunities for social connectedness which were provided by a traditional industry such as mining (Thin, 2012).

Current assessments of wellbeing are not without their criticisms, 'yet are still some of the most influential income-alternatives in the research and policy arena' (Yang, 2018: 456). Nevertheless, many wellbeing assessments rely on objective assessments and neglect subjective dimensions, failing to acknowledge that different cultures understand wellbeing differently (Yang, 2018). Hence, when exploring multidimensional wellbeing, White (2009) argues, as other contributors do in this volume, that wellbeing is often difficult to define and research because it is understood in various ways by different people in different contexts. Therefore, when exploring wellbeing it should be understood as culturally variable embedded in the subjectivities and communities of those being researched.

Using a 3D framework to examine human wellbeing 'shifts our focus beyond incomes and narrow human development indicators to take into account what people can do and be, and how they evaluate what they can do and be' (McGregor and Sumner, 2009: 1). Combining the three dimensions to understand people's perspectives at a time of change reveals how people feel about and respond to different initiatives that impact their lives (Copestake, 2008). Therefore, keeping in mind that there will be many different interpretations as to people's quality of life and how they perceive their own wellbeing, data collection needs to be undertaken in various stages with a stratified sample of different people.

Applying the 3D framework in practice

In this section, we discuss the methodology used in the PhD research (see Table 9.1 and Table 9.2), and the three dimensions of social wellbeing, then focus attention on data related to the subjective dimension of wellbeing. We then consider the uses of a 3D framework for regeneration strategies in Seaham. Table 9.2 illustrates how the methodology maps onto the framework. It operationalizes the

Table 9.1: Table of scale and data type of 3D methods

Data	Material dimension	Relational dimension	Subjective dimension
Type	• Secondary data analysis – Census data and IMDs	• Semi-structured interviews	• Focus groups, • Semi-structured interviews
Scale	• Town level	• Individual level	• Group level, • Individual level

theoretical framework and shows the scale of the collected data. For example, material data was collected via a secondary data analysis on a town level, whereas relational data was collected through interviews on an individual level and subjective data was generated via interviews on an individual level and collected through focus groups. Other research has operationalized the 3D framework in different ways; for example, Camfield et al (2009) used household surveys to explore material wellbeing.

Method 1 – community profile

The fieldwork began with a community profile that provided us with knowledge and understanding of the needs and resources of the community (Hawtin et al, 1995). Often carried out via a mixture of methods from surveys and secondary data analysis to interviews and focus groups (Centre for Community Health and Development, 2016), a community profile generates community involvement from the start of the project (Hawtin et al, 1995). The first method of data collection was split up into three stages – secondary data analysis, focus groups and key person interviews. Ereaut and Whiting (2008) highlighted that there are many different constructions of wellbeing from individual and collective wellbeing to subjective or objective. Therefore, a community profile was undertaken to understand the historical background and social development of the town gaining a sense of the various aspects of wellbeing, and how people talk about their wellbeing in Seaham.

We drew on Hawtin, Hughes, and Percy-Smith's (1995) research on communities to develop a full community profile of Seaham using ethnography, secondary data analysis of census data, Indices of Multiple Deprivation (IMD) as well as focus groups and key person interviews. To understand communities and those who live there 'it is important to know the history of that neighbourhood and the

Table 9.2: Table of the methods process

Method process	Tool	Function	Summarized reflections
1 Community profile	• Focus groups • Key persons interviews	• Contextual input • Icebreaker • Snowball sampling • To build rapport with members of the community.	Good to get to know the town, the people and their history. Helps build a regeneration timeline.
2 Material wellbeing	• Secondary data analysis – Census data and IMDs	• To distinguish what resources people can draw on.	Easy and less time consuming than household survey but lacks individual level detail so limits analysis.
3 Relational wellbeing	• Semi-structured interviews • Example interview question – What are the most important relationships/friendships that have an impact on your capacity to live well?	• To find out the social interactions people engage in and are affected by.	Rich qualitative data gained. Holistic and flexible.
4 Subjective wellbeing	• Semi-structured interview • Example individual interview questions – How satisfied are you with life these days? • In order of importance think of the areas/aspects of your life that are most important for you to be able to live well in the area/community? • What are your hopes and concerns for the future?	• To find out what matters most to people and why. • To see if people felt they had adequate access to the resources available.	Rich qualitative data gained. Holistic and flexible, empowers the respondent to set the interview agenda.
5 Data feedback	• Focus groups	• Feedback data • Generalize findings	Gave community a chance to add to, edit, and discuss findings.

space that people inhabit' (McKenzie, 2015: 19). When researching disadvantaged communities, one must be sensitive to the challenges residents face and how these impact their wellbeing. Therefore, the secondary data analysis at a whole town level gave insights into the history of the community helping us to prepare for the focus groups with community residents.

By immersing oneself in a particular community, ethnography and participant observation helped us gain a nuanced understanding of the distinct way of life of those living in Seaham (Bryman, 2012; Nettle, 2015). This included weekly visits of two to three days over a period of several months, recording daily observations in a diary and identifying and establishing relations with local gatekeepers who helped 'facilitate access to participants by endorsing researchers work' (Crowhurst, 2013: 464). Gatekeepers were important for gaining access to interviewees as they helped foster good relations with community residents and aided snowball sampling techniques.

Community profile – focus groups

Focus groups were a core tool used in community profiling. Six focus groups comprising of three to six participants in each group were organized in three different areas of the town. Held in public buildings such as the library, community centres and the main youth centre the focus groups were sampled via a convenience and snowballing technique in the form of researcher-driven recruitment (Peek and Fothergill, 2009). These events were advertised using posters around the town inviting people to be part of the research. Using focus groups helped generate insights into residents' concerns about social problems such as anti-social behaviour, drugs use, crime, and food poverty. They also uncovered how the town has changed over the past 50 years and generated insights into residents' views on how wellbeing can be improved.

Points on analysis

A thematic-analysis approach was used on the data (Braun and Clarke, 2014), starting from the first two focus groups and continuing until the end of the fieldwork. The initial analysis of stage one also directed the later stages of the fieldwork such as the design of the household interview. Once coded, initial data on different wellbeing factors were broken down into the three wellbeing dimensions to which I added further data as collection methods progressed. The data was analysed in relation to residents beliefs about what was 'good' and 'not so good' about the area, what social, environmental and economic changes had affected the community and people's perceptions about what they needed to 'live well' in Seaham today. These initial categories were then divided into further sub-categories exploring ideas of community, coping, and visions of the future which then fed into the phase two interview schedule. Data regarding the social, environmental, and economic changes that had occurred over the past 50 years was also analysed in relation to the three wellbeing dimensions. Other factors such as having close friends and family nearby were examined as were notions of 'wellbeing successes' and 'wellbeing failures'.

Community profile – key person interviews

Key persons were identified by observing Town and County Council meetings and then arranging semi-structured interviews with attendees from those meetings. Key persons were members of Durham County Council's regeneration team, local business owners and elected town councillors. This stage of the fieldwork helped me understand some of the key social, environmental, and economic changes that have affected the community's wellbeing over the last 50 years and how many of these changes were attributed to the processes of deindustrialization from a key person's point of view. Interviewees were selected based on their knowledge of the previous regeneration of Seaham and future plans which reflected the research questions and their focus on regeneration policies.

Points on analysis

The stakeholder interviews were coded in the same way as other interviews – in relation to the 3D wellbeing framework. Conversations and observations from the ethnographic fieldwork were noted down in a journal. The recorded conversations were then coded into themes alongside the other data and analysed as a whole rather than as a separate data collection phase. This allowed the analysis to be a continuous and fluid process. The stakeholder interviews uncovered a timeline of previous regeneration programmes and also allowed insights into the future directions of regeneration initiatives in Seaham. Discussions with key people also informed questions for later fieldwork stages around such issues as future improvements in wellbeing and how this could be achieved through regeneration strategies.

Method 2: material wellbeing

Establishing a sense of the town's material wellbeing required data on the resources and opportunities enjoyed by residents, how these are patterned and structured the life chances and wellbeing of residents. In some research (Camfield et al, 2009; Western and Tomaszewski, 2016), this information is acquired at a household level, which enables analysis of the relationships between different wellbeing dimensions. For example, do people with a particular level of income, exhibit higher levels of subjective wellbeing? Due to the costs of conducting household surveys I used an alternative approach to material wellbeing, employing data at a town level – utilizing secondary data from the IMD[1] and available Census data[2] on population, housing tenure and economic activity such as employment rates.

Methods 3 and 4 – researching relational and subjective wellbeing using a semi-structured interview

Relational and subjective interviews

Taking inspiration from a 3D wellbeing-methods handbook (Coulthard et al, 2015) the next phase of the fieldwork was a semi-structured interview which used a schedule comprising of 19 in-depth questions that explored people's relational and subjective wellbeing (see Table 9.2). Individual interviews were conducted over a period of days, involving initial meetings then formal interviews at the participant's residence which usually lasted a couple of hours. Twenty participants were interviewed – the sample generated via a maximum variation sampling approach to ensure a wide variation of participants as possible (Palys, 2008; Bryman, 2012). Crouch and McKenzie (2006: 489) argue that using a smaller sample size for qualitative research helps find out 'what things "exist" rather than determining how many such things there are'. Additionally, using a smaller sample size permitted repeated contacts between the researcher and the participants and greater involvement of the researcher that, 'enhance[s] validity and reliability' (Crouch and McKenzie, 2006: 491). The qualitative research and particularly the narrative material offered insights into the complex subjective meanings that people have about wellbeing adding depth and nuance to the data.

Points on analysis

Interview data were coded and the findings were organized into sub-categories derived from earlier focus group analysis – with new themes being added as the analysis progressed. This method allowed the flexibility of an inductive approach by engaging residents in the project and integrating issues that were important to their understanding of wellbeing. I was open to the possibility that there were complex factors that supported and also challenged the wellbeing of participants. This data was mapped onto the 3D framework which highlighted the interlinking connections between different dimensions of wellbeing and helped create the key themes that were emerging from the data.

Method 5 – feedback focus groups

The last phase of the data collection comprised two large-scale focus groups held in a church hall. Posters and diagrams detailing the initial findings of the research were displayed and participants were asked to explore and discuss the preliminary data. I was keen that participants were given an opportunity to reflect on the way I had interpreted the data and developed initial analytical themes. I explored with them the accuracy of my insights into the nature of their wellbeing and how I had documented the three key dimensions of quality of life in their community.

Points on analysis

Once the feedback focus group meetings were completed, their views were treated as additional data and was combined with the data from the other phases of the research. This enhanced the research as it helps draw on a larger set of participants from across the community that were under-represented in the initial sampling (Robson and McCartan, 2016).

Seaham: wellbeing in the wake of deindustrialization

This next section explores some of the findings and emerging themes from the research project. It begins by exploring the interconnectiveness of the wellbeing dimensions while focusing upon the *subjective* accounts of wellbeing. I then examine some of the themes that emerged out of the findings – *feelings of being forgotten and left behind*, *coping*, and *different visions of regeneration*. We finish by discussing the effectiveness of the 3D framework for analysing wellbeing in Seaham.

The final mapping of the data onto the 3D framework suggested that all three wellbeing dimensions were interconnected in some way. For instance, all participants believed good wellbeing required supportive family and friends who lived close by. Many spoke about supportive kin alleviating some of the 'material wellbeing failings' – such as periods of unemployment and low income. Nevertheless, it was found that accessing financial support from friends and family could put a strain on the subjective wellbeing of those both offering and receiving the support. For example, it was mentioned by two participants that borrowing or taking money from friends and family made them feel guilty or sick:

> 'I swear my family think I'm a scrounge, I want to pay them back but don't have the means to at the present minute … Owing money makes me feel sick to the stomach.' [I, 10]

> 'I hate taking money off my sister, she feels bad that I have nowt, so offers, but I feel guilty taking because I know she doesn't have much herself.' [I, 16]

This highlights that not only is there an interrelationship between the dimensions but also uncovers the psychological costs that surrounds the stigma of economic disadvantage which has also been documented in earlier research by McKenzie (2015) and Skeggs (1997).

Those that felt they had access to the relevant material or relational resource reported being satisfied with life:

> 'I am a lot more happier and healthier than previous years. Now I have a good job and great friends, I am very satisfied with life.' [I, 8]

> 'I am quite satisfied with life, in comparison to some, life is fantastic. We have each other, our health, jobs, a roof over our head and good food.' [I, 15]

Whereas those that felt they did not have adequate access to material wellbeing reported being unsatisfied with their present situation:

> 'Some days are too much; it seems like a never-ending battle. Crap job into crap job. I can't seem to get a break like. With

the rising costs of living and my wages not reflecting that, it's hard to get by. Because ya working everyone thinks that you have loads of money, some months it's a tossup between paying the phone bill or car insurance. I need the car to get to work but the phone helps me keep in touch with people. I'm at a loss no matter what I do. Can't even afford to heat the house some weeks. But that's the joy of working in a dead-end job for minimum wage, I wish I could get a better one but it's like looking for gold dust, non-existent.' [I, 16]

'I have the means to live above the poverty line which is more comfortable than most ... I always wish I had more in life or at least done a bit more with my life so I am not really satisfied but I did what I could with what I had.' [I, 19]

This data highlights again that not only are the wellbeing dimensions interconnected but also for good overall wellbeing all three dimensions need to be fulfilled. The interview data also illustrated the significance of culturally specific criteria of what it means to live well. Hence, the social and cultural contexts and their influence on subjective meanings are significant for how people judge their wellbeing. The interviewees often admitted to having very little economically but can see that others in the community have even less. This illustrates that wellbeing evaluations and understandings are embedded in a person's way of life illustrating the essential role of qualitative research for investigating wellbeing.

Data analysis: emerging themes

We used a thematic approach to analyse the data in relation to the adapted 3D framework and this generated a pattern of interlinking themes and sub-themes. The analysis was framed by key questions: 'what people need to live well', 'to what extent people have access to these resources and opportunities' and 'what can people do with what they have'. The analysis highlighted three main themes. The first was that that there were *feelings of being forgotten and left behind* by the local and national government. As we discussed earlier there were two areas in Seaham that were in the 10 per cent most deprived wards in the UK. There was a running narrative among many residents that Seaham was forgotten by central government, particularly by those within these two disadvantaged neighbourhoods. This was supported by the interview and community profile data that suggested residents living within these two neighbourhoods had the least chance of being able to access the resources needed to live well.

The second theme that emerged related to the notion of *coping in hard times*. The interviews illuminated that many people were struggling to cope financially due to the changes to the welfare state brought about by recent government reforms which had left many people in financial turmoil. The negative effects of these changes such as the introduction of Universal Credit and its effect on poverty have been widely documented by The Joseph Rowntree Foundation (Barnard, 2019) and The Trussell Trust (2018). The latter organization reported that '[w]hen Universal Credit goes live in an area, there is a demonstrable increase in demand in local Trussell Trust foodbanks' (Trussell Trust, 2018: 4; Thompson et al, 2019).

By using the 3D framework it was found that many residents used close friends and family as a coping mechanism to get by in hard times drawing on them for financial help or emotional support. This, however, often came at a cost to subjective wellbeing as many people felt they could be a burden on those helping them. Some interviewees, therefore, instead took on extra low-paid work to help alleviate financial hardship and avoid their dependency on others. Interestingly, those that took on extra waged employment also talked about feeling socially isolated because of the long hours they spent at work which impacted on their leisure time and work–life balance.

The third theme that emerged was *different visions of regeneration*. This theme arose from discussions about the future of Seaham with stakeholders (such as local council officials) and residents. We asked: 'what improvements to the area would you think need to be made for future generations to live well in this community'. It was interesting to note how many residents believed there were few regeneration projects that adequately reflected the legacy of the mining industry that had shaped Seaham. Even though the town has a Blue Plaque Heritage Trail, some mining statues, and a Heritage Lifeboat Centre, many participants believed this was insufficient recognition of the mining heritage. On the other hand, the stakeholders, discussed that Seaham's past had been incorporated into previous, current and future regeneration schemes. This narrative from the stakeholders was supported by the ethnographic observations during the research with many roads, buildings and the shopping centre named to reflect Seaham's heritage. The recent Townscape Heritage regeneration plan also aimed to promote this industrial heritage. Tensions between local officials and residents around regeneration is a common one reflecting different perspectives and conflict on what a good community and good wellbeing is (Berkeley and Jarvis, 2004; Jarvis et al, 2012). One strength of the 3D framework was that it allowed me to document these different perspectives and enabled residents to participate and feel engaged in the research process.

When these differing views on regeneration were discussed in interviews it was apparent that the renaming of roads, shopping mall and erection of statues were seen as insufficient to address the problems of deindustrial decline in Seaham. Residents wanted a more tangible way of promoting community solidarity, kinship and better wellbeing. Many respondents talked about the need for funding of local community centres that would bring together older and newer community members, countering the social isolation common in the area. Interviewees also mentioned that community centres could employ local people to establish community savings funds for the many residents who have fallen on hard times – schemes that have been successfully created in other local communities. Despite these calls for further community centres and youth hubs it was emphasized to interviewees that there were existing community centres and churches in Seaham offering food bank facilities. Some respondents mentioned that these were a 'God send' offering residents spaces for adults and children to meet and socialize.

Reflections on using a 3D wellbeing framework

Wellbeing has become an increasingly popular topic among academics and policymakers. Yet how useful is the 3D framework for investigating people's wellbeing in areas of multiple deprivation such as Seaham? By adapting the methods outlined by Coulthard et al (2015), this project uncovered more than just the material factors that are often associated with good wellbeing (see Easterlin, 1974; Veenhoven, 1991). Initial data analysis suggested that relational wellbeing is interwoven with subjective and material wellbeing. By undertaking data collection over several stages allowed first a wellbeing profile to explore collectively what people need to live well drawing on their self-determined criteria. I then investigated whether people have adequate access to these resources and interrogated their views about what they can or cannot do with these resources. The community feedback sessions allowed participants and other residents the opportunity to discuss the findings and further develop the existing data set.

Using multiple focus groups to understand community wellbeing not only allowed different discussions to be had regarding what it meant to live well today, but also it gave the researcher time to familiarize herself with the different areas of the fieldwork site. Furthermore, analysing the data from the focus groups in relation to the 3D framework allowed me to explore the way that relationships and social contexts are significant for subjective experiences of wellbeing.

The town-level data was useful for establishing the context in which residents live which helped with the later research interviews. The community profile data enabled us to understand some of the subtle meanings around the traditions and cultural practices that were distinctive to Seaham. For example, around the cultural significance of mining and the coastal setting for the many residents in the area. By exploring the initial data with people from the town it offered the chance to discuss the preliminary analysis and themes and generate some insights that I may have overlooked. This stage not only helped with bringing the research back into the community but also helped corroborate the initial analysis.

Because wellbeing is a contested concept and can be interpreted in different ways, wellbeing projects can often produce data beyond the initial specific focus of research. In this study, the focus was regeneration, but the things that people talked about were relevant to a wider set of policy issues around social welfare. Hence, I found I could map experiences of wellbeing in relation to some wider national and regional welfare policies. However, there remained the challenge of not losing sight of those connections between structural economic and policy processes and the everyday wellbeing experiences of interviewees.

Implications for regeneration strategies in Seaham

Many different topics emerged from discussions with participants about their wellbeing. There is a fundamental need for policymakers and planners to understand how wellbeing is understood by local residents if regeneration practices are to address wellbeing effectively (Woolrych and Sixsmith, 2013). The emerging themes from the data suggested that some residents felt neglected by governmental bodies and there were different conflicting visions of regeneration of the town. These perspectives on regeneration and different degrees of participation in initiatives can be detrimental to local residents' wellbeing and their longer-term participation in regeneration projects (Woolrych and Sixsmith, 2013). Therefore, the 3D framework, by illuminating the complex experiences of wellbeing and different perspectives on regeneration, can help residents' inclusion in the research, planning and implementation of community development programmes.

During meetings of the recent Townscape Heritage Project there were ample opportunities for Seaham residents to input into the project. However, in reality this process was limited. The many well-publicized meetings about the scheme were poorly attended and few young people participated. As recent research suggests, the 'problem of youth engagement in policy is a global concern' (McCormack and Clayton, 2017: 42). In addition, whereas the project reflected some of the material wellbeing needs of residents such as the regeneration of the main shopping street, some thought it was a little too late while others remarked on previous failed regeneration initiatives. Therefore, using the 3D framework to uncover the community's needs before implementing a regeneration project could help determine the suitability of regeneration strategies in the area. For example, where the Seaham regeneration scheme focused on economic development of the High Street shopping area. Whereas this research suggested a more complex set of relationships and factors were significant for improving wellbeing in Seaham.

Conclusions

This chapter has explored using a 3D framework to investigate people's wellbeing in the wake of deindustrialization and studied its uses for community development. Using the 3D wellbeing framework to research community wellbeing not only considers the 'material, relational and cognitive dimensions; putting resources, relationships and subjective reflections on life satisfaction together as a whole assessment' but also it highlights that all three dimensions strongly interlink and overlap (Britton and Coulthard, 2013: 28). The subjective and relational aspects of wellbeing are clearly as important as material wellbeing for the enhancement of people's lives in Seaham. It was found that poor material wellbeing can be improved by drawing upon relational wellbeing resources; however, this can also be detrimental for subjective wellbeing. Using a holistic 3D framework is beneficial as it reveals the material and relational resources people have access to as well as the ones they do not, as well as highlighting the subjective reasoning behind how people feel about what they can or cannot do with those resources.

Using the 3D framework to understand the needs of the community puts the residents in the centre of the planning but also gives them a voice while mitigating some of the feelings of being forgotten by governmental bodies. In addition, bringing the results back into the community before implementation helps bring the public back into the project allowing findings to be agreed, amended or added. Finally, if shared visions are to be had by regeneration agencies and residents then there needs to be a recognition of the subjective accounts of their wellbeing needs and not just a measurement of objective factors.

Notes
1   The latest Index of Multiple Deprivation (IMD) statistics are available at http://dclgapps.communities.gov.uk/imd/idmap.html
2   Nomis has data available for labour statistics and population at https://www.nomisweb.co.uk/

References

Bache, I. (2018) 'How does evidence matter? Understanding "what works" for wellbeing', *Social Indicators Research*, 142(3): 1153–73.

Bache, I. and Reardon, L. (2013) 'An idea whose time has come? Explaining the rise of well-being in British politics', *Political Studies*, 4(3): 898–914.

Bache, I., Reardon, L. and Anand, P. (2016) 'Wellbeing as a wicked problem: navigating the arguments for the role of government', *Journal of Happiness Studies*, 17(3): 893–912.

Barnard, H. (2019) 'End the benefit freeze to stop people being swept into poverty', *Joseph Rowntree Foundation*, available at https://www.jrf.org.uk/report/end-benefit-freeze-stop-people-being-swept-poverty (accessed 13 September 2019).

Berkeley, N. and Jarvis, D. (2004) *Making Our Voices Heard in Coventry, Communities in Profile Report*, Canley: Coventry Partnership.

Braun, V. and Clarke, V. (2014) 'What can "thematic analysis" offer health and wellbeing researchers?', *International Journal of Qualitative Studies in Health and Well-being*, 9: 1–2.

Britton, E. and Coulthard, S. (2013). 'Assessing the social wellbeing of Northern Ireland's fishing society using a three-dimensional approach', *Marine Policy*, 37: 28–36.

Bryman, A. (2012) *Social Research Methods*, Oxford: Oxford University Press.

Bulmer, M. (1978) 'Social structures and social change in the twentieth century', in M. Bulmer (ed) *Mining and Social Change: Durham County in the Twentieth Century*, London: Croom Helm, pp 15–48.

Camfield, L., Crivello, G. and Woodhead, M. (2009) 'Wellbeing research in developing countries: reviewing the role of qualitative methods', *Social Indicators Research*, 90(5): 5–31.

Centre for Community Health and Development (2016) 'Community Toolbox', University of Kansas, available at http://ctb.ku.edu/en (accessed 6 May 2019).

Copestake, J. (2008) 'Wellbeing in international development: what's new?', *Journal of International Development*, 20(5): 577–97.

Coulthard, S. (2012) 'What does the debate around social wellbeing have to offer sustainable fisheries?', *Current Opinion in Environmental Sustainability*, 4(3): 358–63.

Coulthard, S., Paranamana, N. and Sandaruwan, L. (2015) *Exploring Wellbeing in Fishing Communities (South Asia) Methods Handbook*, Swindon: Economic and Social Research Council.

Crouch, M. and McKenzie, H. (2006) 'The logic of small samples in interview-based qualitative research', *Social Science Information*, 45(4): 483–99.

Crowhurst, I. (2013) 'The fallacy of the instrumental gate? Contextualising the process of gaining access through gatekeepers', *International Journal of Social Research Methodology*, 16(6): 463–75.

Dodge, R., Daly, A., Huyton, J., and Sanders, D. (2012) 'The challenge of defining wellbeing', *International Journal of Wellbeing*, 2(3): 222–35.

Doyal, L. and Gough, I. (1991) *A Theory of Human Need*, New York: Guilford.

Easterlin, R. (1974) 'Does economic growth improve the human lot? Some empirical evidence', in P. David and W. Melvin (eds) *Nations and Households in Economic Growth*, California: Stanford University Press, pp 89–125.

Ereaut, G. and Whiting, R. (2008) 'What do we mean by "wellbeing"? And why might it matter?', *Linguistic Landscape*, available at https://dera.ioe.ac.uk/8572/1/dcsf-rw073%20v2.pdf (accessed 24 August 2017).

Gough, I. and McGregor, A. (2007) *Wellbeing in Developing Countries*, Cambridge: Cambridge University Press.

Hawtin, M., Hughes, G. and Percy-Smith, J. (1995) *Community Profiling: Auditing Social Needs*, Buckingham: Open University Press.

Helliwell, J., Layard, R., and Sachs J. (2017) 'World Happiness Report 2017', *Sustainable Development Solutions Network*, available at https://worldhappiness.report/ed/2017/ (accessed 6 May 2019).

Jarvis, D., Berkeley, N. and Broughton, K. (2012) 'Evidencing the impact of community engagement in neighbourhood regeneration: the case of Canley, Coventry', *Community Development Journal*, 47(2): 232–47.

Karn, J. (2007) *Narratives of Neglect: Community, Regeneration and the Governance of Security*, Cullompton: Willan.

Kerstetter, K. (2012) 'Insider, outsider, or somewhere in between: the impact of researchers' identities on the community-based research process', *Journal of Rural Social Sciences*, 27(2): 99–117.

Kroll, C. (2011) 'Different things make different people happy: examining social capital and subjective well-being by gender and parental status', *Social Indicators Research*, 104(1): 157–77.

McCormack, F. and Clayton, B. (2017) 'Engagement and influence in local policy decisions: an examination of the enabling factors in the negotiations of a youth skateboard community', *International Journal of Sport Policy and Politics*, 9(1): 41–54.

McGregor, A. (2007) 'Researching wellbeing: from concepts to methodology', in I. Gough and A. McGregor (eds) *Wellbeing in Developing Countries*, Cambridge: Cambridge University Press, pp 316–50.

McGregor, A., and Sumner, A. (2009) 'After 2015: "3D human wellbeing"', *IDS in Focus Policy Bulletin*, 9(2): 1–2.

McGregor, A., Coulthard, S. and Camfield, L. (2015) *Measuring What Matters: The Role of Well-Being Methods in Development Policy and Practice*, London: Overseas Development Institute.

McKenzie, L. (2015) *Getting By: Estates, Class and Culture in Austerity Britain*, Bristol: Policy Press.

Ministry of Housing, Communities and Local Government (2015) 'English Indices of Deprivation 2015 – LSOA Level', *OpenDataCommunities.org*. Available at https://www.gov.uk/government/statistics/english-indices-of-deprivation-2015 (accessed 6 May 2019).

NEF (2012) *Well-being and the Role of Government*, available at https://neweconomics.org/uploads/files/4bffe52d926439f033_4im6bntl8.pdf (accessed 24 August 2017).

Nettle, D. (2015) *Tyneside Neighbourhood's Deprivation, Social Life and Social Behaviour in One British City*, Cambridge: Open Book Publishers.

Ochieng, B. and Meetoo, D. (2014) 'Using mixed methods when researching communities', *Nurse Researcher*, 23(1): 16–19.

OECD (2011) *Measuring Well-being and Progress: Well-being Research*, available at http://www.oecd.org/statistics/measuring-well-being-and-progress.htm

OECD (2016) 'Measuring multidimensional well-being and sustainable development', *OECD Insights*, available at http://oecdinsights.org/2016/01/13/measuring-multidimensional-well-being-and-sustainable-development/ (accessed 9 July 2019).

Palys, T. (2008) 'Purposive sampling', in L.M. Given (ed) *The Sage Encyclopaedia of Qualitative Research Methods* (Vol 2), Los Angeles: Sage, pp 697–8.

Peek, L. and Fothergill, A. (2009) 'Using focus groups: lessons from studying day care centres, 9/11, and Hurricane Katrina', *Qualitative Research*, 9(1): 31–59.

Rawls, J. (1971) *A Theory of Justice*, Harvard: The Belknap Press of Harvard University Press.

Robson, C. and McCartan, K. (2016) *Real World Research: a Resource for Users of Social Research Methods in Applied Settings*, Chichester: Wiley.

Sayer, A. (2011) *Why Things Matter to People: Social Science, Values and Ethical Life*, Cambridge: Cambridge University Press.

Scott, K. (2012) *Measuring Wellbeing: Towards Sustainability*, London: Routledge.

Sen, A. (1985) *Commodities and Capabilities*, Amsterdam: North-Holland.

Sen, A. (1999) *Development as Freedom*, Oxford: Oxford University Press.

Shin, D. and Johnson, D. (1978) 'Avowed happiness as an overall assessment of the quality of life', *Social Indicators Research*, 5(1): 475–92.

Skeggs, B. (1997) *Formations of Class and Gender: Becoming Respectable*, London: Sage Publications.

Stiglitz, J., Sen, A., Fitoussi, J-P. (2009) *Report of the Commission on the Measurement of Economic Performance and Social Progress*, available at http://www.stiglitz-sen-fitoussi.fr/documents/rapport_anglais.pdf (accessed 12 October 2018).

Sumner, A., Haddad, L. and Gomez-Climent, L. (2009) 'Rethinking inter-generational transmissions: does a wellbeing lens help?', *IDS Bulletin*, 40(1): 22–30.

The Trussell Trust (2018) *The Next Stage of Universal Credit: Moving onto the New Benefit System and Foodbank Use*, available at https://www.trusselltrust.org/wp-content/uploads/sites/2/2018/10/The-next-stage-of-Universal-Credit-Report-Final.pdf (accessed 13 October 2019).

Thin, N. (2012) *Social Happiness: Theory into Policy and Practice*, Bristol: Policy Press.

Thompson, E., Jitendra, A. and Rabindrakumar, S. (2019) '#5weekstoolong: why we need to end the wait for Universal Credit', *The Trussell Trust*, available at https://www.trusselltrust.org/wp-content/uploads/sites/2/2019/09/PolicyReport_Final_ForWeb.pdf (accessed 15 October 2019).

Veenhoven, R. (1991) 'Is happiness relative', *Social Indicators Research*, 24: 1–34.

Vision Through Time (2017) *Seaham: County Durham*, available at http://www.visionofbritain.org.uk/place/788 (accessed 8 November 2016).

Wallace, J. and Schmuecker, K. (2012) 'Shifting the dial: from wellbeing measures to policy practice', *Carnegie UK Trust*, available at https://d1ssu070pg2v9i.cloudfront.net/pex/carnegie_uk_trust/2016/02/pub1455011624.pdf (accessed 6 May 2019).

Western, M. and Tomaszewski, W. (2016) 'Subjective wellbeing, objective wellbeing and inequality in Australia', *PLoS ONE*, 11(10): 1–20.

White, S. (2009) 'Analysing wellbeing: a framework for development', *WeD Working Paper 09/44*, Centre for Development Studies, University of Bath.

White, S. (2015) 'Relational wellbeing: a theoretical and operational approach', *Bath Papers in International Development and Wellbeing, Working Paper No. 43*.

Williamson, B. (1982) *Class, Culture and Community: A Biographical Study of Social Change in Mining*, London: Routledge and Kegan Paul.

Wiseman, J. and Brasher, K. (2008) 'Community wellbeing in an unwell world: trends, challenges, and possibilities', *Journal of Public Health Policy*, 29: 353–66.

Woolrych, R. and Sixsmith, J. (2013) 'Placing well-being and participation within processes of urban regeneration', *International Journal of Public Sector Management*, 26(3): 216–31.

Yang, L. (2018) 'Measuring well-being: a multidimensional index integrating subjective well-being and preferences', *Journal of Human Development and Capabilities*, 19(4): 456–76.

PART III

Qualitative Research into Happiness/Wellbeing: Methodological Innovations

10

A Board Game Approach to Studying the Multidimensionality of Life Satisfaction

Barbara Holthus and Wolfram Manzenreiter

Introduction

Happiness research has gained extraordinary popularity in recent years, both among scholars and governments as well as the public. Research by anthropologists and sociologists on the topic remains limited in comparison with research by economists and psychologists (see Introduction by Cieslik, this volume). Despite the multitude of studies undertaken, our knowledge about happiness in Japan continues to be limited for a number of problems that boil down to methodology. Large-scale quantitative surveys on happiness and wellbeing that suggest the Japanese are unhappy in comparison with other highly developed societies, often rely on a single-item measurement of 'overall happiness' or in conjunction with objective indicators of 'overall well-being' (Helliwell, Layard and Sachs, 2016; OECD Stat, 2017); and hardly ever is the meaning of happiness and its universal importance in human life questioned (Uchida et al, 2015).

It is desirable, therefore, that sociological research is sensitive to the cultural construction of happiness and its multidimensional nature in Japan. In the two most recent edited volumes on happiness and wellbeing in Japan we presented novel findings from qualitative as well as quantitative researchers (Holthus and Manzenreiter, 2017b;

Manzenreiter and Holthus, 2017b). Yet most contributions focused on singular or select factors, such as age, friendship, parenthood, or political participation, to name but a few. Only Mathews (2017) paid tribute to the diversity of definitions in the understanding of happiness and life satisfaction in Japan.

In the following, we present a three-part innovative approach to studying happiness and life satisfaction. This methodology attempts to be sensitive to the gaps in the literature, as it enquires about definitions of happiness and happiness-related terms, and it allows interviewees to explain their lives and weight elements in their lives as to (1) their importance for living a good life and (2) to their positive and negative evaluation. To test the methodology, we conducted semi-structured interviews with 23 men and women in Japan. Each interview consists of three parts: (a) word association, (b) in-depth conversation on happiness issues using a bullseye structured chart, often referred to by us and the interviewees as a 'board game', together with tokens for visualization of factors of satisfaction and dissatisfaction, and (c) three written quantitative questions on happiness, all to be discussed in-depth with the interviewees thereafter. The data from the study and our reflections on the research process suggest the following:

(1) Happiness is very much an interpretative process, embedded in social networks and across personal biographies. Not one definition exists in people's heads, complicating the interpretation of quantitative surveys.
(2) Happiness is multidimensional, and the relevance of the domains varies by life-course stage and is influenced by numerous life circumstances. Mapping happiness across multiple domains by using visual props allows us to get closer to a more holistic understanding of subjective wellbeing.
(3) 'The happier the better' as the underlying (Western) understanding of happiness in quantitative surveys is shown not to be a universal concept.

In the following section we provide a state-of-the-art overview of the literature on current happiness research within and about Japan, drawing mostly on sociological and anthropological studies. Subsequently, we describe in detail the three-part methodology used in research we conducted in two stages in February and July 2018. We conclude the chapter by discussing some fundamental findings concerning the methodology of happiness research, and the applicability of the research design generally, while critically reflecting on design flaws and methodological improvements.

The concern for culture in happiness research

Despite a decade-long flourishing of happiness research in Japan (Coulmas, 2009; Holthus and Manzenreiter, 2017a), our knowledge about the state of wellbeing of the Japanese is still wanting. A review of the literature generates a compartmentalized debate of often inconclusive and contradictory results, largely due to the incompatibilities of the specific heuristics associated with the agenda of their respective academic fields. The editors of *Cultures of Well-being* (White and Blackmore, 2016) argue that research methods have their own cultures in as far as they produce a generalized view of the world as taken for granted; the rules of the game, as they call it, use specific key terms, reference points, criteria for truth and core routines, rituals, and practices that informs the nature of the research process. Different methodologies do not simply highlight different aspects of happiness, they generate different data and allow different analytical routines and thus actively constitute diverging accounts. On a more fundamental level, unsolved conceptual and methodological issues are at the root of the fragmented nature of happiness research. The vagueness and variety of happiness concepts encompassing similar key terms of the academic debate, such as life satisfaction, wellbeing, or quality of life (for example, the psychologists who originated the Quality of Life Inventory use the terms quality of life, subjective wellbeing, and life satisfaction interchangeably; see Frisch et al, 1992), and the resulting differences in operationalization severely limit the conclusions that can be drawn from these studies (Holthus and Manzenreiter, 2017b).

In the OECD Better Life data from 2017, Japan's life satisfaction score (on a scale from 0 as lowest to 10 as highest) averages at 5.8, which lies below the OECD 35 country average of 6.6 (OECD Stat, 2017). According to the *World Happiness Report 2018*, Japan ranks 54th out of 156 countries (Helliwell et al, 2018: 21, 25). Yet international comparison of happiness and life satisfaction comes with methodological difficulties and limitations. Husser and Fernandez (2018) argue that slight changes in the wording of a question may cause considerable differences in outcome, while others question the ability of respondents to differentiate clearly and consistently between subtle numerical gradients, as evidenced by low test-retest reliability (Krueger and Schkade, 2008). In a rare example of mixed-method research in happiness (Ponocny et al, 2016), the mismatch of respondents' quantitative evaluation with their narrated accounts demonstrated that response biases and semantic variability in the interpretation of happiness constructs and rating scales significantly delimited the explanatory power of numerical self-reported happiness indices. Culture-specific response patterns, such as the tendency by Japanese to avoid extreme ratings in surveys (Chen, Lee and Stevenson, 1995) further question the cross-cultural comparability of measurement rates. Cultural psychologists, for example, have raised doubts about an artificially flattened and problematic understanding of happiness as culturally universal (eg Markus and Kitayama, 1998; Oishi et al, 2013; Uchida et al, 2015). They point out that positive social relationships matter in all societies, but feelings of personal autonomy are of greater importance in so-called individualist societies (Oishi et al, 1999).

In Western societies of Europe and North America where people construe their sense of happiness in relation to the self, self-esteem and other internal references, collectivist societies in Asia place more emphasis on conformity to social norms and mutual social appraisal (Kwan, Bond and Singelis, 1997; Suh et al, 1998; Suh, 2000; Lu and Gilmour, 2004; Kitayama and Markus, 2000; Uchida and Kitayama, 2009). To research happiness in societies like Japan, therefore, one needs rather more social or relational conceptions of wellbeing. The concept of interdependent happiness developed by Hitokoto and Uchida (2015) is based on empirical evidence that wellbeing in Japan is better predicted by emotional support, quality of interpersonal relationships and harmony than by individual achievement and autonomy (Cabinet Office, 2011).

Methodological considerations

Our concern for the cultural distinctiveness of happiness in Japan informed our methodological approach. Our goal was to create a methodology that is culture-sensitive while at the same time flexible enough to be used in a variety of different settings. There are, however, several challenges facing this sort of research.

Intercultural research and issues of intimacy and gender

One problematic is that feelings about happiness and the satisfaction and dissatisfaction with one's life are inherently personal, and might not even be revealed to one's closest peers. Some participants, irrespective of their culture, find face-to-face interviews with strangers as being intrusive. The fact that we as foreigners are researching this topic in Japan is challenging but also advantageous to a certain degree. Being outside the social group of the interviewee, the threshold to reveal personal sentiments to foreigners can be lower, as there is less fear of retribution or other sanctions from one's social group. As outsiders, foreign, Caucasian scholars in rural Japan are able to ask questions naively: it often allows questions that Japanese researchers would be more hesitant to ask, and interviewees might be more open to us outsiders than towards other Japanese. As *gaijin* (foreigners, outsiders), we remain outside the tight-knit community and thus are 'neutral' to the constraints of Japanese society and particularly rural communities and their normative expectations of inhabitants embedded within intricate relationships.

Interview research on wellbeing can always potentially be influenced by interpersonal dynamics such as those around the gender and age of interviewee and interviewer. Even though this cannot always be solved, in our case we approached these issues by conducting research in teams of two, which despite our ethnicity (both researchers are Caucasian), differs in regard to gender, social standing, and personality. As rural Japan even today is a distinctively gendered society, conducting the interviews as a mixed team provided sufficient variance for the interviewees to feel comfortable and forthcoming during the research.

Location: rurality and access to the field

A common hurdle in ethnographic research is gaining access to 'the field', which can be even more pronounced in happiness studies, particularly in rural communities, that explore the sensitive and intimate affairs of individual emotions and subjective experiences. Researchers need participants to reflect on the causes and outcomes of happiness and be willing to communicate their personal histories, values, and ideas about happiness. Yet, Japanese society is more 'tight-lipped' than the 'open-hearted' Western approach for expressing private feelings. In psychological terms, culturally accepted forms of behaviour favour reticency and introspection but not extraversion and self-disclosure (Lebra, 1976; Markus and Kitayama, 1991; Lebra, 2009). This is particularly the case with people outside the limited circle of close friends and family members.

One advantage our research enjoyed and aided our access to people's subjectivities and stories was the history of ethnographic research conducted by our Department of East Asian Studies/Japanese Studies at the University of Vienna. Vienna-based scholars, who spearheaded fieldwork and social sciences research among Continental European researchers of Japan, conducted a first survey in 1968 in the Aso area in Kumamoto prefecture on the southern island of Kyushu. The same area became the focus of a new research project of the Vienna School of Japanese Studies in 2015. The initial researchers are still well remembered in the area, as many local residents had never seen foreigners, giving the researchers at the time an exotic status. All in all, the extensive research history and the careful re-enactment of relations at different levels (locals, officials, governments and scholars) aided access to fieldwork sites and trusting relationships with participants.

Interviewees

We conducted interviews in the Aso region of Japan, among residents of a small rural settlement of about 60 households, as well as among citizens of the town centre 4 km away, which has a population just under 10,000. A large percentage of people in Aso either work in agriculture, services, or are self-employed. Through snowball sampling, we interviewed a total of 23 people. Of these, 13 are male and 10 female, 9 are single and 14 are married, 6 are from the village and 17 are from the town, and ages range from 33 to 75. In total we interviewed 7 people in their 30s, 9 in their 40s, and 7 aged 50 and up. Of these, 12 people have moved into the area at some point during their lives, whereas the other 11 people have been lifelong residents. Some of those had left for a certain period of time in their youth but returned later. Several, particularly the younger interviewees, have moved from outside the region into the town and opened their own businesses. These younger entrepreneurs are well connected with each other, and many of them consider each other as their circle of friends.

Tripartite interview structure

Research was conducted through interviews in a two-step process: 14 interviews in February 2018; 9 in July 2018. The interviews ran on average for 1.5 hours. All interviews were recorded and transcribed, then analysed using MaxQDA analysis software. Interviews were usually held in the interviewees' residences, in some instances in their workplaces and in two cases in public spaces like an unused room of a restaurant in one case, a communal hall in the other. Interviews consisted of three parts, with the second being the main segment.

Part 1: warm-up – associations and definitions

The impersonal completion of a quantitative, anonymous survey away from prying eyes may certainly be the least intrusive form of research on 'happiness' or 'wellbeing'. Yet, a questionnaire leaves many conceptual questions unanswered and presumes respondents to have the same understanding about the meaning of the terms. Curiously, no survey we are aware of provides participants with definitions of happiness or wellbeing to help them complete the questionnaire. Our approach tackles the variations in, or openness of, the concepts around happiness/wellbeing by asking respondents for the meanings associated with these key terms from a 'semantic cloud of wellbeing' at the outset of the interviews. Part 1 of the interviews therefore serves two purposes, as it provides (a) an introduction or warm-up to the topic per se, as well as (b) offering a glimpse into the understandings of the terms used by the interviewees. We began the interviews by naming seven terms, asking interviewees to talk about anything that comes to mind or what they associate with these terms or how they would define them. The seven terms are: happiness (*shiawase*), sadness (*kanashimi*), worries (*nayami*), hope (*kibō*), success (*seikō*), anxiety (*fuan*) and failure (*shippai*).

Part 2: a bullseye view on life satisfaction

This main part of the interviews involved working with props in a board game-style activity. As shown in Figure 10.1, the board is two-coloured, the red side (here shown in lighter grey) meaning satisfaction, the blue side (darker grey) dissatisfaction. Circles radiating from the centre weight the significance of variables that we provided in the form of round tokens. Interviewees were instructed to first place a board game figure representing one's self on the bullseye, and then to arrange the tokens on the board, according to the degree of influence they each have on their lives. By selecting and placing tokens on the chart, people reveal the domains and activities they think are important for living a good life, and whether they are currently satisfied or not with them. If needed we provided interviewees with brief explanations of the aims of the activity during the sessions.

In most cases, the tokens feature an image in connection with the signifying word written in Kanji (Chinese characters) plus the reading in Japanese syllabary script (*hiragana*). Literacy in Japan is high, as indicated by high-school graduation rates of 90 per cent and more; yet functional

Figure 10.1: Bullseye board game

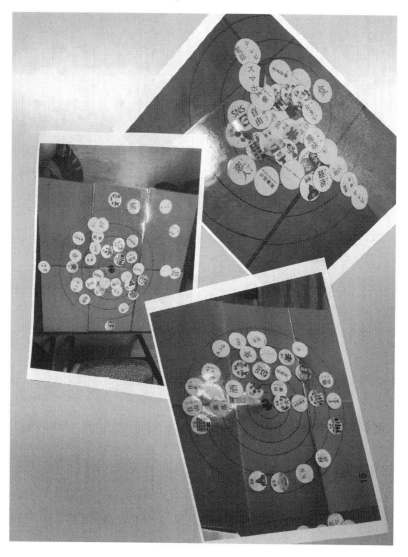

illiteracy is not unheard of, reflecting social deprivation factors, such as low socio-economic status, interrupted educational careers and place of residence at schooling age. By using tokens with visual symbols we could ensure that the task was accessible to those who may have difficulties in reading thus accommodating participants from different social strata and with variations in educational attainment. In addition to the tokens prepared by us, interviewees could label blank tokens with their own terms, giving them some control over the depiction of their wellbeing.

We inscribed the tokens with a variety of terms that reflected our understanding of the state of art of happiness research in Japan. Before the second set of interviews we added a few tokens with concepts and activities that had been raised by participants in the initial interviews. These tokens covered a greater variety of partner relationships, communication devices (social media, internet, mobile phones), and locality labels (district, hamlet). The complete list of tokens is as follows:

> Family (*kazoku*), spouse (*haigūsha*), partner (*pātona*), lover (*koibito*), boyfriend (*kareshi*), girlfriend (*kanojo*), friends (*tomodachi*), work (*shigoto*), colleagues (*dōryō*), freedom/liberty (*jiyū*), time (*jikan*), administration (*gyōsei*), politics (*seisaku*), the economy (*keizai*), money (*okane*), hobbies (*shumi*), TV (*terebi*), purpose of life (*ikigai*), health (*kenkō*), alcohol (*sake*), food/eating (*shoku*), living environment (*seikatsu kankyō*), living/housing (*sumai*), education (*kyōiku*), nature (*shizen*), religion/belief (*shūkyō*), safety/security (*anzen anshin*), village (*mura*), hamlet (*shūraku*), town (*machi*), district [in a town] (*chiku*), internet (*intānetto*), social media (*SNJJS*), old-style mobile phone (*keitai*), smartphone (*sumaho*), and 'community telephone' (*oshirase tanmatsu*).

Once all tokens were placed (tokens identified as irrelevant were to be omitted from the board), we then used the board and the placement of the tokens to start an in-depth conversation about the variables to learn more about the meaning attached to them, the reasons for their placement and their specific realization in the lives of our interviewees.

Part 3: links to quantitative research

As a way of wrapping up the interview, we handed the interviewees one visually appealing sheet featuring three quantitative survey questions on happiness (see Figure 10.2). All three questions offer the same Likert scale from 0 to 10 to answer slightly different questions on subjective wellbeing. In response to the linguistic and cultural variability of terms encompassing issues of happiness, we used suggestive smileys instead of words to identify the extremes of the scales.

Question 1 on the general state of happiness is posed in the same wording as in most large-scale surveys in Japan, asking 'These days, all things considered, how happy do you feel?'. The single-item measurement enables us to relate our study data to traditional quantitative research as well as to understand how interviewees rate their

Figure 10.2: Subjective wellbeing scale

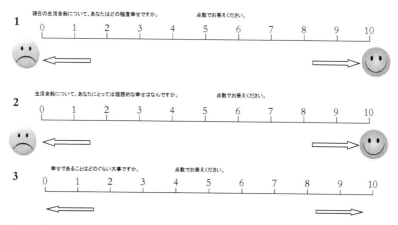

Source: the authors

state of happiness in comparison with others. It helps us put the overall view of life satisfaction as extrapolated from the chart and conversation in part 2 into a wider perspective of research into happiness/wellbeing.

Question 2 'In your opinion, what is the ideal level of happiness?' is important in light of our understanding that the Japanese do not universally subscribe to the Western concept of 'the happier the better' (Uchida, 2014). In contrast to the linearity of the Western concept, which is based on self-esteem, individual achievement and personal attainment, the Japanese idea of happiness is more likely to be seen as fluctuating in a cyclical, sine-wave fashion, in which happiness is a transitory experience, based on interpersonal connectedness and balance between self and others. Cultural psychologist Uchida explains the low levels of happiness among the Japanese in international comparisons by the equally low ideal state of happiness at 6.5 (on a scale of 0 to 10), whereas in the US and Europe it is closer to a 10 (Uchida et al, 2015). She explains this through the desire by Japanese to avoid the top of the sine wave of happiness, as that would mean a decline in happiness in the future. The ideal is to still be on the upswing of the sine wave, as that would signify still a continued increase in happiness for the near future.

Question 3, 'How important is it to be happy?', is an explicit attempt to explore the cultural distinctiveness of Japanese orientations towards happiness and living well. While many studies tacitly presuppose the desire for happiness to be universal, whereby happiness is seemingly the ultimate goal of life, cultural anthropological and cultural psychological research question this universality. Some studies have even shown that under certain conditions happiness can be seen as socially undesirable. Uchida (2014: 483) shows that the desirability of happiness in the US lies at close to 98 per cent among their surveyed population, whereas in Japan, happiness is considered desirable by only 68 per cent.

Findings

Some of the findings from our research interviews about happiness and life satisfaction in rural Japan are discussed in greater detail in Holthus and Manzenreiter (2021). Here we only provide glimpses into the richness of the data and reflect on the methodology we used in our project.

Part 1: diversities of definitions

In this first part, interviewees provided either abstract definitions or general comments on the terms happiness, sadness, anxiety, worries, hope, failure, success, or they shared concrete examples to illustrate their feelings or experiences of happiness, sadness, worry, and so on. These concrete examples ranged from 'large' to 'small' incidents. An example of a 'small' incident was a 33-year-old owner of a small café, who roasts his own coffee, saying he felt happy as he managed to roast a particularly tasty coffee that day. On other days he felt good as his customers were happy with his coffee on that day. A working mother in her late 30s spoke of her happiness through the time spent together with the family in their newly built home, doing everyday things such as dining, playing games or watching TV.

An example of 'large' happiness is often tied to understanding happiness through the interrelatedness of the self to other people and in many instances to family members. 'If everyone is healthy and gets along with anyone else, I can be happy', was a mantra we heard particularly often from elderly interviewees. But also a chef and restaurant owner in his early 40s referred to family health and family time as source of his wellbeing, which he contrasted with his former self that would have sought happiness in rather more fleeting pleasures of surfing, snowboarding, gambling, and gaming.

The idea of happiness as a shared family relationship was intriguing to some interviewees who reflected on alternative lives they could have lived or were anticipating a future yet to be experienced. One woman in her early 60s wondered how life would have become if she had got married, whereas two single men in their 40s fantasized about the increase in happiness if or once they married. And a married woman in her early 30s, although considering herself happy as in a loving relationship, wished for a child, and the further happiness this would bring.

Last but not least, in some instances people would express their sense of happiness in relation to the most basic everyday activities, for example by being appreciative of the simple things in life, living a 'life like everyone around' or a 'normal life', some used the term of *futsū no shiawase* 'normal happiness', or a 'life in which nothing bad is happening', a life 'with the absence of (natural) disaster'. To be happy like the imagined 'everyone', *hitonami no shiawase*, turned up in the conversation with a middle-aged villager who also emphasized nature and social relations as the many invisible things characterizing rural life in stark contrast to city life. He contemplated but could not decide whether the scarcity of things in rural areas or the rich availability of material goods in the city are sources of happiness or unhappiness. For the young wife of a Buddhist priest, however, the joy of the simple things in life and the gift of living a life in ease and free of burden were at the forefront of her thoughts on happiness.

The frequent mentioning of disaster in the context of happiness, anxiety and worries is likely to have been affected by the recollection of the Great Kumamoto Earthquake, which struck the area two years prior to the interviews, severely damaging many homes, facilities, and roads and which disrupted daily life for many residents. With the area dependent on tourism, the effects continue to be felt by many entrepreneurs. One shop owner in his 40s linked his sense of happiness with the 'gratitude for the things you usually take for granted but there is not such a thing, this is something I learnt from the disaster'. Last but not least, a few mentioned at the outset that 'they never really thought about happiness' (75-year-old, married store owner), before providing us with many stories of their experiences of happiness and efforts to formulate definitions of happiness.

The data from the first part of the interviews illustrated how influential everyday personal experiences are for the way that people come to understand their emotions and define their sense of happiness and living well. Happiness is very much an interpretative process, embedded in social networks and across personal biographies. Not one definition exists in people's heads, complicating the interpretation of quantitative surveys.

Part 1 of the interviews was also useful in functioning as an ice-breaker and building some rapport with interviewees. While some participants found it difficult to respond in a concise way, they were usually surprisingly frank and open when it came to personal reminiscences about their wellbeing.

Part 2: the multidimensionality of life satisfaction

The use of the chart and tokens facilitated the conversation with our interviewees, who were often very pleased to see their final arrangement of the board game. Interviewees regarded this visual depiction in the board game as a slice of their current life, and in more than one case people thanked us as they experienced the interviews as enjoyable and as a kind of a psychoanalytic therapy session. For example, we know that in this region of Japan the most significant life domains for a happy life are very likely to be (1) family (respective partner), (2) health, (3) friends, (4) wealth, and (5) a sense of purposeful living (if not food or alcohol). And we also know that for our sample the least important for a happy life are (1) television, (2) politics, (3) religion, (4) education, and (5) the economy.

There were some surprising findings from the research, which is often a feature of ethnographic studies. In informal conversations at the beginning of the fieldwork but prior to our interviews participants told us how important the government-funded free telephone was for the local residents. They said it helped them to stay in contact with family and friends in the region. The ability to see the other person on this particular phone is also valued by local officials as it enables sometimes isolated elderly citizens to access health and social care. So naturally we thought this technology would rank rather high in its importance for life satisfaction, yet we were mistaken. It did not matter much at all to the lives of our interviewees, even though we heard about its convenience from many. Smartphones and the internet take a much more dominant role for the life satisfaction of people – even for older citizens in remote, rural Japan.

To the best of our knowledge, this bullseye chart of 'the self and its life satisfaction' is a first in the application for happiness research – among sociologists at least. It came out of our desire to (a) make the interviews less 'abstract' for the interviewees, to (b) use the chart element as a starting point for detailed questions to follow thereafter, (c) to be able to cover the multidimensionality of happiness and life satisfaction in a comparably short period of time of an hour to hour-and-a-half of interview time, (d) to understand the importance of some elements in people's lives in relation to other elements in their lives, and (e) by making visible and understanding clusters of elements; namely, how some elements are clustered together on the chart by the interviewees, whereas other tokens are placed on the board in far distance from other tokens. All these relationships can be portrayed by giving our interviewees such a visual tool, allowing us to get into complexities of relationships of the different aspects and relationships in their lives. These would have otherwise been extraordinarily difficult to extrapolate from our respondents in such comparably short interview times.

Part 3: happiness as goal – between reality and ideal

The current levels of happiness for our respondents range between 1 and 10 (on a scale between 0–10). A 48-year-old female shop owner, single, who found herself financially exhausted due to the slump in tourism after the earthquake, is the one who rated her happiness the least, whereas a married woman with a ten-year-old son, a fairly satisfying profession, as well as a strong religious household saw herself on the highest rung of the happiness ladder. The majority, however, ranked either a 5 or 8 or in-between these values. For example, a recent in-migrant into the area, a man in his early 30s, has a girlfriend living far away from Kyushu. This long-distance relationship, coupled with his poor financial situation, meant a rating of his current state of happiness at 5, explaining that happy as he is right now, he feels half and incomplete: 'Moving in together with her, building a house and setting up a family, that would be great, and that would make up a full ten.'

Not only do we see great variability in happiness levels, but also in what people consider as ideal levels. Most people would see the ideal level of happiness above their current level, which shows their awareness of something lacking in their current life. Ten of the 23 interviewees saw the ideal level of happiness on the upper extreme of the scale. It is interesting to see that even more people agree that it is very important to be happy (15 out of 23). A finding which does echo some of the research in Western societies about the importance of the pursuit of happiness in popular culture. Nevertheless, despite the many findings that can be drawn from the conversations with interviewees after analysing their three answers, we see that 'the happier the better' understanding of happiness from traditional quantitative survey data is not evident in our small, albeit unrepresentative, sample of interviewees.

Concluding remarks

Due to space limitations it is difficult to elaborate on the culturally specific features of happiness and its many meanings in rural Japan.

Also, we are still developing the links between the three parts of the methodology applied here and this remains an ongoing analytical challenge (see Holthus and Manzenreiter, 2021). Evaluating the benefits of the methodological approach, however, we can say that the quality of findings and ease of conducting the interviews exceeded our expectations by far.

The bullseye chart received much praise from our interviewees, and they became alive and very talkative during the research. We believe this method would be applicable to different cultural contexts beyond Japan and easily adaptable to different social groups. Tokens can easily be designed with different images to reflect cultural differences. The visual symbols on the chart stimulates high-quality conversation and captures different factors for happiness, their strengths or intensity as well as their complex interrelationships. This complexity around happiness could not be grasped without a visual tool. Yet, instructions for the board game are extraordinarily simple, which makes it appealing and accessible for many different types of interviewees. We very much hope that this method will be tried out in many different cultural contexts, with different types of interviewees, the young and the old, those with different levels of education, from different social classes and different walks of life.

What we did not check, however, is the test-retest validity of the chart findings. Would people place the chart the same way the next time they would be asked to? Certainly, the replicability would have to be addressed in future applications. Yet, we envision our method here to be easily adjustable and adaptable to different cultural contexts. It is easy enough to use even in societies with limited education, as the tokens could be images rather than words. Even research with children on their happiness and life satisfaction could be undertaken in this way. We hope that in the future, researchers will adapt this approach to their cultural contexts to improve or test our method. Last but not least, in our increasingly visual world, it is beneficial to have tools like this board game chart which cater for this visual culture, for it is a quick and pleasant entry into happiness research and is a useful tool that can visualize research findings for the wider academic community.

Acknowledgements

We want to thank everyone who we met in the two locations of our research in Kumamoto prefecture. The administration, the shop owners, the residents – they all took us into their homes or offices, they helped smooth the way into the communities, and they were patient with our many questions. We are grateful for the interviewees who shared their very personal stories with us.

Thanks also go to Mariko Konishi and Kumpei Shirai for transcribing the interviews and to both the University of Vienna and the German Institute for Japanese Studies for their financial support of this research project. And last but not least, Barbara would like to express her gratitude to the Minister of State for Happiness and Well-being in the UAE, Her Excellency Ohood Al Roumi, spearheading the Global Dialogue on Happiness and Wellbeing, for inviting me to join an inspiring global network and exchange of like-minded scholars, practitioners and officials, who all strive to understand what essentially makes the world a happier place.

References

Cabinet Office (2011) *Measuring National Well-being: Proposed Well-being Indicators*, available at https://www5.cao.go.jp/keizai2/koufukudo/pdf/koufukudosian_english.pdf (accessed 18 December 2021).

Chen, C., Lee, S. and Stevenson, H.W. (1995) 'Response style and cross-cultural comparisons of rating scales among East Asian and North American students', *Psychological Science*, 6(3): 170–5.

Coulmas, F. (2009) 'The quest for happiness in Japan', DIJ Working Paper 09/1, http://www.dijtokyo.org/publications/WP0901_Coulmas.pdf

Frisch, M.B., Cornell, J., Villanueva, M., and Retzlaff, P.J. (1992) 'Clinical validation of the Quality of Life Inventory. A measure of life satisfaction for use in treatment planning and outcome assessment', *Psychological Assessment*, 4(1): 92–101.

Helliwell, J., Layard, R. and Sachs, J. (2016) *World Happiness Report 2016, Update (Vol. I)*, New York: Sustainable Development Solutions Network.

Helliwell, J., Huang, H., Wang, S. and Shiplett, H. (2018) 'International migration and world happiness', in J. Helliwell, R. Layard and J. Sachs (eds) *World Happiness Report 2018*, New York: Sustainable Development Solutions Network, pp 13–44.

Hitokoto, H. and Uchida, Y. (2015) 'Interdependent happiness: theoretical importance and measurement validity', *Journal of Happiness Studies*, 16(1): 211–39.

Holthus, B., Huber, M. and Tanaka, H. (2015) *Parental Well-being in Japan*, Munich: Iudicium (DIJ Miscellanea Nr 19).

Holthus, B. and Manzenreiter, W. (2017a) 'Making sense of happiness in "unhappy Japan"', in B. Holthus and W. Manzenreiter (eds) *Life Course, Happiness and Well-Being in Japan*, London: Routledge, pp 1–27.

Holthus, B. and Manzenreiter, W. (eds) (2017b) *Life Course, Happiness and Well-Being in Japan*, London: Routledge.

Holthus, B. and Manzenreiter, W. (2021) 'The meaning of place for selfhood and well-being in rural Japan', in S. Ganseforth and H. Jentzsch (eds) *Rethinking Locality in Japan*, London: Routledge.

Husser, J. and Fernandez, K. (2018) 'We are happier than we realize: underestimation and conflation in measuring happiness', *Journal of Happiness Studies*, 19(2): 587–606.

Kitayama, S. and Markus, H. (2000) 'The pursuit of happiness and the realization of sympathy: cultural patterns of self, social relations and well-being', in E. Diener and E. Suh (eds) *Culture and Subjective Wellbeing*, Cambridge, MA: MIT Press, pp 113–61.

Kobayashi, J. and Hommerich, C. (2017) 'Are happiness and unhappiness two sides of the same coin? An analysis of happiness and unhappiness', *Sociological Theory and Methods*, 32(1): 49–63.

Krueger, A. and Schkade, D. (2008) 'The reliability of subjective well-being measures', *Journal of Public Economics*, 92(8–9): 1833–45.

Kusago, T. and Yamamoto, K. (2011) Seikatsu jikkan pairotto chōsa: hitobito no 'shiawase' ya 'fushiawase' o sagutte [Daily life pilot study: searching for people's 'happiness' and 'unhappiness'], http://www2.ipcku.kansai-u.ac.jp/~tkusago/pdf/japdf/reseach/reseach_of_realization.pdf

Kwan, V., Bond, M. and Singelis, T. (1997) 'Pancultural explanations for life satisfaction: adding relationship harmony to self-esteem', *Journal of Personality and Social Psychology*, 73: 1038–51.

Lebra, T.S. (1976) *Japanese Patterns of Behavior*, Honolulu: University of Hawai'i Press.

Lebra, T.S. (2009) 'The cultural significance of silence in Japanese communication', *Multilingua – Journal of Cross-Cultural and Interlanguage Communication*, 6(4): 343–58.

Lu, L. and Gilmour, R. (2004) 'Culture and conceptions of happiness. Individual oriented and social oriented SWB', *Journal of Happiness Studies*, 5(3): 269–91.

Manzenreiter, W. (2018) 'Rural happiness in Japan: contrasting urban and rural well-being in Kumamoto', in R. Lützeler (ed) *Rural Areas between Decline and Resurgence: Lessons from Japan and Austria*, Vienna: Institut für Ostasienwissenschaften/Japanologie, pp 43–64.

Manzenreiter, W. and Holthus, B. (2017a) 'Reconsidering the four dimension of happiness across the life course in Japan', in B. Holthus and W. Manzenreiter (eds) *Life Course, Happiness and Well-Being in Japan*, London: Routledge, pp 256–71.

Manzenreiter, W. and Holthus, B. (eds) (2017b) *Happiness and the Good Life in Japan*, London: Routledge.

Markus, H. and Kitayama, S. (1991) 'Culture and the self. Implications for cognition, emotion and motivation', *Psychological Review*, 98: 224–53.

Markus, H. and Kitayama, S. (1998) 'The cultural psychology of personality', *Journal of Cross-Cultural Psychology*, 29(1): 63–87.

Mathews, G. (2017) 'Happiness pursued, abandoned, dreamed of, and stumbled upon: an analysis of 20 Japanese lives over 20 years', in B. Holthus and W. Manzenreiter (eds) *Life Course, Happiness and Well-Being in Japan*, London: Routledge, pp 189–201.

OECD (2013) *OECD guidelines on measuring subjective well-being*, Paris: OECD Publishing.

OECD Stat (2017) 'Better life index – edition 2017', https://stats.oecd.org/index.aspx?DataSetCode=BLI

Oishi, S., Diener, E., Lucas, R. and Suh, E. (1999) 'Cross-cultural variations in predictors of life satisfaction: perspectives from needs and values', *Personality and Social Psychology Bulletin*, 25(8): 980–90.

Oishi, S., Graham, J., Kesebir, S. and Galinha, I.C. (2013) 'Concepts of happiness across time and cultures', *Personality and Social Psychology Bulletin*, 39(5): 559–77.

Ponocny, I., Weismayer, C., Stross, B. and Dressler, S. (2016) 'Are most people happy? Exploring the meaning of subjective well-being ratings', *Journal of Happiness Studies*, 17(6): 2635–53.

Schwarz, N. and Strack, F. (1999) 'Reports of subjective well-being: judgmental processes and their methodological implications', in D. Kahneman, E. Diener and N. Schwarz (eds) *Well-being: The Foundations of Hedonic Psychology*, New York: Russell Sage Foundation, pp 61–84.

Suh, E. (2000) 'Self, the hyphen between culture and subjective well-being', in E. Diener and E. Suh (eds) *Culture and Subjective Well-being*, Cambridge, MA: MIT Press, pp 63–86.

Suh, E., Diener, E., Oishi, S. and Triandis, H. (1998) 'The shifting basis of life satisfaction judgments across cultures: emotions versus norms', *Journal of Personality and Social Psychology*, 74: 482–93.

Tanaka, R., Hashimoto, S., Hoshino, S. and Skimizu, N. (2014) 'Nōrin chiiki jūmin no kōfukudo ni eikyō suru chiikiteki yōin no shitsuteki chōsa ni yoru tansa: Ishikawa-ken Suzu-shi ni okeru kikitori chōsa o moto ni' [Qualitative inquiry into regional factors affecting the happiness of residents in rural Japan], *Nōson Keikaku Gakkaishi*, 33: 299–304.

Uchida, Y. (2014) 'Collective well-being and a proposal for a sustainable society: a cultural psychological perspective', in G. Trommsdorff (ed) *Interdisciplinary Aspects of Well-Being in Changing Societies*, Konstanz: German-Japanese Society for Social Sciences, pp 480–7.

Uchida, Y. and Kitayama, S. (2009) 'Happiness and unhappiness in East and West: themes and variations', *Emotion*, 9(4): 441–56.

Uchida, Y., Ogihara, Y. and Fukushima, S. (2015) 'Cultural construal of wellbeing: theories and empirical evidence', in W. Glatzer, L. Camfield, V. Møller and M. Rojas (eds) *Handbook of Quality of Life: Exploration of Well-being of Nations and Continents*, Heidelberg: Springer, pp 823–37.

White, S. and Blackmore, C. (eds) (2016) *Cultures of Well-Being: Method, Place, Policy*, Houndmills, Basingstoke: Palgrave Macmillan.

11

'Show Me What Makes You Happy at Work': Visualizing Happiness in the Workplace

Ilona Suojanen

Introduction

What does happiness look like? How can we capture happiness to analyse the complex and often fleeting experience in order to really understand the phenomena? These were the two guiding questions when I started researching workplace happiness for a PhD. Having undertaken earlier quantitative studies into happiness (Suojanen, 2013), I had become convinced that numerical representations of happiness generated by quantitative surveys do not tell us enough about happiness.

I had recently moved to Edinburgh and as I was sharing the exciting, happy moments in the picturesque medieval city by sending pictures to friends abroad, I started thinking of visualizing happiness in research. We live in a visual world and the current accounts of postmodern culture emphasize the increasingly visual aspects of our lives (Buchanan and Huczynski, 2010). As Belk (2017: 79) states, 'the saturation of visual representations in our lives has never been greater'. There are global trends towards a greater role for, and new forms of, visual information. The arts, social media and advertisements 'render the world in visual terms' (Rose, 2012: 2). Also, as the focus in my study was on young employees, who are accustomed to sharing their lives in visual ways via social media (Millennial Impact Report, 2013), a photographic methodology would be an essential part of my data collection.

Despite the popularity of visual methodologies in organizational studies (Shortt and Warren, 2017), few studies had applied them to happiness research, and I noticed various challenges to overcome. An initial revelation was that photos alone were insufficient to understand the complexity of people's accounts of happiness. I wished to hear the actual stories behind the images from people themselves, to provide interpretations of happiness experiences documented by interviewees. Hence, the notion of 'creating synergy' (Warren, 2002: 236) between visual and narrative methods.

When I began my research, happiness was only beginning to be seen as an influential variable in employment relationships. Even though there were many studies on work satisfaction and wellbeing in a broader sense, relatively little attention was paid to workplace happiness (Fisher, 2010: 384; Thin, 2012). Happiness at work, as a distinct concept to job satisfaction and commitment (Van de Voorde et al, 2012), was not widely studied, apart from exceptions, such as Peter Warr's (1987) work on happiness in the workplace.

Since employee wellbeing has been, and still is, often labelled as job satisfaction, it is important to clarify the difference between these two. Fisher (2010: 388) argues that 'happiness at work includes, but is far more than, job satisfaction'. It can include a range of positive experiences and emotions that stem from the formal and informal aspects of employment. According to Locke (1969: 317) job satisfaction is conceived more narrowly in terms of the expectations regarding the job and the degree to which these are met: job satisfaction focuses more on evaluation and judgement than experiences 'in the round'.

Surprisingly, little of the research had found its way into use, particularly within organizational psychology (Judge and Klinger, 2008). Workplace happiness studies were mainly using quantitative self-report fixed questionnaire surveys to address the topic (Fineman, 2004), and alternative approaches were needed to explore the complexity of happiness processes, which are often multifaceted due to the nature of happiness, and embedded in social relationships and specific social contexts. My PhD study focused on a wide range of happiness experiences in the workplace, and although some of these findings are discussed here the key focus in this chapter is on the methodological approach I employed during the research. I discuss the benefits and challenges of using this method, and argue that it can be used to investigate other aspects of happiness in different settings.[1]

First, I will reflect on the literature around the synthesis of narrative and visual methods, then draw on some of my data to explore the challenges and benefits of these methods, and then conclude with the (dis)advantages of this approach. I encourage researchers not only to find alternative ways to use the synergy of visual and narrative methods but also to explore new approaches to happiness studies.

Synergy of narrative and visual studies

My review of the literature suggests that new qualitative approaches to happiness studies are needed. Quantitative studies can surely tell us if the glass is half full, but they fail to tell what the glass contains and how the contents were poured in (Thin, 2012: 327). Using quantitative surveys to generate numerical representations of employment (Godard, 2014: 7) runs the risk of turning people into 'emotional numbers' (Fineman, 2004: 720) neglecting the 'sense of the process of happiness – how it evolves' (Cieslik, 2021). As feelings and emotions are often context dependent and ambivalent (Fineman, 2004), further approaches are needed to complement the proliferation of survey-based happiness research by telling the 'stories behind the numbers' (Thin, 2012; Suojanen, 2013; 2017). As happiness is also an evaluative process, where people, based on their values, reflect the choices they have made (Cieslik, 2015), narratives allow them to explain what led to the experience.

Emotions can be challenging topics to discuss with friends, but even more so when participating in a more rigorous academic study. There are the linguistic challenges associated with capturing subjective experiences and verbalizing physical sensations and automatic or habitual responses to events. The level of emotional awareness and expression can vary greatly between individuals and cultures, while social class and gender may also have an influence on language (Cowen and Keltner, 2017). Not all people are verbally sophisticated, and some might find surveys and interview techniques problematic requiring researchers to utilize other methodologies that employ wider forms of expression and participation (Vince and Warren, 2012: 281).

If narratives are the stories behind the numbers, then how do researchers best access these stories? How do we help respondents remember their experiences, to share them and to form their 'happiness narratives' during fieldwork? I argue that to understand something as intangible as happiness the use of visual data together with supporting narrative analyses can offer a sophisticated approach to wellbeing research (Kunter and Bell, 2006: 177). Photography has been proven to mediate complex and unpredictable work practices (Pritchard and Symon, 2014). This is especially the case when researching happiness across different languages and cultures, not native to the speaker. Visual research can help the sharing of issues difficult to conceptualize in a foreign language, and photos can act as a non-verbal tool to help elicit a variety of associations connected to happiness events. Photography can offer a rich or 'thick' emotional account of wellbeing events that can be comforting or reassuring for respondents exploring deeply felt life events (Day et al, 2003; Johansson et al, 2012). One of the strengths of using visual data, is that they show the phenomenon as it occurs (Buchanan and Huczynski, 2010) and can 'yield a multisensory sense of movement and place' in different circumstances (Pink, 2011: 16).

However, photographs can only provide a fragmented reality, and an outsider might struggle to fully appreciate the meaning of images and their relationship to happiness (Shortt and Warren, 2017). Hence, although the words and images are insufficient on their own, they can 'create a synergy' together to provide valuable insights into happiness experiences (Warren, 2002: 236). With synergy, Warren refers to both images and words being 'inextricably linked in communicating the sensory and aesthetic nature of the experiences'. This syncretic approach takes us further than photo-elicitation techniques that often function more simply as prompts to elicit comments from participants in research settings (Wagner, 1979). An image neither contains all the information respondents can extract from it, nor is it just a prompt (Warren, 2002; Pink, 2011). By allowing the synergy between images and words, new reflections about the nature of happiness can be generated, which reflects the idea of happiness as a collaborative, interpretive process (Cieslik, 2015).

Data collection *with* participants

The qualitative methods used were semi-structured in-depth interviews and 'mindful photography' (Kurtz and Lyubomirsky, 2013) in order to capture happiness moments and to gain deeper understanding into happiness from an employee's point of view. Other similar terms are participant-led photography (Vince and Warren, 2012), participant-employed photography (Lorenz and Kolb, 2009) and PhotoVoice (Migliorini and Rana, 2017). All these terms are variations of participative techniques (Shortt and Warren, 2017) supporting participants to generate their own data, offering discretion over the selection of images and allowing for the sharing of lived experiences. They acknowledge individuals as important knowledge-producers and co-creators (Tinkler, 2013) and promote the sense of ownership and empowerment (Lorenz and Kolb, 2009) over the research process.

The research is hence conducted *with* participants, not *about* or *of* participants.

Three data–collection phases

This study consisted of three research phases. First, the participants took part in a semi-structured interview. The challenge was not to overly guide them in their data-generation activities. So I tried to keep the questions very open and avoided giving any guidance on how to approach the topic.

Second, they were asked to take photographs of work-related happiness moments during a two-week period: to 'show me what makes you happy at work'. As the approach was primarily inductive and the goal was to find new aspects of workplace happiness, they were not given definitions of happiness, but encouraged to decide themselves what was a happy moment. They all suggested to me they knew what happiness was, but found it harder to explain or define it precisely. For some, happiness was about excitement and enjoyment, and for some others was related to a relaxed state. These were all valuable notions and findings, supporting the approach to give participants the freedom to define their own happy moments.

Participants were provided with a Q&A sheet that was planned to help them in a moment of uncertainty during the fieldwork. For example, participants were asked to avoid inventing happiness moments, as authentic experiences were wanted for the research. It was highlighted that the quality of photos was unimportant. If unable to take photos, they were asked to send only the caption explaining the moment. They were also encouraged to send the photo soon after it was taken, to avoid forgetting to do so.

The participants used smartphones to take photos mostly via an app called WhatsApp; some alternatively sent images via email. They were sent a reminder every working day by WhatsApp or email. It was made clear that the reminder was sent automatically every day, regardless of entries received that day or not. The total number of entries received was 226, of which 190 included pictures. Twenty-six was recorded as the highest number of entries from one participant and three the lowest from another.[2]

Third, participants were met in person and asked to 'talk through' the photos, in an unstructured interview format. Questions were asked about the context in which the images were captured to gain further information about the experience, probing for further insights and to help keep interviews on track (Matthews and Ross, 2010: 268). Photos often had a 'can-opener effect' (Walker and Wiedel, 1985) generating insights into happiness from a variety of perspectives as the conversations evolved through discussions. For example, we had discussions on how their happiness at work was influenced by experiences outside employment or earlier in the life course, strengthening the notion that work and personal lives are often inseparable, and happiness is rooted across people's biographies (Cieslik, 2015). This can be seen one of the challenges of workplace happiness studies – how to research different yet interrelated life domains.

After going through each photo separately, participants were shown a collage of their entries and asked to reflect on what they saw. In Sofia's (27, business) case (see Figure 11.1), this led to discussions about freedom, as she noticed that many of her pictures involved her moving around or being flexible in some sense. For her, happiness was deeply rooted in having freedom and not 'just giving yourself to that job because it is required from you'.

In addition to collecting the narratives of the photos, qualitative semi-structured interviews were conducted to deepen the understanding of the context in which the photos were taken.[3] During this interview, they were also asked to reflect on the methods used, its challenges, benefits and usefulness, which are discussed later in the chapter.

Can happiness be photographed? The challenges of using visual methods

Challenges of the method I employed have been divided into those faced by the participants and those I confronted, as a researcher when undertaking the research.

Challenges for the participants

(1) There were difficulties for interviewees in recognizing or choosing when to report or take photos of happiness:

> 'You can clearly tell when you are unhappy, but when something happens that makes you smile, you are like am I happy? Or is it just a good feeling? Happiness, what is happiness?' (Emily, 31, law)

> 'Happiness can come in certain forms that could be completely new to us. How to know something we still do not know about ourselves?' (Sebastian, 33, arts)

Figure 11.1: Sofia's happiness collage

These challenges are not new in happiness studies. They refer to the elastic nature of happiness, which is highly internal and emotional, yet has visible external markers. When something is difficult to define or articulate, it can also be challenging to research.

(2) Although most of the participants enjoyed taking photos of happy moments, it was not always easy. Happiness was seen as something quite intangible and difficult to capture visually, as it was "happening in the head" (Valentina, 28, design):

'Sometimes happiness seemed so abstract, and a photo is such a real thing.' (Ana, 27, finance)

'For example having a good conversation. Or the feeling of nice weather or wind on your skin. Or working in a company that values what you value. You cannot take a picture of it.' (Nathan, 24, banking)

One participant had taken selfies, to emphasize that happiness happened within him. Sometimes participants created something related and took a photo of it. For example, one participant wrote the words 'secondment opportunity' on a piece of paper and took a photo of it (see Figure 11.2).

Not only was the moment often fleeting, but stopping to take a photo of it, in some cases, ruined the flow of the moment:

'Happiness is a moment when you forget everything. Those moments you let go. Then you need to think that

Figure 11.2: Secondment opportunity

you participate and need to take a photo and it takes you out of the moment.' (Karl, 30, education)

McMahon (2006) notes, that classical Greek philosophers acknowledged the risk of ruining happiness by focusing on it (also Diehl et al, 2016). However, by attempting to capture the happy moments in a photo, participants were able to recall their experiences and reflect on them.

(3) Inability to take photos was mainly due to five reasons. (a) Having no access to a camera when experiencing happiness, caused either by cameras not allowed at work, the task requiring full concentration or no time to take photos. (b) Taking photos at work or having mobile phones in work settings is an interruption or part of non-professional behaviour, which made taking photos a challenge. (c) Confidentiality and anonymity provided challenges, mainly concerning other people, such as customers, patients or students:

'The main thing was – obviously with patients – confidentiality. Hospital is not as free as working in an office where you can take pictures.' (Lucy, 28, healthcare)

Confidentiality also related to documents, patents, websites and buildings:

'I couldn't take a picture of it, as it is company's secret, it was their equipment.' (Harry, 33, renewable energy)

(d) Sometimes technical issues (such as the old age of the phone) interrupted taking a photo or made it more complicated. (e) Although only one participant confessed to forgetting to take a picture, this was most likely experienced by some other participants too.

The participants had been advised that if facing a challenge they could take a picture right after the moment or share a verbal entry. This advice was followed by Sofia who took a picture of the ceiling (see Figure 11.3):

'Oh that made me happy, I should take a photo. So I looked around and up and thought oh that is so beautiful, so I just took that.' (Sofia, 27, business)

Whereas Victoria had the opposite approach:

'I was not trying to photograph the most beautiful thing. I was just trying to catch a photo that would remind me of that time.' (Victoria, 32, corporate social responsibility)

Figure 11.3: Skylight in the ceiling

Although both of them aimed and reached the same destination of first capturing the moment and then recalling it afterwards, they had very different approaches to how to represent the moment visually in a photograph.

Some of these challenges led me to conclude that the photos did not always represent a happiness moment. For example, participants took 19 photos of mugs and 28 photos of blue skies and the sun, and barely no pictures of people (Figure 11.4). Had happiness been analysed based on the images, the main conclusions could have been: warm beverages and nice weather make people happy at work; other people have little influence on happiness.

However, the analysis of narrative data gave rather different results, as although nature and the weather were among the main generators of happiness moments, coffee rarely featured in these accounts. The narrative data generated by discussion of the images allowed me to properly interpret these many images of hot drinks. In fact these images actually suggested that it was not coffee per se that was essential to wellbeing but the quality of relationships around the sharing of a coffee with colleagues.

The challenge of capturing visual representations of happiness illustrates the contextual and socially situated nature of wellbeing. It is often difficult to capture this context and the dense social relationships that underpin work-based experiences of wellbeing.

Figure 11.4: Happiness collage

Challenges for researchers

(1) Attempts to please the researcher. There were several examples where respondents felt pressured to complete a promised task. Miguel was experiencing turmoil at work during the mindful photography period, as three of his colleagues were fired unexpectedly, for financial reasons. It meant loosing great colleagues, more work for those who remained, and uncertainty about the future:

> 'Most of the photos I was trying to push. If I had not received your messages I would have not sent anything, because it was really difficult to find something.' (Miguel, 34, oceanography)

This raises questions how authentic his entries were. Another participant was concerned that her pictures were not interesting enough, and failed to convey adequately the emotional intensity of her happiness moments. She started capturing images of plants and trees as they presented flourishing and progressing, which for her were more powerful symbols for happiness. This led her to take images that at times did not capture the empirical detail of happiness moments as they happened but rather documented her more general understanding of happiness experiences (see Figure 11.5). The images she produced were only intelligible with some lengthy commentary and interpretation from her about the experiences they related to.

Figure 11.5: Symbols of happiness

new beginning: boss moving to a new team (happy for her) and I hope
my new manager will have a better management style (happy for me)

At times I felt that participants were perhaps too aware of their
participation in a research study, which resulted in impression
management (Goffman, 1959). They were involved in 'conscious or
unconscious, deceptive or authentic, goal directed behaviour' (Peck
and Levashina, 2017: 1) in order to influence the impressions that
others had of them. Such processes are encouraged by the use of social
media that offers many identity possibilities, opportunities to play
out roles in different settings (Turkle, 2011), and encourages personal
branding and self-marketing (Picone, 2015). Nevertheless, employing
face-to-face interviews rather than utilizing online image feeds perhaps
limited the impression management somewhat. Such problems are
not exclusive to qualitative methods as impression management can
also be an issue for other approaches such as surveys (Lajunen and
Summala, 2003).

(2) The photographs overly directed the discussions in interviews.
As there were sometimes difficulties taking photos of people, there
were some images that did not contain other people yet many of the
narratives on happiness moments focused on interactions with others.

'None of them have people in them, but nearly everything
I talk about is interactions with people. I think if I had just

described the moments I would have talked about people more.' (Dennis, 28, education)

As Dennis suggested, he could have potentially discussed more about people, if the data collection had been undertaken differently (using written text or traditional interviews, for example). As there were inabilities to take pictures in other occasions too, it makes me wonder if people would have talked about slightly different things, had the happiness moments been collected in an alternative way. Were there some aspects of workplace happiness, which were not in the photos – for example, confidentiality reasons – and were hence not discussed during the interviews at all? However, as Dennis pointed out, it did not *stop* him from talking about people – he just talked *less* about them.

(3) Researcher commitment and effort. In contrast to surveys or diary-methodologies, visual methods and qualitative techniques require an ongoing WhatsApp presence, to monitor and manage the data generation. Reminders were sent each day to participants, taking into consideration the different schedules of each participant. Photographs were received at various times across the day and week, and were hence constant reminders of work during a long period of fieldwork.

Although picturing happiness presented difficulties, the combination of visual representations with narrative data from interviews offered a deeper understanding of happiness in the workplace. The benefits of the methodology are discussed next.

'It is second nature' – the benefits of using visual methods in happiness research

When discussing the merits of the methodology used in this research it is useful to examine these in relation to two dimensions: those benefitting the participants and those beneficial for researchers.

Using visual methods: the benefits for the participants

A key reason for choosing a visual methodology was the opportunity it allowed to capture happiness moments in real time as they happened, and so generated insights into the contextual and embedded nature of happiness in the workplace.

(1) Helping participants to recall happiness moments was one of the main advantages of this approach to happiness research, as the

visual record helped participants to discuss these moments during the interview:

> 'I took pictures to remind me of what the moment was. If this wasn't written, I would not remember why I took it.' (Adam, 31, education)

As it was a good attempt to capture a fleeting happiness moment it also made the experience more 'real' for the interviewees, giving them a more rounded insight into happiness events. In particular, the range of visual information in the images conveyed a complexity about the nature of the experience such as aspects of the setting, tasks and time of day:

> 'There is certain immediacy to it. Taking a picture of it makes it a bit more real. It makes it bit more tangible in a sense, that strength of that notion, it made it even more real than it was already.' (Dennis, 28, education)

Revisiting the photos later also had a positive double-effect on happiness:

> 'I see a picture and I am like oh I forgot that happened. So when you take pictures of moments when you are happy and you revisit those moments. It makes you happier.' (Valentina, 28, design)

Other happiness scholars have also noted this in their research. For example, Hyman (2014: 8) concludes in her study that happiness in the present, might well be connected to the past or the future, as: 'present experiences may not be inherently happy per se, but they make happiness from reflection upon happy events or periods from the past'.

(2) A natural way to share information. One of the reasons why visual method was chosen for this study, was that taking and sending photos was a very common way for young people to communicate with each other and did not require the learning of new skills or much effort:

> 'We are so used to taking pictures of ourselves. I guess it is second nature. Like looking into mirror and sending it to you.' (Richard, 27, finance)

> 'I do take photos in my daily life, I use Instagram.' (Sofia, 27, business)

Perhaps, had the sample been older, this would not have been listed as a benefit, but it was certainly a benefit with this focus group.

(3) Ownership of the photos. The photos were taken by the participants and hence they were – and still are – their photos. They had a large amount of control and autonomy over the creation of the images and their dissemination (see also Papaloukas et al, 2017). First, they selected the happiness moments and how to capture these photographically, then which photos to send and then had discretion over the later interview discussion about the images. They were able to raise issues and discuss topics that mattered to them and hence lead the direction of the conversation. This ownership of the images and control of the direction of discussions helped foster good relationships with participants in the interview setting.

(4) Visual methods makes for a more interesting, pleasant and informative research process. The generation of images was a creative process, which added to the enjoyment for participants (and for the researcher too). The most often heard comments were 'it was easy' and 'it was fun':

> 'It actually made me happy. I enjoyed taking the photos and it made me to stop and think, which I don't normally do.' (Charlie, 30, retail)

They also liked to look at happiness images from different perspectives within the interview setting and enjoyed the creative part of capturing happiness:

> 'It does make you think more creatively about "ok I feel happy now, what is it that makes me happy", ok it is that, how can I express it in a picture format?' (Soraya, 33, banking)

Using this method added to the positive experience for both the participants and the researcher. It also provided an easy way to give something back to the participants – making them happy in the process – and not just using them to gain the information needed for the study.

Using visual methods: the advantages for researchers

(1) Using visual methods allowed the development of new insights into the complexity of happiness data. The length of the experiences,

range of emotions and the intensity or duration of happiness moments were discussed in the interviews. The approach also offered researchers some guidance on the original interpretations that interviewees had of the photographs when they were taken (Pink, 2011). This created a dialectical relationship where interviewees moved from image to narrative and back generating a more complex and denser interpretation of the happiness moment than without this synergy approach. Using images also allowed refection on topics with indirect but related associations (Clark-Ibanez, 2004). This is at the core of the synergy between the visual and narrative aspects of the methodology.

The photos also provided information on the participants' surroundings and environments that I would not have had access to otherwise and helped to understand the experienced moments better. As my research approach is associated with the term social constructionism (Saunders et al, 2009: 111) I acknowledge that the interpretations and experiences of individuals are socially constructed. As Illouz (2008: 11) suggests, emotions are formed of and dependent on cultural meanings and social relationships, and therefore 'concern the self and the relationship of the self to culturally situated others'. Therefore, as happiness is a subjectively constructed phenomenon, and given meanings are often contextually specific, we do need some access to the context in which the happiness event occurred, to grasp the meanings associated with it.

(2) A visual methodology offered an approach to happiness that transcended the usual quantitative surveys used to study wellbeing in the workplace.

> 'Happiness is quite complex and it means very different things to different people. I don't think very simplistic staff survey can address those things.' (Charlotte, 26, civil service)

Some of the findings in this study were in line with earlier, quantitative happiness studies, but in addition, this study reached aspects that had not been studied before and allowed a deeper understanding of employees' perspectives and experiences on happiness. For example, instead of just listing happiness enablers, this study provided exploratory narratives on what the underlying issues causing and enabling happiness in different circumstances are, and how happiness is embedded in social relationships. As the participants were not only asked to answer interview questions, but also to create their own entries by capturing happiness moments, the outcomes resulted in deeply felt narratives, instead of banal and shallow answers (Cieslik, 2015: 430).

(3) The photographs stimulated discussion and rapport during the interviews. The focus on the images disrupted the usual face-to face interactions we see in traditional qualitative interviewing, which made the situation more relaxed and helped to focus on the happiness moments. Also, the collage of the visual data allowed participants to examine the relationships between their different images and to reflect on their happiness not only at work but more generally, across other aspects of life. This more holistic approach to happiness would have not been possible with only a narrative or interview method.

Conclusions

The use of a photographic approach to happiness research can contribute to organizational studies, as it illuminates the relationships between employees and employers (Pritchard and Symon, 2014) and invites us to listen to the happiness stories behind the numbers (Thin, 2012; Suojanen, 2017). Visual information may be especially suitable in situations where there are constraints on language-based data collection; for example, in cross-cultural research and with diverse sample membership. However, it may be less useful where participants are unfamiliar with online/phone technologies or where interviewees have difficulties expressing their thoughts and emotions through images. Also, although most of the participants found the methodology pleasant, some spoke of being forced to take pictures of the external markers of happiness, when the feeling or emotion was more internal, psychological or embodied. Hence, the need to provide opportunities for participants to interpret the meanings around these images.

The analyses of just the photos themselves could be open to misinterpretation as we saw earlier with the many images of cups of coffee that were taken to represent happiness moments. Hence, by combining the two methods of visual/narrative data collection it allowed people to reflect on their happiness experiences in a more considered way than is possible in a one-off interview or survey.

The research showed that the visual and narrative data may be subject to impression management as interviewees work to create socially desirable narratives. In these instances researchers can only stress the importance of authenticity, highlight the participants' expertise on their own happiness and create a sense of trust between participants and researchers. This approach, by using lengthy interviews and visual data, can help establish good rapport between researchers and participants (Papaloukas et al, 2017), which in turn can encourage the creation of more authentic data.

Table 11.1: The advantages and disadvantages of the synergy approach

Advantages	Disadvantages
Captures happiness in the moment	Happiness is hard to capture
Captures the context and surroundings	Intrusive and interruptive of the flow of events
Participants choose the happiness moment	Challenges in selection of photos
Images help participants to recall the moments later	Challenges with taking pictures in situations where other people are present
Highlights the visual culture and image sharing	Risk of impression management
Participants are able to see and reflect on their happiness, both at the moment and on the 'bigger picture'	Happiness as an internal feeling might be hard to externalize in a photo
Provides an alternative way to interview	Risk of images influencing and reframing the narratives conducted later in interviews
Provides an alternative way to participate and to conduct research	Can be a challenge to less tech-savvy people
New insights emerging from looking at the photos	Time consuming, requires effort from both the researcher and participant

New insights and lines of inquiry evolved as the photos and experiences were analysed. On the downside, the amount of resources spent on interviewing and analysing the data does limit the scope and generalizability of this approach which are common issues for qualitative research. The advantages and disadvantages of this approach are presented in Table 11.1.

To provide robust information on something as mobile, context dependent, ambivalent, subjective and multifaceted as happiness is challenging but also rewarding. For example, as this chapter has shown, photos and narratives together can create a synergy (Warren, 2002) and reduce misinterpretations of the complex meanings around happiness (Papaloukas et al, 2017). This synergy can inform our understandings of happiness and fill the gaps left by quantitative methods. It can also help when creating survey questions, as more nuanced features can be captured, providing new insights into happiness. Visual approaches can also be a useful method to capture and reflect on a range of emotions such as safety, fear and trust, or experiences related to health conditions.

Returning to my initial question on 'How can we capture happiness and analyse this complex and often fleeting experience to really understand it?' I am convinced that asking people to take photos when experiencing happiness provides good data to help answer this question. Visualizing happiness in the workplace is possible and provides opportunities to explore this phenomenon – opportunities that are often lacking in quantitative survey research.

As Belk (2017: 93) writes, 'the current generation of "born digital" consumers have come to expect visual images and quickly become bored with purely textual information'. By using visual approaches in happiness research we can make it more interesting and informative for ourselves, our colleagues and for the wider population as well, hence fulfilling our responsibility for knowledge-sharing outside academia too.

I would also encourage researchers to ask themselves how do they make sense of their own experiences and emotions, what are they passionate about and how those could help them to best reflect and express their own happiness, when words and numbers are insufficient. This way we could create new methods to study happiness, as well as making the whole process more meaningful and enjoyable for both the participants and for ourselves. Science can flourish only when creativity and a sense of play are present, as the painter David Hockney remarked:

> Without sense of play there is not much curiosity either.
> Even a scientist has a sense of play.

Notes

[1] Thirty young professionals, based in Edinburgh, participated in this study in 2015. They were all employed individuals from different organizations (in both the private and the public sector) born between 1979 and 1994. Fourteen were women and 16 men and all had at least a university degree. One half of the participants were of British nationality, the other consisted of a variety of nationalities from Europe, Latin America, North America, Asia and Oceania. Snowball sampling was used to find volunteering participants. The sample is of a middle-class professionals and hence offers particular insights into graduate jobs and employment, rather than more general work experiences.

[2] The number of entries was not necessarily related to the level of happiness or unhappiness of the participant, but was sometimes explained by the incapability/ challenges they faced taking photos at work, as we see later on in this chapter.

[3] All interviews were audio-recorded and transcribed and imported into NVivo9 for data management and coding. General principles of thematic analysis were used (Matthews and Ross, 2010).

References

Belk, R. (2017) 'Collaborating in visual consumer research', in M. McCabe (ed) *Collaborative Ethnography in Business Environments*, London: Routledge, pp 105–23.

Buchanan, D.A. and Huczynski, A.A. (2010) *Organizational Behaviour* (7th edn), Essex: Pearson Education.

Cieslik, M. (2015) '"Not smiling but frowning": sociology and the "problem of happiness"', *Sociology*, 49(3): 422–37.

Cieslik, M. (2021) 'Sociology, biographical research and the development of critical happiness studies', in N. Hill, A. Petersen and S. Brinkmann (eds) *Critical Happiness Studies*, London: Routledge.

Clark-Ibáñez, M. (2004) 'Framing the social world with photo-elicitation interviews', *American Behavioural Scientist*, 47(12): 1507–27.

Cowen, A.S. and Keltner, D. (2017) 'Self-report captures 27 distinct categories of emotion bridged by continuous gradients', *Proceedings of the National Academy of Sciences*, 114(38): 7900–9.

Day, K., Stump, C. and Carreon, D. (2003) 'Confrontation and loss of control: masculinity and men's fear in public space', *Journal of Environmental Psychology*, 23: 311–22.

Diehl, K., Zauberman, G. and Barasch, A. (2016) 'How taking photos increases enjoyment of experiences', *Journal of Personality and Social Psychology*, 111(2): 119–40.

Fineman, S. (2004) 'Getting the measure of emotion – and the cautionary tale of emotional intelligence', *Human Relations*, 57(6): 719–40.

Fisher, C.D. (2010) 'Happiness at work', *International Journal of Management Reviews*, 12(4): 384–412.

Godard, J. (2014) 'The psychologisation of employment relations?', *Human Resource Management Journal*, 24(1): 1–18.

Goffman, E. (1959) *The Presentation of Self in Everyday Life*, New York: Random House.

Hyman, L. (2014) 'Happiness and memory: some sociological reflections', *Sociological Research Online*, 19(2): 1–9.

Illouz, E. (2008) *Saving the Modern Soul: Therapy, Emotions, and the Culture of Self-Help*, Berkeley, CA: University of California Press.

Johansson, K., Laflamme, L. and Eliasson, M. (2012) '"Adolescents" perceived safety and security in public space – a Swedish focus group study with a gender perspective', *Young*, 20: 69–88.

Judge, T. and Klinger, R. (2008) 'Job satisfaction: subjective well-being at work', in M. Eid and R. Larsen (eds) *The Science of Subjective Well-Being*, New York: The Guildford Press, pp 393–413.

Kunter, A. and Bell, E. (2006) 'The promise and potential of visual organizational research', *M@n@gement*, 9(3): 177–97.

Kurtz, J. and Lyubomirsky, S. (2013) 'Happiness promotion, using mindful photography to increase positive emotion and appreciation', in J.J. Froh and A.C. Parks (eds), *Activities for Teaching Positive Psychology*, Washington: American Psychological Association, pp 133–6.

Lajunen, T. and Summala, H. (2003) 'Can we trust self-reports of driving? Effects of impression management on driver behaviour questionnaire responses', *Transportation Research Part F: Traffic Psychology and Behaviour*, 6(2): 97–107.

Locke, E.A. (1969) 'What is job satisfaction?', *Organizational Behaviour and Human Performance*, 4(4): 309–36.

Lorenz, L.S. and Kolb, B. (2009) 'Involving the public through participatory visual research methods', *Health Expectations*, 12(3): 262–74.

Matthews, B. and Ross, L. (2010) *Research Methods. A Practical Guide for the Social Sciences*, Essex: Pearson.

McMahon, D.M. (2006) *Happiness: A History*. New York: Grove Press.

Migliorini, L. and Rania, N. (2017) 'A qualitative method to "make visible" the world of intercultural relationships: the photovoice in social psychology', *Qualitative Research in Psychology*, 14(2): 131–45.

Millennial Impact Report (2013), http://casefoundation.org/wp-content/uploads/2014/11/MillennialImpactReport-2013.pdf (accessed 14 April 2015).

Papaloukas, P., Quincey, K. and Williamson, I.R. (2017) 'Venturing into the visual voice: combining photos and interviews in phenomenological inquiry around marginalisation and chronic illness', *Qualitative Research in Psychology*, 14(4): 415–41.

Peck, J.A. and Levashina, J. (2017) 'Impression management and interview and job performance ratings: a meta-analysis of research design with tactics in mind', *Frontiers in Psychology*, 8: 201, DOI: 10.3389/fpsyg.2017.00201

Picone, I. (2015) 'Impression management in social media', in *The International Encyclopedia of Digital Communication and Society*, Wiley Online Library, https://www.researchgate.net/profile/Ike_Picone/publication/314361839_Impression_Management_in_Social_Media/links/59ef8b9c0f7e9baeb26ac3f8/Impression-Management-in-Social-Media.pdf (accessed 16 May 2018).

Pink, S. (2011) 'Sensory digital photography: re-thinking "moving" and the image', *Visual Studies*, 26(11): 4–13.

Pritchard, K. and Symon, G. (2014) 'Picture perfect? Exploring the use of smartphone photography in a distributed work practice', *Management Learning*, 45(5): 561–76.

Rose, G. (2012) *Visual Methodologies: An Introduction to Researching with Visual Materials*, London: SAGE.

Saunders, M., Lewis, P. and Thornhill, A. (2009) *Research Methods for Business Students* (5th edn), Harlow: Pearson Education.

Shortt, H.L. and Warren, S.K. (2017) 'Grounded visual pattern analysis: photographs in organizational field studies', *Organizational Research Methods*, online first, DOI: 10.1177/1094428117742495

Suojanen, I. (2013) *Work for Your Happiness – Defining and Measuring Happiness at Work*, CreateSpace, Independent Publishing Platform.

Suojanen, I. (2017) *Young Professionals and the Pursuit of Happiness*, University of Edinburgh, Doctoral Thesis.

Thin, N. (2012) 'Counting and recounting happiness and culture: on happiness surveys and prudential ethnobiography', *International Journal of Wellbeing*, 2(4): 313–32.

Tinkler, P. (2013) *Using Photographs in Social and Historical Research*, London: Sage.

Turkle, S. (2011) *Alone Together: Why We Expect More from Technology and Less from Each Other*, New York: Basic Books.

Van De Voorde, K., Paauwe, J. and Van Veldhoven, M. (2012) 'Employee well-being and the HRM–Organizational Performance Relationship: a review of quantitative studies', *International Journal of Management Reviews*, 14: 391–407.

Vince, R. and Warren, S. (2012) 'Participatory visual methods', in *Qualitative Organizational Research, Core Methods and Current Challenges*, London: Sage, DOI: 10.4135/9781526435620.n16

Wagner, J. (ed) (1979) *Images of Information*, Sage: London.

Walker, R. and Wiedel, J. (1985) 'Using photographs in a discipline of words', in R. Burgess (ed) *Field Methods in the Study of Education*, Falmer Press: London pp 191–216.

Warr, P. (1987) *Work, Unemployment, and Mental Health*, Oxford University Press: Oxford.

Warren, S. (2002) 'Show me how it feels to work here: using photography to research organizational aesthetics', *Ephemera*, 2(3): 224–45.

Index

Page numbers in *italic* refer to figures and page numbers in **bold** refer to tables.

'good works' 102–3
government policy 76–7, 78, 186–7, 189, 190
Graham, Carol 38
Greatest Happiness Principle 23
Great Kumamoto Earthquake 210
guilt 124, 125, 185

H

habitus 96–7, 98, 102, 103
Haidt, Jonathan 75, 76, 77–8, 84
Hannah, respondent 74–5
happiness definitions 4–6, 50–2, 94–5, 209–11
happiness industry 5, 168
happiness in the workplace *see* workplace happiness
happiness lens 21, 22, 36–8, 40, 41, 85–6
happiness levels 199–214
happiness, national *see* national wellbeing
'happiness turn' 49
Harry, interviewee 227
Hawtin, M., Hughes, G. and Percy-Smith, J. 179
health, physical 114, 211
Hebridean Connections 140–1
Hedonia 6, 52, 95
helplessness 82–3
heritage, cultural 13, 133–51
  and aging populations 138, 144
  and capital 133, 141–2, 143–6, 148, 150
  and community identity 143, 145, 146, 147, 149
  and community leadership 143, 144, 146
  and community participation 142, 143, 144–5
  and economic growth 138, 145
  and marginalization 142, 146–7
  and sense of place 146–9, 150
  and tourism 138, 149
  and tradition 135–9, 141, 142, 148
  and volunteering 138, 140, 143, 144, 146, 148
heritage, industrial 187–8
'hermeneutics of suspicion' 48
Hill, Nicholas 12–13, 47–64
history, local 139–41, 145, 146–7, 179
Hitokoto, H. and Uchida, Y. 202
Hockney, David 237
holism 22, 31, 180
Holloway, W. 85
Holmes, Mary 54
Holthus, Barbara and Manzenreiter, Wolfram 11, 14, 199–214
hope 165–7

humanness 117
Husser, J. and Fernandez, K. 201
Hutcheson, Francis 23
Hyman, L. 232
'hysteresis' 97–8, 104

I

Ian, respondent 75
identity 2, 9
  and biographical research 58–60, 62, 106, 107, 121, 122–3
  community/cultural identity 143, 145, 146, 147, 149
  and embodiment 116, 121, 122–3
  and life experiences 59, 62
'Ikigai' 4
Illouz, E. 234
imaginary, social 51, 63
impression management 7, 230, 235, *236*
improvement, cumulative 28
improvement, social 23
inclusion, social 33, *35*, 143
incomers 144, 148–9, 150
Index of Multiple Deprivation (IMD) 177
individualism 14, 75, 81, 82–3, 103, 202
industrial towns 175–91
  deindustrialization 14, 184–8
  industrial regeneration 187–8, 190
  and social relationships 177–8, 185, 187, 188, 190
  unemployment in 176, 177
inequality, social and economic 37–8, 74, 75–7, 79, 97
  poverty 185–6, 187, 188
Ingrid, interviewee 50–1, 52
innovation 28, *35*
insecurity 104, 108
institutional reform 77
intangibility of experiences 127–8
interconnectedness 185, 186, 188, 190
interdependent happiness 202
interpretations of happiness 234
interviewing 60–3, 96, 162, 182–4
  and embodiment 119, 127
  Japanese culture 200, 202–4
  and the workplace 223–4, 237n1
  see also biographical research methods
Iranians 159
isolation, social 51, 101, 188

J

Jackson, M. 161
  and Piette 163
Japanese culture 11, 14, 199–214
  and social relationships 204, 209–10, 211